国家职业教育改革发展示范校建设成果

苏州景点导游

苏州导游人员英语类现场考试指导用书

主编 吴晓群

编者 沈 宏　朱 勇　任文莺
　　　　伍 静　李昕白

苏州大学出版社

图书在版编目(CIP)数据

苏州景点导游：苏州导游人员英语类现场考试指导用书 / 吴晓群主编. —苏州：苏州大学出版社，2015.4（2024.1重印）
国家职业教育改革发展示范校建设成果
ISBN 978-7-5672-1252-7

Ⅰ. ①苏… Ⅱ. ①吴… Ⅲ. ①导游－英语－职业教育－教材 Ⅳ. ①H31

中国版本图书馆 CIP 数据核字(2015)第 077691 号

苏州景点导游

吴晓群　主编

责任编辑　沈　琴

苏州大学出版社出版发行
（地址：苏州市十梓街 1 号　邮编：215006）
广东虎彩云印刷有限公司印装
（地址：东莞市虎门镇黄村社区厚虎路20号C幢一楼　邮编：523898）

开本 787 mm×1 092 mm　1/1　印张 15　字数 374 千
2015 年 4 月第 1 版　2024 年 1 月第 8 次印刷
ISBN 978-7-5672-1252-7　定价：38.00 元

苏州大学版图书若有印装错误，本社负责调换
苏州大学出版社营销部　电话：0512-67481020
苏州大学出版社网址　http://www.sudapress.com

编写说明

　　为了培养学生的语言综合运用能力，成功通过苏州英语导游资格现场口试，并能用英语自如地与游客沟通，不仅需要有高质量的专业英语教材，而且要有配套的课堂教学模式。只有这样，学生才有机会得到真实的对客服务的训练，提高现场应变能力和专业技能。

　　作为江苏省职业教育教学改革研究课题"高职导游专业英语课程实境化教学的研究与探索"的配套教材，本书根据《导游服务技能》、《景点导游》以及苏州市旅游局编写的《导游资格现场考试手册(苏州)》要求而设置。每个模块以不同项目为引导，大量充实与项目内容相关的知识，并设置相应的课前课后任务、课堂实践活动和实训实践活动，实现课程教学目标。

　　教材内容主要包括导游工作程序、苏州文化、苏州主要景点讲解三个模块。学生可以熟练掌握导游职业素养和工作程序相关的基本知识，重点讲解苏州地区的名胜古迹、园林文化、寺院古镇等，全面了解苏州的吴地文风、民风节俗、饮食文化、艺术风采、丝绸刺绣、茶艺等文化知识，同时也锻炼了学生英语的表达能力以及与人沟通能力。

　　本书由吴晓群主编，参加编写的有：模块一为沈宏、吴晓群，模块二为朱勇、任文莺，模块三为伍静、李昕白。

　　由于编写时间仓促，书中肯定还存在着许多需要改进的地方，我们真诚希望广大师生在使用过程中能发现问题，并提出批评和建议。

编写组
2014 年 11 月

Preface

The aim of this book is to further develop students' English language abilities and fluency in listening and speaking in tourism industry. It helps them to communicate better with the tourists in English and facilitate the daily customer service in tour guiding.

	Learning outcomes
Listening	Be able to understand the tourists' inquiries and requests: 1. inquires about the information of tour or other tourism services 2. common instructions in the workplace
Speaking	Be able to conduct dialogues with the tourists to fulfill the tasks in the tours, reflecting fluency of language, correct pronunciation, context and grammar usage: 1. fulfill regular service procedures 2. introduce the city and its culture, hotel facilities, hotel service items and tourist attractions in detail 3. be confident in communication with the tourists 4. express personal viewpoints on some issues concerning the tourism industry and put forward at least two particular examples to back up 5. provide sufficient information about the inquiries on shopping, entertainment, dining, etc.
Reading & Vocabulary	Be able to read English articles concerning hospitality industry and master useful words and expressions of about 3,500: 1. narrative articles on daily life and simple correspondences 2. job-related notice, message, forms and memorandum 3. brief description of the objects' usage and job responsibility in the hotel 4. constructive articles on conflict resolution 5. constructive articles on staff behavior norm 6. articles on different cultures and tourist attractions in China

Table of Contents

Module I　Working Procedures as a Tour Guide ······················· 1

　Project 1　Meeting Guests at the Airport ································ 1
　Project 2　On the Way to the Hotel ······································ 8
　Project 3　Hotel Accommodations ······································ 16
　Project 4　Itinerary Planning ·· 24
　Project 5　On the Way to the Scenic Spot ······························ 32
　Project 6　Dining in Suzhou ·· 39
　Project 7　Farewell ·· 47

Module II　Suzhou Culture ·· 54

　Project 1　Wu Culture ·· 54
　Project 2　Silk and Embroidery ·· 62
　Project 3　Art Culture ·· 69
　Project 4　Folk Customs and Festivities ································ 77
　Project 5　Food Culture ·· 83
　Project 6　Tea Culture ·· 90

Module III　Main Tourist Attractions in Suzhou ······················ 97

　Project 1　The Tiger Hill ·· 97
　Project 2　The Humble Administrator's Garden ······················ 116
　Project 3　Suzhou Gardens ·· 145
　Project 4　Old City Center Canal Cruise ······························ 159
　Project 5　Zhou Zhuang ·· 187
　Project 6　Tongli ·· 213

References ·· 232

Module I Working Procedures as a Tour Guide

Project 1 Meeting Guests at the Airport

Learning Objectives:
- be able to recognize the tour group at the airport
- be able to communicate with guests for the first time
- be able to deal with unexpected problems

Task 1 Warm-Up

1. Before the arrival of the tour group, what preparation and reception work should be made by the guide?
2. How can the local guide identify the tour group at the airport?
3. What documents and relevant material should the tour guide carry before the reception?

Task 2 Words and Expressions

lobby	[ˈlɒbi]	n.	（机场）大厅
guide	[ɡaɪd]	n.	导游
Los Angeles	[ˌlɒsˈændʒəliːz]	n.	[美]洛杉矶市
tired	[ˈtaɪəd]	adj.	累的,疲劳的
nevertheless	[ˌnevəðəˈles]	conj.	然而,不过
jasmine	[ˈdʒæzmɪn]	n.	茉莉,淡黄色
luggage	[ˈlʌɡɪdʒ]	n.	行李
manage	[ˈmænɪdʒ]	v.	设法对付,做成
travel agency			旅行社

shuttle bus	班车
parking lot	停车场
jet lag	时差病

Task 3 Dialogues

Dialogue 1

Scene: In the Hongqiao Airport lobby, Li Ping (Susan), a young tour guide from China International Travel Agency, is greeting a tour group from the United States headed by Mr. James White. (S = Susan, J = James White, E = Emily White)

S: Excuse me! Are you Mr. White from Los Angeles?

J: Yes, I'm James White.

S: Nice to meet you, Mr. White. I'm Li Ping, your local guide from China International Travel Agency. Just call me Susan.

J: Nice to meet you, too.

S: (Li Ping shakes hands with Mr. White and other guests) Welcome to China!

J: We're so glad that you've come to meet us at the airport, Susan.

S: Did you have a good trip, Mr. White?

J: Yes, quite pleasant. But we feel a bit tired after the long flight, especially those two children.

S: Yes, you must. You all need a good rest first.

J: Nevertheless we are so excited that we've finally arrived in the country that we have been wishing to see for years.

S: You will have plenty of time to see all the interesting places here. Is everyone in the group here?

J: Yes, a party of six. We have two ladies with two children and two gentlemen. This is my wife, Emily.

S: Hello, Mrs. White! Nice to meet you!

E: Nice to meet you, too! Please call me Emily!

J: This is Michael and Sophia, my friends. Those are my children, Kate and Tom.

S: Hello, everyone! Welcome to Suzhou! Good. Can we go now? Shall I help you with your luggage, Emily?

E: No, thanks. I can manage.

S: Please follow me, ladies and gentlemen! The shuttle bus is just waiting in the parking lot.

J: That's fine. Hurry up, guys!

S: This way, please.

Dialogue 2

Scene: Lily (the local guide) is waiting for a couple from Britain. (L = Lily, B = Mr. Brown, MB = Mrs. Brown)

L: Excuse me. Are you Mr. Brown from Britain?
B: Yes, I am. Are you our local guide here?
L: Yes. My name is Lily. Welcome to China.
B: Thank you.
L: Is there anyone else who accompanies you?
B: Yes, this is my wife. We come together.
L: Glad to meet you.
MB: Glad to meet you, too.
L: How many pieces of luggage do you have?
B: 3 pieces in all.
L: Mr. and Mrs. Brown, you look a bit tired.
B: Yes, we are tired from the jet lag.
L: I think you need a good rest. Well, let's get on the bus right now, and we'll stay in the Jasmine Holiday Inn, which is located in the downtown of Suzhou. I'm sure you will like it.
B: How long will it take to get to the hotel?
L: Around 3 hours. Please take a rest on the bus.
B: OK.

Task 4 Useful Sentences

1. I'm Li Ping, your tour guide from the Youth Travel Service.
2. Did you have a good trip, Mr. White?
3. You will have plenty of time to see all the interesting places here. Is everyone in the group here?
4. The shuttle bus is just waiting in the parking lot.
5. Is there anyone else who accompanies you?
6. How many pieces of luggage do you have?
7. Hello, everyone. Welcome! How was your flight? I'm glad you enjoyed your flight.
8. You can relax now, and leave all your worries to me / we are at your service!
9. I'm really looking forward to talking more with you, but for now, I think you must be tired after this long flight and we'd better go straight to the hotel, where you can get settled.
10. There are rest rooms in the baggage area which you're free to use, but please remain in the area, as we hope to leave the airport as quickly as possible.
11. Have you all got your baggage? Good, now let's go to the motor coach. Please follow me and

my flag. Your baggage will be put on another vehicle. Don't worry about it.

Task 5 Listening

You will hear five sentences. Listen carefully and put down the whole sentences.

1. _____.
2. _____.
3. _____.
4. _____.
5. _____.

Task 6 Dialogue-Completing

Lily:	_____. But are you Mr. William Smith?
Mr. Smith:	Yes, I am.
Lily:	How do you do, Mr. William Smith?
Mr. Smith:	_____! I guess you must be Lily, _____.
Lily:	Yes, Mr. Smith. _____. I am Lily from China International Travel Service, Suzhou branch.
Mr. Smith:	Glad to meet you.
Lily:	_____. You have a group of 25, right?
Mr. Smith:	Yes, everyone of the group is here.
Lily:	_____?
Mr. Smith:	48 and here they are. Shall we take them to the bus?
Lily:	No, you needn't. _____.
Mr. Smith:	Thank you very much.
Lily:	Ladies and gentlemen, attention, please. Our bus is waiting outside. Now please follow me to the bus.
Lily:	(*After they get on the bus, Lily counts the tourists. And then they will head for the hotel.*) May I have your attention please? I wonder _____.
Mr. Smith:	Sorry, but Jenny is not on. Ah, here she comes.
Lily:	Since everybody is on the bus, shall we go now?
Mr. Smith:	Yes.

Task 7　Role-Play

Situation 1: The local guide from China Youth Travel Service is at Pudong Airport to meet a travel group from Canada. Mr. Bellow is the tour leader.

Local guide:
- Greets Mr. Bellow and extends welcome to him.
- Asks about the flight.
- Thinks that Mr. Bellow is possibly tired.
- Asks Mr. Bellow if all members of his party are here.
- Offers to help with the baggage.
- Says a bus will send them to the hotel.

Mr. Bellow:
- Greets the local guide.
- Says the flight was a bit long.
- Answers that he had some sleep during the flight.
- Tells his wish for this trip.
- Tells the number of people in the group.
- Expresses thanks. Says he can take care of his baggage himself.

Situation 2: Zhang Ming, from China International Travel Service, is waiting for his tourist Mr. Black from London in the lobby of Hongqiao Airport.

Task 8　Translation

Put the following passage into Chinese.

Procedures to remember:
- Come to the airport at least 30 minutes in advance; check the arrival terminal to confirm the actual arrival time and arrival gate.
- Walk to the gate, establish a meeting/waiting site for the group, and note the location of the baggage claim area.
- Receive the group and offer a friendly greeting, inquire about their trip, and give brief but clear instructions as to the immediate procedures.
- Help tourists when they collect their luggage, and remind them to check if there is any damage. And then transfer the luggage to the vehicle.
- Escort the tourists to their motor coach.

Task 9 Supplementary Reading

The Role of a Tour Guide

1. The tour guide should do everything possible to ensure that tour members obtain the maximum enjoyment and satisfaction from the tour.
2. The tour guide should pay particular attention to the health and safety of the tour members.
3. The tour guide should supervise the transporting of the tour members' luggage.
4. Assist the tour members in their dealings to the airlines, hotels and other principals. For example, if a tour member's luggage is lost or damaged, help the tour member file a complaint to the airline or the department connected.
5. Coordinate all arrangements in cooperation with the hotels and local tour guide(s). If a tour needs a single room on his/her own, the tour guide should check with the hotel first and pays a single supplement on the spot.
6. Do everything possible to become knowledgeable about the cities and sites included in the itinerary of each trip he/she leads.
7. File complete and accurate trip reports.

Questions:
1. What is a tour guide?
2. What's the development trend of tourist service?
3. Narrowly speaking, what people are included in one tour service collective?
4. In China, what are the classifications of tourist guides?
5. What is the main work of the tour guide at each station?

Tips for Tour Guides

Preparation and reception work before the arrival of the tour group:
- Check the schedule of tourism activities.
- Contact Tourism Vehicle Company or team to implement the travel vehicles.
- Learn the phone number of relevant units, departments and staff.
- Make sure of housing and meals, get familiar with the location and general condition of the hotel, number and level of the rooms for tourists and confirm group meals in every situation.
- Learn general situation of unfamiliar attractions, such as the opening hours, the best sightseeing routes, toilets and so on.

Identifying the tour groups at the airport:
- Raise a reception board at a recognizable place (or travel agency flag) and wait for the tour

leader, the tour guide (or tourists) to come to contact.
- Take the initiative to tell tourists from their national identity, clothes, logo and approach tactfully to ask and find their tour.
- Make clear which country (region) they come from, travel agency of the source, the name of tour leader and tour guide, etc.
- In the absence of its leader and tour guide, the local guide should check the name of the tour group, country (region) and the names of the members. Only when everything is consistent can the local guide make sure of the tour group.

Project 2 On the Way to the Hotel

Learning Objectives:
- be able to present a special welcome speech
- be able to introduce the city and its culture briefly
- be able to explain the scenery along the way to the hotel

Task 1 Warm-Up

1. What should a guide introduce when conducting the first tour on route?
2. What kinds of items should be included in a welcome speech?
3. What aspects should the local guide pay attention to when introducing the scenery along the way?

Task 2 Words and Expressions

enjoyable	[ɪnˈdʒɔɪəbl]	adj.	愉快的,开心的
memorable	[ˈmemərəbl]	adj.	值得怀念的
cultivation	[ˌkʌltɪˈveɪʃn]	n.	栽培;养殖
coach	[kəʊtʃ]	n.	车厢,经济舱
furnishing	[ˈfɜːnɪʃɪŋ]	n.	供给(装备)
extensive	[ɪkˈstensɪv]	adj.	广泛的
facility	[fəˈsɪləti]	n.	设备,设施
heaven	[ˈhevn]	n.	天空,天堂
entertain	[ˌentəˈteɪn]	v.	娱乐
scene	[siːn]	n.	情景,场景
cruise	[kruːz]	n.	巡航,漫游
hence	[hens]	adv.	因此;由此
fertile	[ˈfɜːtaɪl]	adj.	(土地)肥沃的
schedule	[ˈskedʒuːl]	n.	时间表
buffet	[ˈbʊfeɪ]	n.	自助餐
industrial	[ɪnˈdʌstrɪəl]	adj.	工业的

embroidery	[ɪmˈbrɔɪdəri]	n.	刺绣品
unique	[juːˈniːk]	adj.	独特的
characterize	[ˈkærəktəraɪz]	v.	赋予……特色
variety	[vəˈraɪəti]	n.	多样
consummate	[kənˈsʌmət]	adj.	完美的
artisan	[ˌɑːtɪˈzæn]	n.	技工
efficient	[ɪˈfɪʃnt]	adj.	效率高的
leisure	[ˈleʒə]	n.	闲暇, 休闲
paradise	[ˈpærədaɪs]	n.	天堂
population	[ˌpɒpjuˈleɪʃn]	n.	人口
time-honored	[ˈtaɪmˈɔnəd]	adj.	历史悠久的
ancient	[ˈeɪnʃənt]	adj.	古老的
water-alley	[wɔːtəˈæli]	n.	水巷
settle	[ˈsetl]	v.	解决, 定居
craft	[krɑːft]	n.	工艺, 手艺
institute	[ˈɪnstɪtjuːt]	n.	学院
elegant	[ˈelɪgənt]	adj.	优雅的
stitch	[stɪtʃ]	n.	一针
craftsmanship	[ˈkrɑːftsmənʃɪp]	n.	技术
marvelous	[ˈmɑːvələs]	adj.	非凡的
fasten	[fɑːsn]	v.	扎牢
do one's best			尽某人最大努力
Jasmine Holiday Inn			茉莉花假日酒店
long for			渴望
license plate number			车牌号
thanks to			幸亏, 由于
the Land of Fish and Rice			鱼米之乡
artistic style			艺术风格

Task 3   Dialogues

Dialogue 1: Itinerary Planning

Scene: Susan, the guide, meets the tour group at the Hongqiao Airport and they are driving to the Jasmine Holiday Inn, which is in the downtown of Suzhou Shilu District. (S = Susan, J = James White)

S: Is everybody on the bus?

J: Yes, I think so.

S: Shall we go now?

J: Yes, please.

S: (*to all the tourists on the coach*) Welcome to China, ladies and gentlemen. Let me introduce myself to you first. My name is Susan. I am a tour guide from China International Travel Agency. I'll be your guide during your stay in Suzhou. And this is Mr. Wang, our driver. He has been a driver for more than 10 years. Our bus license plate number is Su E K4865. We will do our best to make your trip more enjoyable and memorable. I hope you will have a very pleasant stay here in Suzhou. Thank you very much! Now, we are driving straight to the hotel, the Jasmine Holiday Inn.

J: Well, how far is it to the hotel?

S: It'll take us about three hours. It's one of the best four-star hotels in the city. It is located in Shilu downtown of Suzhou. There is warm and efficient service with extensive leisure facilities. Well known for its comfortable furnishings and excellent service, it has long been the first choice of many guests from all over the world. I hope you will enjoy your stay there.

J: That's great. It is said that just as there is paradise in heaven, there are Suzhou and Hangzhou on earth.

S: Yes. Suzhou is a famous city in China with 2,500 years. The population is 6.2 million. It is a pleasant place to visit as well as to do business, shop, dine, or be entertained. Classical gardens, time-honored towns, water scenes, 1,000-year-old ancient city, modern attractions, scenic Taihu Lake, night cruise, water-alley houses, all these bring you the tourism image of Suzhou, which is Paradise Suzhou, Eastern Watertown. Thanks to its fertile soil and warm climate, it is the major rice production and fresh-water fish cultivation base of China, hence it has got the name "the Land of Fish and Rice".

J: We are really longing for a visit.

S: Now, I would like to give you a brief outline of your schedule for the next few days. After we check in and get settled, we will meet for supper in the buffet restaurant. In the first 2 days we'll visit Suzhou classical gardens and museums. On the third day, the Industrial Park will show you what modern Suzhou looks like.

J: Excuse me, I wonder if we have a chance to go to any arts and crafts factory.

S: Of course, I will arrange you a visit to Suzhou Embroidery Institute. You know, Suzhou embroidery has a long history of more than two thousand years. It has developed a unique artistic style and been characterized by its beautiful patterns, elegant colors, variety of stitches and consummate craftsmanship. There you can see the artisans making one piece.

J: Marvelous.

S: You must be tired after the long trip. I'm afraid you need a good rest first.

J: That's very kind of you.

S: Remember to fasten your seat belt; we'll arrive in 3 hours. Have a good rest now.

J: Thanks for your suggestion.

(*3 hours later*)

S: Well, ladies and gentlemen, here we are. Let's get off and go to the reception desk.

J: OK.

Dialogue 2: A Welcome Speech

Good morning, ladies and gentlemen, welcome to paradise Suzhou. Allow me to introduce myself. My name is Huang Lan. Huang is my surname, so you may call me Xiao Huang. I'm a guide from Suzhou China Travel Service. And this is Mr. Deng, our driver. He has 20 years of driving under his belt, so you're in very safe hands. We're glad to have all of you here.

I'll be with you during your five-day tour in this city and we'll be at your service at any time. We'll do everything possible to make your visit a pleasant experience. If you have any problems or suggestions, please don't hesitate to let us know.

The hotel where you stay is the Shangri-La Hotel. It offers the best services in this city. We shall meet at the hotel lobby at 7:00 a.m. for our first visit tomorrow. Please remember the number of our bus. It's Su E KL459. Thank you.

Now we are on the Xihuan overhead road. It's in the Suzhou New District. We'll reach the hotel soon. We hope you'll enjoy your stay in this city.

Task 4 Useful Sentences

1. Let me introduce my team to you first.
2. We will do our best to make your trip more enjoyable and memorable.
3. It's one of the best four-star hotels in the city.
4. Thanks to its fertile soil and warm climate, it is the major rice production and fresh-water fish cultivation base of China. Hence it has got the name "the Land of Fish and Rice".
5. Excuse me, I wonder if we have a chance to go to any arts and crafts factory.
6. He has 20 years of driving under his belt, so you're in very safe hands.
7. On behalf of my travel agency, I would like to welcome you, our distinguished guests, to our city.
8. I sincerely wish you a pleasant and comfortable stay and a wonderful vacation here.
9. I will do my best to make everything easy for you.
10. If you have any questions, please don't hesitate to ask me.
11. We will have a 50-minute ride to the hotel, so please sit back and relax. Thank you.

Task 5 Listening

You will hear five sentences. Listen carefully and put down the whole sentences.

1. _____.
2. _____.
3. _____.
4. _____.
5. _____.

Task 6 Dialogue-Completing

James: Look, there are so many cars and bicycles over there. Why?

Susan: _____. We are on the Beihuan overhead viaduct which connects _____. Now please look straight ahead on your right, which is _____.
_____.

James: Are we going to visit the Tiger Hill?

Susan: Yes, we will. Now we are in the Shilu Downtown. _____.
_____. Look at that tall building.
That's the Jasmine Holiday Inn. _____.

James: Shall we go shopping here?

Susan: _____.

James: Can you recommend some local souvenirs to us?

Susan: _____.

James: It's marvelous. I will go and have a try. Thank you so much.

Susan: _____.

Task 7 Role-Play

Situation 1: You are an English tour guide who is meeting a Canadian tour group at the Pudong Airport. On the way to the hotel, you are supposed to:

- make a welcome speech;
- say something about the hotel;
- introduce the city briefly;

♦ explain the scene along the way.

Situation 2: Suppose you are a local guide, Mr. White is the tour group's national guide from Canada. Make a welcome speech:
♦ to extend a warm welcome to the tourists;
♦ to introduce your team;
♦ to give a brief account of tour arrangements;
♦ to make sure you'll be always at their service;
♦ to tell them the time difference;
♦ to give best wishes to them.

Task 8   Translation

Put the following passage into Chinese.

Suzhou, my hometown, has been known as a historical city of cultural renown. And it is also known as a city of gardens, a town of canals, the land of fish and rice, the metropolis of arts and crafts, and the home of silk. In 514 BC, King Helv of State Wu ordered to build its capital. His prime minister Wu Zixu inspected the water and soil conditions, surveyed the terrains, made astrological telling, and on the basis of land planning, built the Great City of Helv. At that time the city was 23.5 km in circumference with eight land gates and eight water gates. That began the history of Suzhou.

Now there exist four land gates and two water gates. The city provides a rare specimen of an ancient Chinese city with its streets and canals on close parallel. Such scenes are still apparent today along its 35-km-long canals and some 168 bridges within the old city area. Totally there are 487 historical and cultural sites that have been listed as national, provincial or municipal monuments. Known as a typical garden city, Suzhou preserves 68 classical gardens. In 1997, UNESCO inscribed Suzhou Gardens on the world cultural heritage list.

Covering an area of 14.2 sq km, the old city proper surrounded by the moat lies in the center with the Sino-Singapore Cooperative Industrial Park of 70 sq km to the east and both the new urban area and the high-technological development zone of 60 sq km to the west.

Task 9   Supplementary Reading

Suzhou—a Famous Historical and Cultural City

Suzhou is not only a famous historical and cultural city in China, but also a scenic and tourist city of great importance. Suzhou reminds people naturally of the elegant gardens, towering pagodas and scenes of families living along the canals and bridges in fine drizzle. The city leads you to the great appreciation of the beautiful scenery of mountains and lakes, the galaxy of gardens and places of historical interests, the exquisite folk arts and crafts and famous Wu School of Painting. The unique grace and glamour of this city of cultural renown will make a deep impression on you.

Suzhou covers a total area of 8,488 sq km. The municipal seat covers an area of 40.48 sq km, in which the old city proper covers an area of 14 sq km. It now administrates 5 urban cities. The total population of Suzhou is 6 million with the residents of Suzhou city proper being 1 million.

The history of Suzhou is more than 2,500 years. The long history has left Suzhou many charming humanistic historic sites and the Suzhou gardens must be the most stylish ones. Most of them were built in Song, Yuan, Ming and Qing Dynasties. It was recorded that there were about 271 large or small gardens in Suzhou, of which over 60 are well protected and 19 are open to public officially.

Unlike the imperial gardens, Suzhou gardens were built as private resorts of local officials, wealthy scholars of absentee landlords. A classical Suzhou garden is a comprehensive art form, a harmonious embodiment of the artistic traditions of Chinese Painting, literature, architecture, arts and crafts.

In the long history, Suzhou shapes its own special culture—Wu Culture. In Suzhou, Kunqu Opera, Ballad Singing and Story Telling in Suzhou Dialect, Wu School of Painting and classical architecture hold high places in history. During the long history, Suzhou also has developed special local arts and crafts, with unique artistic value. The most famous are Suzhou silk embroidery, Suzhou fans, Suzhou carvings and jade carving.

Questions:
1. What are the characteristics of classical Suzhou gardens?
2. What is the population of present Suzhou and what is the tourism image of Suzhou?
3. It is said that the economy in Suzhou has been rapidly growing. Can you say something about that?
4. What honorary titles has Suzhou city received?
5. What are the rewarding tourism products in Suzhou? Please give a brief introduction.

Tips for Tour Guides

First en route speech includes:
- A welcome speech.
- The introduction of time difference and the adjustment of the time.
- The general introduction of the city: local conditions, climate conditions, population, administrative divisions, social life, cultural traditions, native products, history and so on,

timely introduction of local cities and development condition and important buildings, streets and so on along the way.
- Scenery guides: choose apporpriate scenery introductions right along with the tourists' viewing.
- The introduction of hotel: The basic condition of the hotel, such as the name, location, the distance from the airport (stations, port), star level, scale, major facilities and equipment.

A welcome speech includes:
- Giving the tourists a warm welcome on behalf of the travel agency.
- Making self-introduction, and introduce the driver and brief schedule, and express the hope of getting tourists' cooperation.
- Expressing a sincere desire to provide services.
- Wishing the tourists a pleasant journey.

Project 3 Hotel Accommodations

Learning Objectives:
- be able to help the guests with the check-in procedure
- be able to introduce the hotel facilities briefly
- be able to deal with problems and special requests from the tourists

Task 1 Warm-Up

1. What main work should be done by the local guide when the tourists arrive at the hotel?
2. What should a guide do if tourists want to exchange rooms?
3. After checking in a hotel, the tour group in the rooms of the hotel meets the fire affairs at midnight. The fire spreads quickly to the floors occupied by the tour group. At this moment, what should the guide do?

Task 2 Words and Expressions

registration	[ˌredʒɪ'streɪʃn]	n.	注册，登记，挂号
cooperation	[kəʊˌɒpə'reɪʃn]	n.	合作，协作，协同作用
passport	['pɑːspɔːt]	n.	护照，手段
unforgettable	[ˈʌnfə'getəbl]	adj.	难忘的
departure	[dɪ'pɑːtʃə]	n.	出发，离开
gratitude	['grætɪtjuːd]	n.	感激，感谢
receptionist	[rɪ'sepʃənɪst]	n.	接待员
concerned	[kən'sɜːnd]	adj.	关心的，关切的，有关的
certificate	[sə'tɪfɪkeɪt]	n.	执照，证(明)书
		vt.	认可，批准
opportunity	[ˌɒpə'tjuːnəti]	n.	机会，时机
schedule	['skedʒuːl]	n.	时间表，计划表
belongings	[bɪ'lɒŋɪŋz]	n.	所有物
feast	[fiːst]	n.	宴会，酒席
accommodate	[ə'kɒmədeɪt]	v.	容纳

heartfelt	[ˈhɑːtfelt]	adj.	衷心的
upset	[ʌpˈset]	adj.	心烦的
effort	[ˈefət]	n.	努力
organize	[ˈɔːgənaɪz]	v.	组织
stupid	[ˈstjuːpɪd]	adj.	愚蠢的,笨拙的
property	[ˈprɒpəti]	n.	财产
calm	[kɑːm]	adj.	平静的
description	[dɪˈskrɪpʃn]	n.	描述
tag	[tæg]	n.	标签
handle	[ˈhændl]	n.	把手
deliver	[dɪˈlɪvə]	v.	递送,发表
attach	[əˈtætʃ]	v.	附上
appreciate	[əˈpriːʃieɪt]	vt.	欣赏
approximately	[əˈprɒksɪmətli]	adv.	大约
relax	[rɪˈlæks]	v.	休息,放松
absolutely	[ˈæbsəluːtli]	adv.	完全地,绝对地
bellman	[ˈbelmən]	n.	行李员
sort	[sɔːt]	v.	分类,协调
hold dear			看重,珍视
standard room			标准客房;标准间
travel agency			旅行社
hand in			交上,递交
on behalf of			代表
make-up			化妆品

Task 3　Dialogues

Dialogue 1

Scene: Susan, the local guide, has led a tour group to the hotel. Now they are at the reception desk of the Jasmine Holiday Inn. Susan should work together with the tour leader, Mr. James White, to make sure that all the guests are well accommodated at the hotel. The following dialogue is between them and the receptionist of the hotel. (R = Receptionist, S = Susan, J = Mr. James White)

R: Good afternoon. Welcome to the Jasmine Holiday Inn. May I help you?
S: Good afternoon. I'm Susan from China International Travel Agency. We have booked three standard rooms.
R: Just a moment please. Let me check the reservation record. (*After a short while*)

S: Well, yes. Your travel agency has booked three standard rooms for a group of 6. This group will stay for four days at our hotel. Will you please fill in the registration forms?

S: OK. Please give these forms to me and I will hand them out.

R: Thank you. And here you are.

(The local guide receives the forms and hands them out to the tourists. Several minutes later, they hand in the forms to the local guide.)

S: These are our registration forms.

R: Good. May I have a look at your passports?

J: No problem. Here they are.

R: I'd like to confirm your departure date. You are going to leave next Tuesday, October 10th, right?

S: Yes. And we have to start early tomorrow morning because of the busy schedule, I'm afraid.

J: No problem. At what time should we start?

S: At least 8:30.

J: OK. Let's settle on 8:30.

R: Excuse me, Susan, here are the room keys. The bellman will show you up to your rooms.

S: Thank you.

(The local guide receives the keys from the receptionist. She hands them out to the tourists.)

J: Susan, let me help you to hand out these keys.

S: Thanks a lot. Please make sure that all the tourists get the right keys to their rooms.

J: I'm in Room 601. The telephone numbers are the same as your room numbers. Please call me if you need something. Now Susan will speak to you.

S: Attention please. Since we have very busy schedule tomorrow, we have to start early. Departure for the visit to Tiger Hill tomorrow is at 8:30. The morning call is required at 7:30. Wish you all have a nice night.

Dialogue 2

Scene: The last day, the tour group will leave the hotel at 10:00 in the morning. They have packed all the baggage, and are checking out at the front desk.

(C = Front Desk clerk, S = Susan, B = Bellman, J = Mr. James White)

S: Good morning, everybody. Please leave all the baggage at the post over there. The bellman will take them to the bus.

J: OK.

S: Excuse me. Here is all the baggage of our group. The bus is waiting outside. The plate number is K4865. Thank you.

B: I see. Leave it to me.

S: Is everyone here? *(Counting the number)* Please check your own belongings again. Don't leave behind your travel certificates. Now I will help you check out.

C: Good morning, your room keys, please.
S: Here you are.
C: Wait a moment, please. I'll check with the department concerned.
C: Sorry to have kept you waiting. Everything is OK. Here is your final bill. Please sign your name here.
S: That's fine. Please get on the bus. Mind your steps. (*Check the number again*) Ladies and gentlemen, your current visit to Suzhou is drawing to a close. I would like to say a few words before you leave. There is an old Chinese saying, "Even the finest feast must break up at last". I hope you have enjoyed all your stay. If there's anything that you are not satisfied with, please do tell me so that I can do better in the future. And here, I'd like to take this opportunity to thank you all for your understanding and cooperation. I sincerely hope that you'll come to visit Suzhou again.
J: Thank you very much, Susan. On behalf of the whole group, I'd like to express our heartfelt gratitude to you for your efforts and excellent services. We certainly have had a wonderful time in the past four days and will always hold dear this unforgettable journey.

Dialogue 3

Scene: On the way to the next hotel, a tourist has left a personal item in their former hotel room. (S = Susan, T = tourist)

T: Oh, Susan. I'm so upset. I've just discovered my make-up bag is missing and I've left it behind in the bathroom at the hotel.
S: I'm sorry to hear that. I know your feeling. However, don't worry too much. I'm sure we can organize its safe return.
T: I feel so stupid.
S: Now don't be too hard on yourself. People often leave things behind. Trust me. Any item, however small left in a room is always sent to the lost property department of the hotel.
T: Thanks, Susan. I feel I can calm down now.
S: Yes, you can. I will ring the hotel immediately. Now I need a description of it and your room number.
T: Well, it's dark blue and opens at the top. It has a side pocket and two handles. The name tag is attached to one of its handles, Emily White.
S: I've got all the details. I'll make the call now.
 (*A few minutes later.*)
S: Emily, everything is sorted. Yes, your make-up bag was in the bathroom and the hotel is making arrangements now for it to be delivered to our new hotel tonight. It should arrive approximately at 7 p.m.
T: Thank you so much. I really appreciate your effort and I apologize for the trouble I've caused.

S: Absolutely no problem. It's my pleasure to help. Now just relax and enjoy your day.
T: OK. I will!

Task 4 Useful Sentences

1. We have to start early tomorrow morning because of the busy schedule.
2. Please make sure that all the tourists get the right keys to their rooms.
3. Departure for the visit to the Tiger Hill tomorrow is at 8:30.
4. Your room number is 244 on the second floor.
5. Please check your own belongings again, and don't leave behind your travel certificates.
6. Ladies and gentlemen, your current visit to Suzhou is drawing to a close.
7. There is an old Chinese saying, "Even the finest feast must break up at last."
8. I'd like to take this opportunity to thank you all for your understanding and cooperation.
9. On behalf of the whole group, I'd like to express our heartfelt gratitude to you for your efforts and excellent services.
10. We certainly have had a wonderful time in the past 7 days and will always hold dear this unforgettable journey.
11. If you have anything for the laundry, just leave it in the laundry bag in your room.
12. The shopping arcade is opposite the information desk. They offer a good selection of things there.

Task 5 Listening

You will hear five sentences. Listen carefully and put down the whole sentences.

1. _____.
2. _____.
3. _____.
4. _____.
5. _____.

Task 6 Dialogue-Completing

R: May I help you?
G: My name is Zhang Chen. I'm from China International Travel Agency. _____.

R: Just a moment please ... Yes, they are all on the 11th floor, all facing the south.
G: Good.
R: Here are some registration forms _____.
G: _____. Is that all right?

Task 7 Role-Play

Situation 1: You lead a group from the United States. Now you are at the hotel front desk, helping the group to check in.
- to check the number of the group
- to hand out the registration forms
- to collect all the tourists' passports
- to set morning call for each room
- to assign rooms

Situation 2: You take three individual travelers to Bamboo Grove Hotel without having booked in advance.
- to ask for two rooms and tell the receptionist the duration of their stay
- to ask the travelers whether they like a room facing the street
- to check the rate for the room
- to check whether meals are included in the rate for the room

Task 8 Translation

Put the following sentences into English.
1. 请把我们结账时间改为早上8点。
2. 贵团人数有没有变化?
3. 这些是我们的护照。
4. 我们可以领取房间钥匙了么?
5. 大家请注意。

Put the following passage into Chinese.

All hotels do not serve the same clientele, that is, the same kind of guests. In fact, hotels can be classified into four categories. The first is the commercial hotel, which provides services essentially for transients, many of them traveling on business. The second category is resort hotels, which are located in vacation areas. They provide recreational facilities of their own. The third type of hotel aims its services largely at the convention trade. And the fourth category is the resident hotel.

Task 9 Supplementary Reading

To Accommodate a Guest in a Hotel

After tourists arrive at the hotel, you, as the tour guide, should help them check in and introduce them to the locations of the main facilities of the hotel. After the luggage arrives, you should help the tour leader put the room number on the luggage and have it sent to the room as soon as possible. If tourists find their rooms dirty and in disorder, or they are having some other problems, you should inform the floor attendant immediately and actively assist him in solving the problem. You should show tourists to the dining hall when they have their first meal in the hotel, and tell the waiters of the restaurant how many people are in the group, who the tour leader is and whether there are any special requirements. You should also tell the tourists when they are to have the meal, and inform them about any special arrangements for Chinese and Western meals and the supply of drinks, etc.

Before a tour group leaves a hotel, you should remind the tourists to settle their bills. If the tour group is leaving the country, you should remind the tourists to have their passports, plane (or train) tickets and customs declaration forms put in their carry-on bags in preparation for going through the Customs. The local guide should tell the tourists when and where to collect luggage, and check the number of pieces of luggage along with the national guide, the tour leader and the bellboy.

After tourists get on the bus, the guide should remind them to check their carry-on bags and see if they have left anything behind. The bus can leave the hotel only after you are sure that everybody is on the bus.

Questions:
1. What are the formalities you usually go through when you register at the reception desk in a hotel?
2. An overseas tour group has arrived in China. On the second day, a tourist wants to exchange his room because the tourist in his room snores loudly and he can't go to sleep at night. What should the guide do then?
3. Before leaving for the scenic spot, a tourist doesn't feel well and he wants to stay in the hotel and have a rest. What should the guide do?
4. The newlyweds in a tour group want to change their room into deluxe suite when they arrive at the hotel, what should the guide do?
5. Introduce the facilities of a hotel.

Tips for Tour Guides

When the tourists arrive at the hotel, the local guide should:
- Accompany and assist the tour leader or the tour guide to make check-in procedures.
- Introduce the main hotel facilities such as restaurants, entertainment venues, hotel shops, foreign currency exchange offices, and so on.
- Lead the tour group for the first meal.
- Announce today or tomorrow's activities.
- Discuss with the team leader about wakeup call time, and request the tour leader to inform the whole group, the local guide shall also notify the hotel desk or floor desk.

Fire emergency:
- The guide should assist the hotel personnel to evacuate the tourists.
- He should warn the tourists not to take elevators or jump off the building at random.
- If the body is on fire, the tourist should roll himself on the floor or use heavy clothing to cover and stop the flame.
- If the tourist must pass through smoke, he should wrap his body in the wet clothes, and crawl close to the group with his mouth and nose covered.
- If one can not escape from the fire when the door is closed, he should wet the clothing and bedding to stop the crack in the door or cool the door by water.
- Then he should wait for rescue and shake colorful clothing to call for rescuers.

Project 4 Itinerary Planning

Learning Objectives:
- be able to discuss the itinerary with the tourists
- be able to negotiate the difference or the change in the itinerary
- be able to recommend some scenic spots to the tour group

Task 1 Warm-Up

1. What should the local guide do if the tourists request to change the itinerary or add new tour items?
2. What should a local guide do when there appears a great difference between the local guide's travel schedule and that of the tourists', national guide's or the tour leader's?
3. What does the local guide do if the tourists' request differs from the itinerary and the reception specifications?

Task 2 Words and Expressions

itinerary	[aɪˈtɪnərəri]	n.	旅行计划,旅程
spacious	[ˈspeɪʃəs]	adj.	宽敞的,广阔的
cozy	[ˈkəʊzi]	adj.	舒适的,惬意的
tentative	[ˈtentətɪv]	adj.	不确定的,暂时的
detail	[ˈdiːteɪl]	n.	细节,琐事,枝节
tight	[taɪt]	adj.	紧的,密集的
brand	[brænd]	n.	烙印,商标,牌子
pagoda	[pəˈgəʊdə]	n.	宝塔
wonton	[ˈwɒnˈtɒn]	n.	馄饨
assemble	[əˈsembl]	v.	集合,收集,装配
miracle	[ˈmɪrəkl]	n.	奇迹
fiddle	[ˈfɪdl]	n.	小提琴
exploration	[ˌekspləˈreɪʃn]	n.	探险,探索
nightfall	[ˈnaɪtfɔːl]	n.	傍晚,黄昏

Venice	[ˈvenɪs]	n.	威尼斯
orient	[ˈɔːrɪənt]	adj.	东方的
knowledgeable	[ˈnɒlɪdʒəbl]	adj.	博学的
arcade	[ɑːˈkeɪd]	n.	拱廊,游乐中心
wharf	[wɔːf]	n.	码头
urban	[ˈɜːbən]	adj.	城市的,都市的
leisure	[ˈleʒə]	n.	闲暇,休闲
bestselling	[ˌbestˈselɪŋ]	adj.	畅销的
highlight	[ˈhaɪlaɪt]	n.	加亮区,精彩部分
advanced	[ədˈvɑːnst]	adj.	先进的,高级的
giant	[ˈdʒaɪənt]	adj.	巨大的
wheel	[wiːl]	n.	方向盘,车轮
theme	[θiːm]	n.	主题,题目,主旋律
splendid	[ˈsplendɪd]	adj.	极好的,辉煌的
reputation	[ˌrepjuˈteɪʃn]	n.	好名声,声誉
Pan-Fried Steamed Bun			生煎馒头
be dedicated to			致力于,献身于
scenic spots			景点
can't wait to do sth.			迫不及待地要做某事

Task 3 Dialogues

Dialogue 1

Scene: Susan knocks at the door of Mr. James White's room in the hotel. She is going to talk with him about the itinerary. (S = Susan, J = James White)

S: Excuse me, may I come in?

J: Who's it?

S: It's Susan. I'd like to discuss the itinerary with you.

J: Come on in.

S: How about this room?

J: It's spacious and cozy. We all like it very much. Sit down, please.

S: Thank you. This is the tentative itinerary I've worked out. Would you please go over the details?

J: Sure. (*Going over the itinerary*)

S: The tour to the Tiger Hill will start at 9 o'clock tomorrow morning and last about one and a half hours.

J: Don't you think one and a half hours is a bit tight? We've heard that there're a lot of scenic spots with many historical stories. And we also expect to have a close look at the pagoda, for which the Tiger Hill is well known.

S: In that case, I'll offer you one more hour.

J: That's great. By the way, What time should we be ready?

S: Please be ready at 8:30. We'll meet outside the hotel entrance at about 8:45. Is that OK?

J: OK, no problem! Here (*pointing to the itinerary*), why don't we try a local flavor restaurant instead of this Pearl Restaurant?

S: I've thought about that. There is a famous brand local flavor restaurant which is near Shantang Street. We could stop there for lunch. Some of the tour members may enjoy walking along the street.

J: I'm sure all the tour members would like that.

S: Absolutely, while walking in Shantang Street, you'll have a chance to enjoy our local snacks, such as Pan-Fried Steamed Bun, Wonton.

J: It sounds good. It makes my mouth water.

S: Is there anything you'd like to have a change?

J: Nothing!

S: OK, have a nice dream then. See you tomorrow.

J: See you.

Dialogue 2

Scene: Susan is talking about the 4-day itinerary with the Whites and their friend Michael.
(S = Susan, J =James White, M =Michael Smith)

S: Excuse me, Mr. White. May I take up some of your time to discuss the next 3-day itinerary in Suzhou?

J: No problem, we are all longing for the exploration of the city.

S: Tomorrow we are going to see the Humble Administrator's Garden, the Master-of-Nets Garden and the Lingering Garden.

J: Nice, the classic gardens are Michael's favorite.

M: Yes, I'm a great fan of Chinese classic gardens. I have been to Jichang Garden in Wuxi, Ge Garden in Yangzhou, Yu Garden in Shanghai, as well as Summer Palace in Beijing.

S: Well, Suzhou gardens will leave you a new image for its elegance.

J: What about the third day?

S: Have you ever heard of Zhou Zhuang?

M: Of course, Zhou Zhuang boasts the reputation of the "Venice of the Orient".

S: You're quite knowledgeable. On the third-day morning, we'll take a bus to Zhou Zhuang and visit the ancient water town of southern China, where you can enjoy street arcade, water gates, wharf and corridor, Shen's House, Double Bridge, Zhang Hall, etc.

J: Shall we have a chance to experience the modern Suzhou?

S: The last day we will visit Suzhou Industrial Park (SIP). Through over 10 years' exploration, SIP has gradually shaped the brand of urban tourism and leisure travel, and fashion is the bestselling highlight.

J: Well, what kind of places will we visit then?

S: First we'll drive to Suzhou Culture and Art Center, where you can experience the most advanced IMAX film. Then we'll have our lunch in Li Gong Di. After lunch, we'll have a happy hour in the Ferris Wheel Theme Park. At night, you can have a walk in the Times. Jinji Lake in SIP appears more splendid and attractive at nightfall. I'm sure that you'll fall in love with SIP.

J: It sounds terrific. I can't help having a sightseeing there.

Task 4 Useful Sentences

1. While walking in Shantang Street, you'll have a chance to enjoy our local snacks, such as Pan-Fried Steamed Bun, Wonton.
2. This is the tentative itinerary I've worked out. Would you please go over the details?
3. Have you got anything special in mind that you would like to see?
4. It might be a good idea to arrange a three-day program.
5. I think we'd better make it 8:30, in case we get caught in the traffic.
6. We have a number of private gardens that are worth a visit.
7. Through over 10 years' exploration, SIP has gradually shaped the brand of urban tourism and leisure travel.
8. Jinji Lake in Suzhou Industrial Park (SIP) appears more splendid and attractive at nightfall.
9. I can't wait to have a sightseeing there.
10. Zhouzhuang boasts the reputation of the "Venice of the Orient".

Task 5 Listening

You will hear five sentences. Listen carefully and put down the whole sentences.

1. _____.
2. _____.
3. _____.
4. _____.
5. _____.

Task 6 Dialogue-Completing

G: _____, everyone.
T: Morning, Xiao Li.
G: Unfortunately, the weather is not going to improve. Our proposed tour of the Summer Palace and Beihai Park is not _____ in this heavy rain today.
T: We'd like to visit _____. Is this possible?
G: No problem! The Pan Market is protected from the weather and _____ its huge range of Chinese craft works and antiques. Bargain hard, everyone.
T: Cool. _____ hours do we have for shopping?
G: _____.
T: Fantastic.
G: OK. Let's go. Happy bargain hunting, everybody!

Task 7 Role-Play

Situation 1: Mr. Smith, a foreign teacher working in Soochow University, intends to have a sightseeing in Suzhou Industrial Park. He comes to you for suggestions.
- to tell him the landmark buildings in SIP
- to ask him what he'd like to see and do
- to work out a brief route and recommend some restaurants and places to visit

Situation 2: A group of American students headed by Professor White arrived in Suzhou during this summer vacation. Li Ming, the national guide of the group, invited Professor White to discuss the travel arrangements for the group.
- to find out what the visitors would like to see in Suzhou
- to make some suggestions about places of interest
- to lead the students who want to visit a university to Soochow University to experience the campus life of Chinese students

Task 8 Translation

Put the following sentences into English.
1. 让我们来讨论一下为期三天的行程计划。
2. 到苏州不到虎丘乃憾事也。
3. 逛山塘街时,你可以尝一下当地的小吃。

4. 我口水直流。

5. 科文中心有着完善的设备。

Put the following passage into Chinese.

The Tiger Hill is said to be the most interesting spot historically in Suzhou. Thirty-four meters above sea level, 630 meters in circumference and some 20 hectares in area, it used to be called the Hill of Emergence from the Sea. It is the burial place of Helv, King of State Wu, who founded the city of Suzhou in 514 BC and made it his capital.

Task 9 Supplementary Reading

Tourism and Travel Tour Guides

The success of travel agencies in the field of tourism lies in the tour guide. In fact, tour guides are part of the tourist product. They often contribute to the tourists' likes or dislikes of the package tour. So it is important to understand what tour guides do and what roles they play in the package tour. A tour guide refers to a person who is officially accredited by the tourism authority and assigned by a travel agency, and who offers guiding, interpretation and other relevant tourist services for tourists. Western tour guides have a variety of terms like local guides, city guides, and step-on guides in the industry. Outside the industry, tour guides are used to describe those who guide people. They include tour managers, docents, and interpreters. In China, tour guides also refer to all those who guide and manage the tour group. But the names for tour guides vary a bit from those in Western countries. There is national guide, local guide, interpreter/ spot guide, and tour manager/ tour escort.

Itinerary

An itinerary is a detailed plan of the tour. Dates and times of arrivals and departures should be very clearly set out.

(1) All flight details included.
- The number and name of the flight
- Flying time
- Airline reference
- The seat class
- Name of the city and terminal airport
- Final report at the airports is clearly stated in time
- Everyday activities arrangement

(2) There will be a check-list of documents required for the trip.
- Airline Ticket
- Valid Passport

- Applicable Visas
- Completed departure card
- Departure tax—prepaid

(3) The Baggage allowance per person will also be noted, e. g. 20 kg.

A 2-Day Itinerary of Suzhou

Day 1—Shanghai → Suzhou (L)

Visits: Garden of the Master of the Nets (Wang Shi Garden), Lingering Garden (Liu Yuan)

In the morning, head for the railway station and take a safe, fast and comfortable train ride to Suzhou. In the afternoon visit the Lingering Garden, then go to the Garden of the Master of Nets and have a class of traditional Chinese horticulture. After that, enjoy a short cruise along the historic Grand Canal.

Day 2—Suzhou → Tongli → Shanghai (B, L)

After enjoying your breakfast set for No. 1 Silk Factory. It is founded in 1926 as a state-owned factory. With this tour, you can get the knowledge of the whole life of a silkworm. After lunch you will be transferred to Tongli by private car. You will be transferred to Shanghai by private car. In the morning your excursion starts from Chongqing to Langzhong through Yulin Highway.

Questions:
1. What issues should be avoided during the guiding process?
2. What information should an itinerary include?
3. Please work out a special tour in Suzhou itinerary (such as leisure tour, business tour, culture tour, farmhouse tour, etc.).
4. If you take a boat tour of Jinji Lake at night, what scenic spots can you appreciate?
5. Why is Suzhou called "the Land of Fish and Rice"?

Tips for Tour Guides

When there appears a great difference between the local guide's travel schedule and that of the tourists':

- Consult with his travel agency about the differences.
- Make appropriate adjustments after the obtaining approval from the travel agency.

When the tourists request to change the itinerary or add new tour items:

- Report it to the travel agency as soon as possible.

- If the change is reasonable and feasible, usually the guide should arrange and make the appropriate adjustments.
- If there are some additional costs, the local guide should make it clear to the tour leader or the tourists and charge the service according to the relevant regulations.
- If it is difficult to satisfy the tourists' need, the local guide should be patient and explain the reason in detail.

When the tourists' request differs from the itinerary and the reception specifications:
- Usually the local guide should decline politely and explain that one part can not fail to carry out the contract.
- If there is some special reason and the tour leader makes the request, the local guide should contact with the travel agency, and make a decision as the case may be.

Project 5 On the Way to the Scenic Spot

Learning Objectives:
- be able to do a good job of along-the-way guiding and introduction
- be able to arrange tour activities of scenic spots
- be able to deliver a presentation of scenic spots

Task 1 Warm-Up

1. On the way to scenic spots, how can the local guide do a good job of along-the-way guiding and introduction?
2. Before the tour, what points of attention should the guides explain to tourists?
3. How can the guide prevent the tourists from being lost in the travelling process?

Task 2 Words and Expressions

classical	[ˈklæsɪkl]	adj.	古典的
architect	[ˈɑːkɪtekt]	n.	建筑师
calligraphy	[kəˈlɪgrəfi]	n.	书法
craftwork	[ˈkrɑːftwɜːk]	n.	工艺（品）
display	[dɪˈspleɪ]	n.	显示，陈列
mention	[ˈmenʃn]	vt.	提到
variety	[vəˈraɪəti]	n.	多样，种类
pastry	[ˈpeɪstri]	n.	面粉糕饼
confection	[kənˈfekʃn]	n.	甜食，糖果
dedicate	[ˈdedɪkeɪt]	vt.	致力于
miracle	[ˈmɪrəkl]	n.	奇迹
absolutely	[ˈæbsəluːtli]	adv.	绝对地
personal	[ˈpɜːsənl]	adj.	私人的
assemble	[əˈsembl]	v.	集合
temple	[ˈtempl]	n.	庙宇
sticky rice			糯米

The Humble Administrator's Garden	拙政园
time-honored brand	老字号
downtown business district	城市商业区
The Dragon Boat Festival	端午节
fit as a fiddle	非常健康
The Lingering Garden	留园
tourist attraction	旅游胜地

Task 3　Dialogues

Dialogue 1

Scene: In the parking lot, Susan helps the tourists get on the coach. They are starting …
(S = Susan, J = James White, E = Emily, M = Michael, K = Kate)

S: (*After recounting the number of the tourists*) Hello, friends, I will reconfirm the itinerary for today. Firstly we'll go to the Humble Administrator's Garden, then, move on to Suzhou Museum. We'll have lunch at 12:00 in Da Hong Yun Restaurant. After lunch, you'll have free time in the Guanqian Street. You can do some shopping there; along the street you'll find a lot of Suzhou's time-honored brand shops, such as Huang Tian Yuan, Ye Shou He, Cai Zhi Zhai. The dinnertime is 6:00 in the evening, at De Yue Lou Restaurant. Then we'll go back to the hotel. Now, we're leaving for the Humble Administrator's Garden.

J: I've heard the Humble Administrator's Garden is one of the four classical gardens in China.

S: Yes, it's also the largest of the four famous classical gardens in Suzhou.

M: Is the Suzhou Museum designed by world-famous architect Ieoh Ming Pei?

S: Yes. This museum draws a lot of people from home and abroad every year.

E: What are collected in the museum?

S: China, jade, painting, calligraphy, craftwork, silk, and so on.

M: We'll feast our eyes on its display.

J: Look, the street is very busy. Is it Guanqian Street?

S: Yes, we'll have lunch in this street. It is the downtown business district of Suzhou.

E: Susan, you mentioned that there were many time-honored brand shops in this Street. I wonder what kind of things they are famous for.

S: Huang Tian Yuan is noted for its variety of pastries made from sticky rice. If you want to buy some local confections, Cai Zhi Zhai is without doubt the best place to go. Wu Fang Zhai is famous for its Zongzi. Do you know what Zongzi is?

K: I know. My classmate Rose, who comes from China, once told me that Chinese always eat Zongzi on Dragon Boat Festival.

S: Quite right. We eat Zongzi to memorialize great poet Qu Yuan.

M: Look, is that the garden we'll visit?

S: Yes, here we are, the Humble Administrator's Garden.

Dialogue 2

S: Good morning, everyone! Can all of you hear me?

J: Yes, very clearly.

S: How are you doing today?

J: We are fit as a fiddle! Thank you!

S: So are you ready for touring?

J: Yes, of course.

S: Let's get to business. First of all, let me tell you the itinerary today. We'll start today's trip with a visit to the Tiger Hill. It is always said that it is a great pity if visit Suzhou without the Tiger Hill. Now we're heading for it.

J: How long will the bus trip take to get there?

S: About a quarter. The tour will start at 9 o'clock and will last two hours. Then we'll have a lunch nearby. This afternoon is dedicated to the Lingering Garden. And then in the evening we'll have a chance to enjoy Suzhou Pingtan in a famous tea house in our schedule. I hope all of you have a wonderful trip today.

J: Susan, what is the name of this road? It looks very busy.

S: It's Tongjing Road. Along this road, there exist a lot of tourist attractions of Suzhou. Xiyuan temple, the Lingering Garden, etc. This is a famous restaurant named Little De Yue Lou, and we'll have today's dinner here.

J: It must be a great miracle!

S: Absolutely!

(*A quarter later.*) OK, here we are. It's time to get off the bus. Before you go, please take care of your personal belongings.

Attention, please! Now, we're going to visit the Tiger Hill. Please do remember that we will assemble at the main gate at 11:30. Thank you.

J: What's the plate number of the bus?

S: It's K4865. Have a nice trip!

Task 4   Useful Sentences

1. You can do some shopping there; along the street you'll find a lot of Suzhou's time-honored brand shops.

2. It's also the largest of the four famous classical gardens in Suzhou.

3. This museum draws a lot of people from home and abroad every year.

4. Huang Tian Yuan is noted for its variety of pastries made from sticky rice.
5. It is the downtown business district of Suzhou.
6. We are fit as a fiddle!
7. Now we're heading for it.
8. We'll have a chance to enjoy Suzhou Pingtan in a famous tea house in our schedule.
9. Please take care of your personal belongings.
10. Do remember that we will assemble at the main gate at 10:30.

Task 5 Listening

You will hear five sentences. Listen carefully and put down the whole sentences.

1. _____.
2. _____.
3. _____.
4. _____.
5. _____.

Task 6 Dialogue-Completing

(G = Guide, T_1 = 1st tourist, T_2 = 2nd tourist)

G: _____.
T_1: Wonderful! We have been waiting for it so long.
T_2: What's the length of the Shan Tang Street?
G: About 3,600 meters. We always call it "_____".
T_1: The buildings here are quite different from modern architecture.
G: Yes, Shan Tang Street has _____, about 1,100 years. It fully appears as a street with historic characteristics and typical Suzhou outlook.
T_2: It looks like a good place for _____.
G: Absolutely. While wandering on the street, you could view many old temples, halls, etc. and taste the traditional Suzhou food.

Task 7 Role-Play

Situation 1: You are a local guide with a tour group of 20. Now you are on the way to Zhou Zhuang.

The local guide:
- to give a brief introduction of Zhou Zhuang
- to introduce views in sight (Suzhou SIP): the Modern Avenue; the Times Plaza; Suzhou Crowne Plaza, the Jinji Lake
- to mention the tourist attractions in the vicinity

Tourists:
- to ask the location of Zhou Zhuang
- to ask name of the lake (Jinji Lake)
- to ask the specialties of Zhou Zhuang

Situation 2: Mr. Smith is going to visit the Panmen Gate. It is one of the eight gates of Suzhou built by Wu Zixu, the general of the Wu State of Warring States Period (403 −222 B.C.). Then he will visit No. 1 Silk Factory. The factory tour will show how the silk is processed from the silk worm to the final woven cloth. Susan is on the coach and will explain something before getting to the destination.

Task 8 Translation

Put the following sentences into English.
1. 沧浪亭以它宁静的环境和简约的建筑风格而闻名。
2. 苏州是我国最古老的名城之一。
3. 苏州不愧为人间天堂啊!
4. 留园以它的镂空窗而闻名。
5. 苏州园林甲天下。

Put the following passage into Chinese.

  For the history and culture enthusiast we invite you to start with our classic gardens, great canals, and ancient city gates to discover the legends of Suzhou and its people. Perhaps you're an arts and crafts enthusiast? In Suzhou take the time to visit the museums and handicraft institutes where you will find the great Suzhou Embroidery, skillful carving works, and Chinese paintings. Or, you could pay a visit to the silk factories to see how the silk is produced. If you're an outgoing person, Suzhou also has plenty of places for you, such as restaurants, bars, clubs, shopping districts, amusement parks, and golf courses.

(http://www.classicsuzhou.com/PageItem/Default.aspx? PageID =1)

Task 9 Supplementary Reading

Suzhou Museum by I.M. Pei

I visited Suzhou Museum on Dec 3. The museum is designed by I. M. Pei, and we had the honor to attend a behind the scene tour conducted by Bobbie Pei. Bobbie was so kind to talk about the design philosophy of his uncle. That tour was one of the highlight of the trip.

Symmetry is the key. Symmetry is one of the very key elements of the Chinese architecture. It is also the symbolic sign of I. M. Pei's design.

The interesting thing is, there are two wings of the museum. The intention of the designer is to ask people turn left and see the west wing first and then leave the museum from the east wing. Pei didn't put a large sign at the entrance "Turn left please". He made the west wing a little big longer (seems more interesting), and had a water fall at the end of the hall way, so the sounds of water can be very attractive to visitors. At least, I turned left without a thought. That is the beauty of good design. It is the same principle in usability: if you need a label to explain something, the design may be already failed.

Architects always face challenges. Just as triangle site Pei faced in the design of National Gallery East Wing in Washing D. C. , this big white existing wall at the entrance is not easy to handle. Pei used stone to form a scene according to painting in Song Dynasty.

This is a great museum. The museum itself is a piece of art.

Suzhou is beautiful. The icon color gray and white made the gardens so unique. However, this town started 2,500 years ago, and many of the architectures were built 300 years ago.

(http://home. wangjianshuo. com/archives/20071206_suzhou_museum_by_im_pei. htm)

> Questions:
> 1. Try to make a brief introduction of Suzhou Museum.
> 2. Introduce some famous buildings in Suzhou.
> 3. What are the world heritages of Suzhou?
> 4. On the way back, what should the tour guide do in general?
> 5. What measures should be taken to prevent the visitors from getting ill in travelling?

Tips for Tour Guides

Making introduction on the way to scenic spots:
- Reaffirm activities, name of scenic spots, weather conditions, report major news at home and abroad.

- Seize the opportunity to introduce the scenery along the way, answer inquiries from tourists.
- Introduce briefly the general situation of the scenic spots before arrival so as to arouse tourists' interest.
- If the journey takes too much time, the guide can warm up atmosphere by various forms of entertainment.

Points of attention explained by the guide to tourists before the tour, on the bus or in front of scenic sketch map:
- The tour route, time needed, time and place of gathering.
- Coach models, colors, signs, wagon number and parking locations.
- The points of attention during the sightseeing tours.

Project 6　Dining in Suzhou

Learning Objectives：
- be able to reasonably arrange the first meal for the tour group
- be able to provide standard dining service for the tourists
- be able to solve the problems during the dining service

Task 1　Warm-Up

1. How can the local guide lead the tourists to enjoy the first meal?
2. What does a guide do when a tourist prefers to have meals alone?
3. What does the guide do if the tourist tries to taste flavor at his own expense?

Task 2　Words and Expressions

reservation	[ˌrezəˈveɪʃn]	n.	预订
confirm	[kənˈfɜːm]	v.	确定
flavor	[ˈfleɪvə]	n.	风味
chopsticks	[ˈtʃɒpstɪks]	n.	筷子
finger	[ˈfɪŋgə]	n.	手指
thumb	[θʌm]	n.	拇指
tip	[tɪp]	n.	尖端，顶端
sour	[ˈsaʊə]	adj.	酸的
vivid	[ˈvɪvɪd]	adj.	栩栩如生的
crackle	[ˈkrækl]	v.	发噼啪声
aroma	[əˈrəʊmə]	n.	浓香，香气
buffet	[ˈbʊfeɪ]	n.	自助餐
decorate	[ˈdekəreɪt]	v.	装饰，布置
array	[əˈreɪ]	n.	排
compliment	[ˈkɒmplɪmənt]	n.	称赞
congee	[ˈkɒndʒiː]	n.	粥
pickle	[ˈpɪkl]	n.	腌汁，泡菜

croissant	[krəˈsɑːnt]	n.	羊角面包
toast	[təʊst]	n.	吐司,烤面包
column	[ˈkɒləm]	n.	圆柱
chill	[tʃɪl]	v.	(使)变冷
soybean	[ˈsɔɪbiːn]	n.	大豆
diner	[ˈdaɪnə]	n.	用餐者
sausage	[ˈsɔːsɪdʒ]	n.	香肠,腊肠
bacon	[ˈbeɪkən]	n.	培根
chafing dish			火锅
in charge of			负责
bird's-eye view			鸟瞰
Mandarin Fish Shaped as Squirrel			松鼠鳜鱼
White Shrimps			白虾
Whitebait Fish Soup			银鱼羹
Stir-Fried Eels			响油鳝糊
index finger			食指
cater to			迎合

Task 3 Dialogues

Dialogue 1

Scene: Susan and the tour group led by Mr. White are now in the dining hall. They will have their first meal in the Pearl Hall. (S = Susan, J = James White, T = Tom, W = Waiter)

S: We have a table reservation at 7:30, and would like to confirm it, please.
W: May I have your name, please?
S: Susan. I'm in charge of an American group.
W: There are 6 of you.
S: Right.
W: This way, please.
    Here we are. Are you satisfied with the table by the window?
J: We like it very much. I can have a bird's-eye view of Suzhou.
T: Dad, what shall we eat today?
S: Tom, today, you'll try Suzhou local flavor.
W: Mandarin Fish Shaped as Squirrel, Quick-boiled White Shrimps and Whitebait Fish Soup, Stir-Fried Eels.
J: Susan, would you like to teach Tom how to use chopsticks?

S: Sure. Tom, put this chopstick between your middle and ring fingers. Put the other chopstick between your middle and index fingers, and hold it with your thumb. Only this chopstick is moved when you pick up food. Open the tips of the chopsticks and try to pick up food with them. Yes, that's done, clever boy!

T: Dad, Susan, you see, I got the fish. Oh, it's delicious, a bit sweet and a bit sour. Why do you call this fish a squirrel?

S: Because after frying the fish is shaped as a squirrel in the forest, the chef add the tomato sauces on it, which makes a sound like squirrel.

J: What a vivid name!

T: Excuse me, the dish of the eels, does it have a Chinese name?

S: Of course, we call it Xiang You Shan Hu. It is so named as it crackles when the hot oil is poured onto eels. When Xiang You Shan Hu is taken on the table, you can still hear it crackles and smell the mouthwatering aroma.

T: Quite interesting.

(*An hour later*)

J: Susan, we are full now. Shall we settle the bill?

S: OK. Waiter, the bill, please.

Dialogue 2

Scene: On the second day morning, Susan and her group are having a buffet breakfast in the cafe. (S =Susan, E =Emily, K =Kate, W =waiter)

W: Good morning, sir and madam. A table for 6?

E: Yes.

W: I'll show you to your table. Come this way, please. We serve buffet here. Our buffet price is 50 yuan for each person.

E: We like it.

W: Please help yourselves to the buffet.

S: Emily, look at the buffet table. It's well decorated and well organized.

K: And there is an array of fancy dishes.

W: Thank you for your compliments. The buffet is an international one which caters to the taste of diners both from home and abroad. Allow me to introduce our buffet to you here. In the middle is a set of chafing dishes which include noodle, congee, smoked fish, bacon, ham, sausage and pancakes. Near the window are cold dishes, that is, salad, pickles, fresh vegetables and so on. Next to the window is the bread table including croissant, Danish bread, French toast and rolls. Around the column are chilled and hot drinks such as hot and cold milk, coffee, black tea, chilled juices and soybean milk.

E: Thank you. We'll be sure to have a good breakfast here.

W: I hope you will.

Task 4 Useful Sentences

1. I'm in charge of an American group.
2. I can have a bird's-eye view of Suzhou.
3. It is so named as it crackles when the hot oil is poured onto eels.
4. Shall we settle the bill?
5. When Xiang You Shan Hu is taken on the table, you can still hear it crackles and smell the mouthwatering aroma.
6. Please help yourselves to the buffet.
7. The buffet is an international one which caters to the taste of diners both from home and abroad.
8. I'm sorry. There isn't any table right now. There will be a wait of about 20 minutes.
9. May I suggest the chef's Sichuan-style sour soup?
10. They accept American Express, MasterCard, Visa, and Diner's Club.

Task 5 Listening

You will hear five sentences. Listen carefully and put down the whole sentences.

1. _____.
2. _____.
3. _____.
4. _____.
5. _____.

Task 6 Dialogue-Completing

(W = Waiter, G = Guest)

W: Good evening, sir. Can I help you?
G: I'd like to _____, but I _____ about Chinese food. Can you give me some suggestions?
W: Well, there are different _____.
G: Can you give me _____?
W: Four styles of food are especially known throughout China. They are Shandong cuisine,

Cantonese cuisine, Sichuan cuisine, and Huaiyang cuisine.
G: What is the Cantonese cuisine _____?
W: It is _____.
G: How about Shandong cuisine?
W: It's _____.
G: And what about the Huaiyang cuisine?
W: It's _____.
G: The last one, Sichuan cuisine is?
W: Sichuan dishes are _____.
G: Oh, really. I like hot food. _____?
W: The famous Sichuan dishes are Mapo bean curd and shredded meat in chili sauce.
G: I'll _____.

 Task 7　Role-Play

Situation 1: There are three Moslems in the group and another member who has high blood pressure and must have no salt in his diet. It is already five o'clock and the group is scheduled to have dinner at the Beijing Duck Restaurant.

Tour guide:
- To reserve a table of 10.
- To tell the clerk who is in charge of the reservation that there are Moslems, who can't eat pork.
- To tell the consumption standard for each person.
- To ask for recommendation.

Hotel clerk:
- To greet the guide.
- To ask for requirements of the reservation.
- To recommend some dishes.
- To confirm the dishes.

Situation 2: Most of the tour members don't know how to use chopsticks. You come over to demonstrate and tell them the history of Chinese chopsticks.

Task 8   Translation

Put the following sentences into English.
1. 你觉得这里的饭菜如何？
2. 中国菜可分为四大菜系，分别是山东菜、广东菜、四川菜和淮扬菜。
3. 苏州小吃值得一尝。
4. 中餐和西餐进餐时最为不同的是中餐使用筷子。
5. 这里的自助餐迎合了国内外宾客的需求。

Task 9   Supplementary Reading

Dining in China

China has a long history of cuisine and culinary arts. Her dishes enjoy world popularity. Many tourists visiting China make special requests to dine in the local restaurants purely for the enjoyment of specialty dishes. Travel agencies usually arrange to include local delicacies once or twice in the overall itinerary of most package tours.

In recent years, more and more independent tourists have come to China. These tourists often ask the travel agency only to arrange transportation, accommodations and tour guides, while they would rather choose their own dining places. They do so because they want to try the local flavors and satisfy their curiosity about the delicacies, also because the local snacks are cheaper. Therefore, tour guides should be well prepared to take the initiative and willingly introduce the special culinary characteristics, including the major cuisines, and renowned dishes.

When dining with tourists at the same table, tour guides should be polite and respect their guests. They should never do anything against their guests' will, such as forcing drink or food on them. When invited to a banquet given by tourists, or when trying local flavors on a "Go Dutch" basis, tour guides should not take the initiative to place servings of food on their guests' plates, to persuade them to drink or to eat, or propose toasts. They should try to avoid usurping the host's role. Remember, never outshine the host.

Suzhou Snacks

Suzhou snacks are also worth trying since they are no less famous than Suzhou Cuisine. At present, there are a number of featured old-brand restaurants and cakes and pastries shops in Suzhou City. Just like the authentic Suzhou dishes, pastries and confectionery in Suzhou are also eaten according to season. Scones with sweet fermented rice in spring and moon cakes stuffed with fresh meat in autumn will certainly satisfy your appetite.

Huang Tian Yuan is noted for its variety of pastries made from sticky rice. Address: No. 86, Guanqian Street, Pingjiang District, Suzhou City. Average cost: CNY10-CNY20 per person.

If you want to buy some local confections, Cai Zhi Zhai is without doubt the best place to go. Developing from a roadside booth into a century-old establishment, it serves consumers with a variety of good quality products. Address: No. 91, Guanqian Street, Suzhou City. Opening hours: 08:30-21:00 from Monday to Thursday, 08:30-22:00 on Friday, Saturday and Sunday.

Nearby Cai Zhi Zhai, Ye Shou He is also noted for its various Suzhou pastries. Recommendation: Wa Di Su (crisp cake in the shape of sole of socks), Suanmei Tang (plum juice), Doufu Gan (dried bean curd). Address: No. 69, Guanqian Street, Pingjiang District, Suzhou City. Average cost: CNY20-CNY50.

Lu Gao Jian Recommendation: Jiangrou (braised pork with soy sauce), Jiangya (duck seasoned with soy sauce), Wuxiang Niurou (spiced beef). Address: No. 8, Guanqian Street, Pingjiang District, Suzhou City. Average cost: CNY20-CNY30 per person.

Xi Sheng Yuan Recommendation: Wonton, Xiao Long Bao (small cage package). Address: No. 43, Fenghuang Jie, Canglang District, Suzhou City. Average cost: CNY10-CNY20 per person.

Wu Fang Zhai Recommendation: Zongzi (glutinous rice dumpling). Address: No. 1, Taijian Nong, Pingjiang District, Suzhou City. Average cost: CNY20-CNY30.

Yaba Shengjian Recommendation: Yaba Shengjian (pan-fried bun), Wonton. Address: Donghuan Lu, Suzhou Industrial Park, Suzhou City. Average cost: CNY10 per person.

Yi Pin Xiang This is one of the old brand restaurants in Suzhou city, noting for its various kinds of steamed stuffed bun and the other authentic Suzhou snacks. Its chain branches can be found easily in Suzhou. Average cost: CNY5-CNY20 per person.

Famous Restaurants in Suzhou

Maybe, autumn is the time most yearned for by the population, because it is time to enjoy the delicious steamed crabs and nutritious Bafei Soup (barbel soup). As well as these famous dishes, Songshu Guiyu (mandarin fish, stewed and fried), which was praised by Emperor Qianlong of the Qing Dynasty, is considered to be the ultimate Suzhou dish, and it is highly recommended that you try it during your visit. Following are two recommended century-old establishments where you will be able to sample these famous dishes:

De Yue Lou Resulting from four hundred years of culinary experience, De Yue Lou serves dozens of famous and authentic dishes to visitors both from home and abroad. Address: There are two restaurants located on Taijian Nong. Opening hours: 11 am-2 pm and 5 pm-9 pm.

Pine and Crane Restaurant Having more than 200 years' history, good and authentic Suzhou cuisine here is noted world wide. The Songshu Guiyu cooked here is highly recommended. Address: No. 141, Guanqian Jie. Opening hours: 11 am-1:30 pm and 5 pm-8:30 pm.

Additionally, there are a number of other restaurants where authentic Suzhou cuisine is cooked, too. Shijia Restaurant, which has more than 200 years' history, is especially famous for its Bafei Soup.

(www. busisi. com)

Questions:
1. Tell the differences in dining between package tours and independent tourists.
2. Briefly introduce the food in Suzhou.
3. The lunch for an overseas tour was Chinese food, but the tour asks for changing into Western food half an hour before the meal. What should the guide do then?
4. A contradiction occurred between the tourists in a tour group, and the tourists want to eat separately. In that case, two tables have to be divided into four tables. What should the guide do then?
5. After lunch, the symptoms of food poisoning and diarrhea occur among half of the tourists in one tour group. What should the guide do then?

Tips for Tour Guides

Issues cared by guides, as for the food and beverage services:
- Guests should be arranged to have meals at fixed restaurants.
- During meal period, guides should ask their guests of their food requirements and introduce the features of the meals, supervise and see whether the restaurants provide services consistent with the food standard.
- After meals, the local guide should truthfully fill out a final settlement according to the actual number of diners, the standard and the number of drinks consumed.
- If the guide finds the restaurants do not fulfill the dinner contract, he should timely report to the relevant authorities.

When the tourists ask for changing food:
- Sometimes the tourists may ask for changing food, such as change Chinese dishes into Western dishes or light meal into flavor meal.
- If the tour group requests to change the food just 3 hours ahead of mealtime, the guide should consult with the restaurant and deal with it upon relevant rules.
- If the tour group requests to change the food just before mealtime, the guide should graciously decline the request and give explanations. But if the tourist insists on changing the food, the guide may suggest the tourist order and pay the dishes himself.
- If the tourist requires for more dishes or drinks, he should pay himself.

Project 7　Farewell

> **Learning Objectives:**
> - be able to deliver a farewell speech properly
> - be able to go through standard departure procedure
> - be able to deal with special request from tourists or issues during the seeing off

Task 1　Warm-Up

1. On the way to the railway station, airport or the wharf, the tour group encounters a traffic jam. What should the guide do?
2. Before leaving the country, a tourist requests to extend his travel time, what should the guide do?
3. What information shall a farewell speech include?

Task 2　Words and Expressions

board	[bɔːd]	v.	登(飞机、车、船等)
conclude	[kənˈkluːd]	v.	结束
luggage	[ˈlʌɡɪdʒ]	n.	行李
opportunity	[ˌɒpəˈtjuːnəti]	n.	机会
construction	[kənˈstrʌkʃən]	n.	建设
express	[ɪkˈspres]	v.	表达
fee	[fiː]	n.	费用
security	[sɪˈkjʊərəti]	n.	安全
communication	[kəˌmjuːnɪˈkeɪʃn]	n.	沟通
personnel	[ˌpɜːsəˈnel]	n.	职员
merely	[ˈmɪəli]	adv.	仅仅，只不过
receipt	[rɪˈsiːt]	n.	收据
evaluation	[ɪˌvæljuˈeɪʃn]	n.	估价，评价
farewell	[ˈfɛəˈwel]	n.	告别
comment	[ˈkɒment]	n.	评论

Task 3 Dialogues

Dialogue 1

Scene: The Whites are leaving for home; Susan is seeing them off at the airport. (J = James White, S = Susan, the local guide)

S: Here we are at the airport. Is everything in order now?

J: Yes. When will the plane take off?

S: At ten. Would you please wait for me for a few seconds? I am going to get the boarding passes and luggage claim cards for you!

J: OK, take your time.

(*Susan comes back.*)

S: Thank you for waiting. Here are boarding passes and luggage claim cards. Please check them. And take care of your suitcases.

J: Thank you very much. It's so considerate of you. During our trip in the past four days, you've shown great concern for us in every aspect.

S: It's my pleasure. Hope you will come to China again if possible. You will have a better understanding of China.

J: It's a pity we haven't enough time for many other places. I will come if there is another opportunity.

S: Welcome to China. You're always welcome.

J: Fantastic. Keep in touch.

S: I think so, too. It's time for boarding. Shall we go for the security-check now?

J: OK. Let's go.

S: Here we are. These are the airport security personnel.

J: Yes, here you are.

S: Now please get your plane ticket, group visa and boarding pass ready.

J: Thank you for your help.

S: It's my pleasure. Have a wonderful journey home.

Dialogue 2

Scene: The Whites' tour of Suzhou is drawing to a close, they are on the way to the airport, and Susan is giving a farewell speech on the way.

Farewell Speech (On the Way to the Airport)

Ladies and gentlemen,

Now that you have concluded your tour of Suzhou, you'll be leaving for Shanghai. When we get to the airport, I will be busy taking care of your luggage, your boarding passes, and will help you with any last minute problems. If the plane takes off on time, we will have little time to say goodbye So, let me take this opportunity to express my hearty thanks for your cooperation.

It is my great pleasure to have had the opportunity to work as your guide. What I learned from our communication is not merely your culture, but also your way of looking at things. When you cooperate with me and help each other in the tour group, I am deeply touched.

Here are some evaluation forms, postage-paid. Please fill them out and drop them in the mailbox before you board the plane. We hope you will leave with us your comments, as well as your friendship.

Finally, let me wish you all a pleasant journey and an enjoyable stay in Suzhou.

Thank you!

Task 4 Useful Sentences

1. I am going to get the boarding passes and luggage claim cards for you.
2. Please produce your receipt for the airport construction fee.
3. Let me take this opportunity to express my hearty thanks for your cooperation.
4. When you cooperate with me and help each other in the tour group, I am deeply touched.
5. Here are some evaluation forms, postage-paid.
6. Finally, let me wish you all a pleasant journey and an enjoyable stay in Suzhou.
7. I would like to tell you that it has been a great pleasure for me to spend the last few days as your guide.
8. Your trip to Suzhou is drawing to a close.
9. At this time, I would like to say a few words on behalf of Suzhou CITS.
10. I would like to welcome you back, sometime in the future, for return visits.
11. Nothing is more delightful than to meet friends from afar.

Task 5 Listening

You will hear five sentences. Listen carefully and put down the whole sentences.

1. _____.
2. _____.
3. _____.
4. _____.
5. _____.

Task 6   Dialogue-Completing

(G = Guide, T = Tourist)

G: Is everything in order now?
T: Yes, _____?
G: At eleven thirty. There is still half an hour to go. _____.
T: Mr. Hu, during our trip in the past 3 days, you've helped us a lot. I really don't know how to express my gratitude.
G: _____.
T: Before I came here, I only had an understanding of China from books and papers, television and films. Now I've seen China with my own eyes.
G: _____.
T: It's a pity we haven't got enough time for many other places.
G: _____. You're always welcome.
T: Wonderful. I hope we'll keep in touch.
G: _____.
T: Goodbye, Mr. Hu. Thank you very much.
G: _____!

Task 7   Role-Play

Situation 1: Zhang Lan is the local guide of a tour group. She is saying goodbye to an American tour group at the airport. Mr. David is the tourist.

Zhang Lan:
- Asks to gather the baggage.
- Helps check in.
- Reminds to put the passport, credit card and travelers check in the suitcase so as to go through the security check.
- Tells that the airport tax is included in the air ticket.
- Expresses great honor to serve Mr. David.
- Hopes that Mr. David enjoys his trip home.
- Welcomes him to China again.

Mr. David:
- Thanks to accompany to the airport.
- Asks about the airport tax.
- Thanks for all having been done for him.
- Appreciates every minute of his stay here.

♦ Wishes everything goes well.

Situation 2: A Canadian tour is now on the way to the airport. The tour guide is bidding farewell to her guests. They all feel regretful at parting because they all had a memorable experience.

Task 8   Translation

Put the follwing sentences into English.
1. 请照管好您的机票。
2. 这是您的行李牌和登机牌,上飞机时您需要出示它们。
3. 这是意见征询表,麻烦您填一下。
4. 我们要提前一小时到达机场,这样我们才有充足时间办理各种手续。
5. 希望我们再见面。

Task 9   Supplementary Reading

Farewell

Bidding farewell to guests marks the end of a tour guide's service. Wherever it is arranged to be, it is of equal importance to the greeting and should be conducted with sincerity. If anything undesirable happens at the last minute, it may ruin the entire experience of a tour. Therefore, a qualified tour guide should be thoughtful and enthusiastic throughout his service and try to make the farewell impressive and everlasting.

A farewell speech, formal or informal, is often necessary. It may be delivered at the dinner table, or at other places such as the airport, seaport, railway station, etc. The contents of the speech depend very often on the special features of a specific group, but the speech is usually flooded with beautiful memories and good wishes.

There might be some inadequacies in the service, and it is always wise to make apologies for the service and to invite criticism for improvements. Evaluation forms should be given out before your guests' departure.

A Formal Farewell Speech

Respected president of the Sino-American Friendship Association, distinguished guests:

Time has gone by quickly and your trip to China is drawing to a close. Tomorrow morning you will be leaving for home. At this time, I would like to say a few words on behalf of China International Travel Service.

First, we want to thank you for coming. The duration of your stay in our country has been about two weeks. This is not long of course, but it is long enough for us to have a better understanding of our two countries. While your delegation has been here, you have met with some of our government leaders as well as some ordinary people; visited some of our largest cities, as well as some of our most beautiful landscapes. Some of you have exchanged views with your Chinese counterparts. All this is certainly beneficial to further economic development and business cooperation between our two countries.

Next, we want to express our sincere appreciation for your friendship. While you are in China, all of the delegation members have showed great patience, cooperation and understanding, which have made our job much easier.

Lastly, we would like to welcome you back, sometime in the future, for return visits. Nothing is more delightful than to meet friends from afar. This is only the beginning of our friendship. We believe that it will continue to grow in the future.

"Parting is such sweet sorrow", but we all have to accept it.

Upon your arrival in the States, please send our best regards to your family members, your relatives, your friends, and your colleagues.

Let's remember these words well:

Make new friends,

But keep the old,

One is silver,

And the other gold.

Now I propose a toast:

To the friendship between the peoples of our two countries;

To this successful visit of the delegation to China.

Cheers!

An Informal Farewell Speech

Ladies and gentlemen,

I would like to tell you that it has been a great pleasure for me to spend the last few days as your guide. I have had the opportunity to meet and get to know you, and we have spent a great deal of time together. I hope you have enjoyed these days as much as I have. We have tried to make your stay here in Suzhou as pleasant and enjoyable as possible. We sincerely hope that you have enjoyed being here and that one day in the future you will return to visit us again. If there is ever anything we can do to make this possible, please feel free to call on us. We look forward to seeing you all again soon.

I wish to thank you all for your cooperation and support you have given us in the past several days. You have kept good time on all occasions, which made things easier for us.

Several days ago, we met as strangers; today, we bid farewell to each other as friends. I hope you'll take back happy memories of your trip to Suzhou and welcome you back sometime in the future.

Once again, thank your for your cooperation and support.

Bon voyage!

Questions:
1. What are the key points you should mention in a farewell speech?
2. Please compare the different styles of farewell speech.
3. Try to make a farewell speech.
4. What should be done when the local guides are going through departure procedure?
5. If the tourists blame all the difficulties and trouble on the guide, what should the guide do?

Tips for Tour Guides

A farewell speech should:
- Review the whole tour activities, and express thanks for tourists' cooperation.
- Express feelings of friendship and farewell.
- Sincerely ask the tourists for suggestions about the reception work.
- If tour activities are not smooth or travel services are less than satisfactory, the guides can take this opportunity to apologize once again to tourists and express good wishes.

On the way to the railway station, airport or the wharf, when the tour group encounters a traffic jam:
- It depends on the time.
- If the traffic jam can not be cleared in a short time, the guide should make a detour round it so as to arrive at the station, airport or the wharf on time.
- If the tour group is caught in the traffic jam, the guide should ask for help from the traffic police.
- If possible, the guide should report the traffic jam to the travel agency and ask for instructions.

Module II Suzhou Culture

Project 1 Wu Culture

Learning Objectives:
- be able to deliver a presentation of Suzhou City
- be able to explain the essence of Wu Culture
- be able to introduce some famous people of Suzhou

Task 1 Warm-Up

1. Can you say something about Wu Culture?
2. Do you know I. M. Pei?

Task 2 Words and Expressions

inscribed	[ɪnˈskraɪbd]	adj.	印刻的
architecture	[ˈɑːkɪtektʃə]	n.	建筑,建筑物
stele	[ˈstiːli]	n.	石柱,石碑
steel	[stiːl]	n.	钢铁
engrave	[ɪnˈgreɪv]	vt.	雕刻
pyramid	[ˈpɪrəmɪd]	n.	金字塔
vying	[ˈvaɪɪŋ]	adj.	竞争的
bead	[biːd]	n.	汗珠,露珠
controversy	[ˈkɒntrəvɜːsi]	n.	争论,辩论
inscribe	[ɪnˈskraɪb]	vt.	刻,雕刻
fragrant	[ˈfreɪgrənt]	adj.	芳香的

bluestone	[ˈbluːstəʊn]	n.	硬黏土
skyscraper	[ˈskaɪskreɪpə]	n.	摩天楼
reign	[reɪn]	n.	统治,支配
numerous	[ˈnjuːmərəs]	adj.	许多的
depict	[dɪˈpɪkt]	vt.	描绘,描写
prestigious	[preˈstɪdʒɪəs]	adj.	有名望的
storehouse	[ˈstɔːhaʊs]	n.	仓库
residence	[ˈrezɪdəns]	n.	居住,住宅
descendant	[dɪˈsendənt]	n.	子孙
extant	[ekˈstænt]	adj.	现在的,尚存的
ideal	[aɪˈdɪəl]	adj.	完美的
precious	[ˈpreʃəs]	adj.	宝贵的,珍贵的
decline	[dɪˈklaɪn]	vi.	下降,衰退
miracle	[ˈmɪrəkəl]	n.	奇迹
internal	[ɪnˈtɜːnəl]	adj.	内部的
foundation	[faʊnˈdeɪʃn]	n.	基础,基金
struggle	[ˈstrʌgl]	n.	奋斗,斗争
successive	[səkˈsesɪv]	adj.	连续的,依次的
fierce	[fɪəs]	adj.	凶猛的
reconstruction	[ˌriːkənˈstrʌkʃn]	n.	重建,复原
disgust	[dɪsˈgʌst]	vt.	厌恶,憎恶
chessboard	[ˈtʃesbɔːd]	n.	国际象棋棋盘
ambition	[æmˈbɪʃn]	n.	雄心,抱负
perspective	[pəˈspektɪv]	n.	展望,远景
hermit	[ˈhɜːmɪt]	n.	隐士
conventional	[kənˈvenʃənl]	adj.	普通的,惯例的
military	[ˈmɪlɪtəri]	adj.	军事的
dialect	[ˈdaɪəlekt]	n.	方言
strategist	[ˈstrætɪdʒɪst]	n.	战略家
architect	[ˈɑːkɪtekt]	n.	建筑师
retreat	[rɪˈtriːt]	n.	隐退
native	[ˈneɪtɪv]	adj.	天生的,本土的
Pritzker Prize			普利兹克奖

Task 3　Dialogues

Dialogue 1　City Planning & Design

Scene: It's Mr. James White's first trip to Suzhou. Ms. Li, the tour leader, is introducing the city's plan to him in the Museum of Inscribed Steles. (J = James White, L = Ms. Li)

J: Ms. Li, what's this? It looks like a map.

L: Yes, it really is a map. We call it Pingjiang City Map.

J: Isn't it Suzhou City Map? Why you call it Pingjiang City Map?

L: Actually, Suzhou was called Pingjiang in the history.

J: Oh, I see. Can you introduce Pingjiang City Map to me?

L: Sure. The stele of Pingjiang City Map is 2.76 m high and 1.45 m wide. On the head is engraved a pattern of double dragons vying to get a bead, and in the middle is inscribed three characters in official script that means Map of Pingjiang. The stele is made of a single block of bluestone, engraved in the second year (1229) of the Shaoding reign of the Southern Song Dynasty. In the upper part is engraved a picture of the whole Pingjiang (today's Suzhou City). The picture depicts in detail the whole layout of Suzhou, its appearance, its main office buildings, temples, gardens, shops, colleges, storehouses and residences, etc. and the mountain chains, lakes, bridges and so on. There are more than 50 temples, 12 ancient towers and 65 cross-street houses in the picture. It is the earliest and most complete city plan extant in China, providing a very precious material data for the study on Suzhou City in the Song Dynasty. Through 2,500 years, Suzhou, yet in the original map layouts, is a miracle in the world history.

J: Yes. Why is Suzhou City still on the earlier site after 2,500 years?

L: Surrounding the ancient city are moats and crisscross waterways, which make a strong network to help keep the basic framework of the city, and also lay a strong foundation for the successive reconstructions.

J: But I still didn't understand Suzhou's pattern. Can you explain simply?

L: Of course. In brief, the old city of Suzhou is "small bridges, running water and households". The outdoor moat is also surrounded by rivers within the double chessboard layout of "water and land in parallel, canal and street in neighbor".

J: Oh, I see. With our today's traffic perspective, it is combined design of conventional road network and high-speed road network. Is it right?

L: Absolutely. This is a creative city pattern in Chinese history.

J: I agree with you. The design of ancient years is not only practical, convenient, but also brings the city beautiful charming style, forming a unique artistic characteristics of Suzhou city. Oh, I like Suzhou even more now.

L: We are going to visit Ancient Xumen Gate and Suzhou Urban Planning Exhibition Hall later.

J: OK. But why is it called Xumen Gate?

L: Xumen Gate was named after Wu Zixu, and also because it connects the Xu Jiang and faces west. And you know Xu pronounces like west in Suzhou dialect.

J: Is that far from Ancient Xumen Gate to Suzhou Urban Planning Exhibition?

L: No, not far. Wannian Bridge connects the ancient Xumen Gate Square and Suzhou Urban Planning Exhibition Hall, which connects Suzhou's yesterday and today.

J: Let's go. I'm looking forward to having a look.

Dialogue 2 Famous People in Suzhou History

Scene: Mr. James White and Mrs. White are visiting Suzhou Museum. Li Lan (local guide) and Mr. White are discussing the famous people in Suzhou history. (L = Li Lan, J = James White)

L: Here we are. Suzhou Museum. It was designed by Ieoh Ming Pei.

J: Ieoh Ming Pei? I've heard of him. He is a famous Chinese American architect.

L: Exactly. He was a native of Suzhou, born in Canton, China and raised in Hong Kong and Shanghai. Pei drew inspiration at an early age from the gardens at Suzhou. But in 1935, he moved to the United States and learned architecture.

J: He designed a glass-and-steel pyramid for the Louvre Museum in Paris.

L: Yes, In the early 1980s, Pei was the focus of controversy when he designed it for Louvre Museum.

J: Did he design any other building in China?

L: Yes. He returned to China for the first time in 1974 to design a hotel at Fragrant Hills, and designed a skyscraper in Hong Kong for the Bank of China fifteen years later.

J: I saw the Bank of China tower when I was in Hong Kong. But I didn't know it is designed by I. M. Bei.

L: During his career, Pei and his firm have won numerous architecture awards. He won the prestigious Pritzker Prize in 1983.

J: He was a great man. Are there any other famous people in Suzhou history?

L: Sure. Sun Wu was a native of the State of Qi during the Spring and Autumn Period. Being a descendant of generations of generals, Sun Wu had unique and ideal conditions under which he studied the art of war.

J: Did he have relationship with Suzhou history?

L: Yes. When Sun Wu was in his teens, the State of Qi began to decline, and internal struggles for power within the court became increasingly fierce. Disgusted with these internal struggles, Sun Wu decided to go to a place far from home in order to realize his ambitions. Then he chose the State of Wu, which was the origin of the name Suzhou.

J: What did he do in Suzhou?

L: In the State of Wu, Sun Wu lived a hermit's life deep in the mountains and summarized the results of his research in his 13-chapter book *The Art of War*.

J: *The Art of War*? This book is very popular in America.

L: Really? But most of Chinese can't understand it. Do you like it?

J: Of course. It's my favorite. You know most of business men like this book.

L: Yes, he was a great military strategist. I think you will be interested in Qionglong Mountain.

J: Why do you say that?

L: Because Sun Wu had his retreat life there and wrote the book *The Art of War*.

J: Oh, I want to go to Qionglong Mountain.

L: OK, we are going to visit there tomorrow. Let's go.

Task 4 Useful Sentences

1. Suzhou is the birthplace of the flourishing Wu Culture.
2. As one vital part of the Chinese traditional civilization, the Wu Culture has a long history which may be traced back to 10,000 years ago.
3. The Wu Culture mainly adopted the essence of the central Chinese civilization.
4. After the Qing Dynasty, Suzhou City was one of the most prosperous Chinese cities, both in agricultural production and domestic and foreign trade.
5. The historic Wu Culture has left Suzhou City with a series of attractive heritages, including the classical gardens and water townships, the melodic rhythm of Kun Opera and Pingtan (Suzhou ballad), the Wumen Fine Arts School, the Suzhou handcrafts and the Jiangsu Cuisine.
6. Being the cradle of Wu Culture, Suzhou plays a vital role in Chinese cultural history.

Task 5 Listening

You will hear five sentences. Listen carefully and put down the whole sentences.

1. _____.
2. _____.
3. _____.
4. _____.
5. _____.

Task 6 Dialogue-Completing

Dialogue 1

Mr. Smith: Lily, _____?
Lily: _____.
Mr. Smith: _____?
Lily: _____ and it shows Suzhou's Pattern.
Mr. Smith: Well, _____?
Lily: Sure. _____
_____.
Mr. Smith: Oh, I see. And now it is combined design of conventional road network and high-speed road network.
Lily: Absolutely. _____
_____
_____.
Mr. Smith: It's amazing.
Lily: Now, we're going to visit Suzhou Urban Planning Exhibition Hall.
Mr. Smith: _____!

Dialogue 2

Mr. Smith: Lily, as Suzhou is compared to Paradise, there must be many famous people born in Suzhou. _____?
Lily: Sure. Many notable people in history are native Suzhounese. Such as _____.
Mr. Smith: Ieoh Ming Pei? _____.
Lily: Exactly. He was _____.
Mr. Smith: Well, _____?
Lily: Sure. _____
_____.
Mr. Smith: Really?
Lily: Absolutely. _____
_____.
Mr. Smith: Oh, he was a great man!

Task 7 Role-Play

Situation 1: Mr. Brown and his granddaughter are visiting Suzhou Museum. Mr. Brown is amazed by the design and he is asking questions about the designer.

Situation 2: It's Ms. Miller's first trip to Suzhou. She is interested in the city planning and design of ancient Suzhou City. The local guide Ms. Li is explaining to her:
- brief introduction
- geographical location
- history
- cultural background

Task 8 Translation

Put the following passage into Chinese.

As an important part of traditional Chinese culture, Wu Culture has a long history and can be dated back to the San Shan Mountains Culture of the late Paleolithic Period more than ten thousand years ago. In a very long period, Wu Culture mainly absorbed the Central Plain's culture, and disseminated Wu Culture itself overseas. From the mid-Ming Dynasty, Wu Culture gradually absorbed foreign culture more and communicated with the Central Plain's culture, which led to a unique style of the Wu Culture.

As basic academic study in all cultural and academic researches in Suzhou, researches on Wu Culture have the oldest and most extensive coverage, which include: geography, history, characteristics, connotation, resources development of Wu Culture and so on. In recent 50 – 60 years, it has formed a diversified layout in Wu Culture researches, which combined with protection, exploitation, utilization and development in research ideas and achieved a lot of fruitful results.

(http://61.155.22.86/list_en.aspx? id = 39)

Task 9 Supplementary Reading

Famous People in Suzhou

Suzhou, known as "Paradise on Earth", has been a cradle of talented people for thousands of years.

Many notable people in history are native Suzhounese, such as the politician and litterateur Fan Zhongyan, who expressed his political ideal as "Be the first to bear hardships, and the last to enjoy themselves"; the philologist and geographer Gu Yanwu, who advocated that everybody be responsible for the rise and fall of the country; Yan Yan, one of Confucius' ten disciples; the script-sage Zhang Xu; the top sculptor Yang Huizhi; the great poet Lu Guimeng; Fan Chengda, one of the four great poets in Southern Song Dynasty; the famous artists, such as Huang Gongwang, Shen Zhou, and Tang Bohu; Kuai Xiang, the supervisor of the construction of Tiananmen Gate; Astronomer Wang Xichan; the famous writer Feng Menglong; the noted physician Ye Gui; Weng Tonghe, a Chinese Confucian scholar and imperial tutor of the Qing Dynasty; Liu Yazi, Chen Qubing, Ye Shengtao, the famous scholars of modern times.

As an old saying goes "the water and soil of one region raise the people of the region", a large number of talented, especially the Imperial Number One Scholars, were emerged in Suzhou. In the Qing Dynasty, there were 26 Imperial Number One Scholars, accounting 22.81% of the total in the whole country, and 53.06% in Jiangsu Province, which made Suzhou rank No. 1 of average and absolute quantity in the country.

With the fast development in science, a quite large number of scientific and technical elites are needed. So far, Suzhou has 83 academicians of the Chinese Academies of Sciences and Engineering, who have forged ahead in the forefront of world science researches, making important contributions to the development of science and technology in China. Having these great people, Suzhou got profound culture; having these great people, Suzhou became famous all of the world: Suzhou is much proud of having these great people.

(http://www.suzhouculture.cn/list_en.aspx? id = 37)

Project 2　Silk and Embroidery

Learning Objectives:
- be able to provide some information about silk and its history
- be able to offer some suggestion and advice on how to select silk fabrics
- be able to illustrate the characteristics of Su Embroidery and recommend its products to the tour group

Task 1　Warm-Up

1. Can you say something about Suzhou silk?
2. Do you know how to choose Su embroidery?

Task 2　Words and Expressions

embroidery	[ɪmˈbrɔɪdəri]	n.	刺绣
superb	[suːˈpɜːb]	adj.	极好的
fabric	[ˈfæbrɪk]	n.	结构，织物
workmanship	[ˈwɜːkmənʃɪp]	n.	手艺，技巧
stroll	[strəʊl]	n./v.	闲逛，漫步
elegant	[ˈelɪɡənt]	adj.	优雅的，雅致的
scarf	[skɑːf]	n.	围巾
decor	[deɪˈkɔːr]	n.	装饰，陈设
shawl	[ʃɔːl]	n.	披肩，围巾
corporate	[ˈkɔːpərət]	adj.	公司的
gown	[ɡaʊn]	n.	长袍，长外衣
collectable	[kəˈlektəbl]	adj.	可收集的
authentic	[ɔːˈθentɪk]	adj.	真正的
crown	[kraʊn]	n.	王冠，顶点
cocoon	[kəˈkuːn]	n.	茧，茧状物
embody	[ɪmˈbɒdi]	v.	代表
silkworm	[ˈsɪlkwɜːm]	n.	蚕

realm	[relm]	n.	领域,王国
fade	[feɪd]	v.	褪色,凋谢
apply	[əˈplaɪ]	vt.	应用
colorfast	[ˈkʌlə fɑːst]	adj.	不褪色的
binding	[ˈbaɪndɪŋ]	n.	镶边
knot	[nɒt]	n.	结,节
lukewarm	[ˈluːkˈwɔːm]	adj.	微温的
thread	[θred]	n.	线,细丝
rinse	[rɪns]	v.	清洗,冲洗
needle	[ˈniːdl]	n.	针
rub	[rʌb]	v.	摩擦,搓
vertical	[ˈvɜːtɪkl]	adj.	垂直的
wring	[rɪŋ]	v.	拧,绞出
punched	[pʌntʃt]	adj.	穿孔的
symbolize	[ˈsɪmbəlaɪz]	v.	象征
raw	[rɔː]	adj.	生的,未加工的
traverse	[ˈtrævɜːs]	v.	横贯,穿越
rim	[rɪm]	n.	边,框
camel	[ˈkæml]	n.	骆驼
neat	[niːt]	adj.	整洁的
caravan	[ˈkærəvæn]	n.	商队,大篷车
dense	[dens]	adj.	密集的
mystical	[ˈmɪstɪkl]	adj.	神秘的
harmonious	[hɑːˈməʊnɪəs]	adj.	和谐的
grotto	[ˈgrɒtəʊ]	n.	洞穴,岩穴
even	[ˈiːvən]	adj.	平坦的
magnificent	[mægˈnɪfɪsnt]	adj.	壮丽的
barely	[ˈbɛəli]	adv.	几乎不,刚刚,勉强
feature	[fiːtʃə]	n.	特征,特色
stitch	[stɪtʃ]	n.	针法,针脚
visible	[ˈvɪzəbl]	adj.	看得见的
naked	[ˈneɪkɪd]	adj.	裸体的,无掩饰的
shrink-proof			防缩

Task 3 Dialogues

Dialogue 1 Suzhou Silk Fabrics

Scene: Ms. Li is giving some suggestions to Mrs. White on how to choose gifts for their families and friends. (W = Mrs. white, L = Ms. Li)

W: Ms. Li, I'd love to take some gifts home for our families and friends. What would you suggest?

L: How about silk fabrics? You know, Suzhou is famous for silk production.

W: I am not familiar with it. Can you take me to have a look?

L: Of course. Let's go.

(They are taking a stroll in a street full of Suzhou silk fabrics.)

L: Here! Mrs. White. Silk fans, silk scarf, silk shawl, silk shirt, silk nightgown. Is there anything you like?

W: Oh, they are beautiful. Why didn't you take me here early?

L: You can have a free choice now. You know Suzhou is the silk capital of China.

W: Yes, I'd like to have a silk nightgown for my mother, and one for myself. What is the silk produced from, Li Lan?

L: Authentic Suzhou silk is produced from the cocoons of silkworms.

W: You see, how nice it is! Hum, I wonder if the color will fade in washing.

L: It's colorfast and shrink-proof. But please wash it in lukewarm water amount of special detergent for silk washing and rinse it well. Don't rub or wring it.

W: Wonderful. And this silk tie is suitable for my father! Can you tell me more about silk culture?

L: Of course. Suzhou silk has the history of more than 3,000 years.

W: I have heard of the Silk Road, which symbolized the communication between the east and the west in Chinese history.

L: Exactly. The Old Silk Road, the road on which the earliest Eastern and Western exchanges took place, was surrounded by vast deserts, traversed by camel caravans, site of mystical stone grottoes, ancient temples, and magnificent passes.

W: Thank you for telling me so much about Suzhou silk.

L: My pleasure, Mrs. White.

Dialogue 2 Su Embroidery

Scene: Mrs. White is visiting Suzhou Embroidery Museum. Ms. Li (local guide) is introducing Su embroidery to her. (W = Mrs. White, L = Ms. Li)

W: Ms. Li, I have heard Suzhou embroidery is very famous. And I'd like to buy some for gifts. Can you give me some suggestions?

L: Sure. Su embroidery is one of the four major styles of Chinese Embroidery. It already has a history of 2,000 years.

W: What are the features of Su embroidery?

L: Su embroidery is praised as "the pearl of oriental art" for its beautiful designs, varied stitches, superb workmanship and elegant colors. Su embroidery paintings are a unique wall art, an ideal choice for home, office, hotel wall decor, an unusual gift idea that satisfies both personal and corporate needs. It is highly collectable and its value doubles with its age.

W: That's interesting. What's this? Why are the two sides the same pictures?

L: That's called Double-sided embroidery. Double-sided embroidery is a pearl in the crown of China Su embroidery, and it embodies the skill level of Su embroidery.

W: Look here, why do the two sides have different pictures?

L: Double-sided embroidery has developed into tri-embroidery, with difference colors, different shapes, and different stitches on both sides. These bring embroidery to the realm of magic.

W: How do they do that?

L: An embroiderer embroiders the pattern of a cat on one side and the pattern of a dog on the other side. She applies binding stitches instead of tying knots. The end of the thread is hidden. She uses the needle in a vertical way so that the thread on the other side won't be punched.

W: It's magical. Can you embroider? How about the girls in Suzhou, can they embroider?

L: No, I can't. Actually, in ancient times, nearly every family raised silkworms and embroidered here. Even today, you can find the street name which is related to the Su silk fabric, such as Yang Can Li, Gun Xiu Fang, Xin Luo Xiang, Sun Zhisha Xiang, Jin Fan Road, Bei Ju, etc.

W: Is it handmade or by machine?

L: Su embroidery is 100% handmade embroidery made with raw silk threads on silk satin. You know, Ms. Shen Shou, a famous embroidery lady, won the highest honor at Italy's Turin International Fair (1911), and at the Panama-Pacific International Fair (1915).

W: Oh, Ms. Li, I love Su embroidery. Now, I'd like to choose some for my friends. I am sure they will like Su embroidery. But how can I know which is better?

L: OK, let me show you. Look at this one, please. The surface must be flat, the rim must be neat, the needle must be thin, the lines must be dense, the color must be harmonious and bright, and the picture must be even. The thin thread is divided into up to 48 strands that are barely visible to the naked eye.

Task 4 Useful Sentences

1. Suzhou, famous for its rich silk, is regarded as the "Hometown of Silk".
2. From the Tang Dynasty, silk is considered to be articles of tribute.
3. Silk and embroidery were the main products transported along the ancient Chinese Silk Road.
4. The Chinese silk products are peculiar to the Chinese nation and representatives of international fashion as well.
5. Shen Shou was called "Sage of Embroidery" and the "Lifelike Embroidery Style" created by her is well known all over the world.
6. Several thousand years ago, the silk trade first reached Europe via the Silk Road. It brought with it not only gorgeous silk apparel and decorative items, but also the ancient and resplendent culture of the East.
7. Suzhou embroidery originated in Suzhou, with more than 2,000 years history.
8. Su embroidery is famous handicrafts in China, renowned for its delicacy home and abroad, and has been presented to foreign guests as national presents many times.

(http://handembroidery.cn/SE.html)

Task 5 Listening

You will hear five sentences. Listen carefully and put down the whole sentences.

1. _____.
2. _____.
3. _____.
4. _____.
5. _____.

Task 6 Dialogue-Completing

Mrs. Smith: Ms. Li, _____?
Ms. Li: I suggest you buy some silk clothes for your daughter, Mrs. Smith.
Mrs. Smith: _____. She would love them. _____?
Ms. Li: Well, there're lots of shops near here.
Mrs. Smith: Great! But _____?
Ms. Li: OK, let me show you. _____

Mrs. Smith: _____.

Task 7 Role-Play

Situation 1: Mr. Bentley is visiting Suzhou now. He is interested in Suzhou silk and he wants to buy some as souvenir for his wife. The local guide Ms. Zhang is helping him.

Situation 2: Alice is an Australian university student. She is amazed by Su embroidery. Now the local guide Ms. Wang is introducing Su embroidery to her.

Task 8 Translation

Put the following sentences into English.
1. 我想给我祖母买件丝绸的睡衣。
2. 我想为我的朋友买点纪念品,你有什么推荐吗?
3. 我听说苏州的丝绸制品非常有名,能给我介绍下吗?
4. 请问,丝绸制品会褪色吗?
5. 谢谢你的讲解,实在太有意思了。我想买副双面绣回家,能帮我挑选下吗?

Put the following sentences into Chinese.
1. Su embroidery accessories are known as foreign trade artworks all over the world.
2. Chinese silk is light as a breeze and soft as a cloud.
3. Xi'an, the starting point of the ancient Silk Road, was capital intermittently for many dynasties in the Chinese history.
4. A silk worm spins all its silk till its death/a candle won't stop its tears until it is fully burnt. This Tang poem accurately describes the property of the silkworm.
5. Su embroidery accessories are exquisite artworks.

Task 9 Supplementary Reading

Tips on Buying Silk

When visiting China, many visitors would like to buy some souvenirs. The smooth silk product is certainly the best choice. Before buying them, it is always wise to learn the common sense of the silk product including the function, identification and maintenance.

The most common methods to identify real silk are handling, eye observation, inflammation and chemical coloring.

Observe the length and uniformity of the fiber: silk is slim and long; cotton fiber is short; fleece is longer and more curled than cotton fiber; the long chemical fiber is long, and the short chemical fiber is short and trim.

Observe the handling and strength of fiber: the handling of silk is moderate; terylene, nylon yarn and viscose feel very similar to silk; the flax and cotton are hard and the fleece is soft.

Observe from the appearance: silk fiber has special sheen, bright but not harsh glare; chemical fiber does not have this property.

The best way to wash real silk is to dry-clean, or wash it with neutral soap or detergent specially used for silk product. Do not wash it under high temperature. It is good to wash silk alone. It is bad to scrub it hardly or wash it in the washing machine.

The dyed silk product should be put in dry and cool place to avoid direct sunlight. It is not suitable to wring it after wash. When ironing, the temperature of the electric iron should not be too high and interfacing is suggested to put on it to keep the silk from being damaged.

Project 3　Art Culture

> **Learning Objectives**：
> * be able to arrange an art show for the tour group
> * be able to introduce Kunqu Opera and its development and achievements
> * be able to deliver a presentation of Pingtan and the importance of Suzhou Dialect

Task 1　Warm-Up

1. What do you know about Kunqu Opera in Suzhou?
2. Do you play any musical instrument? Can you describe one of them?

Task 2　Words and Expressions

peony	[ˈpɪəni]	n.	牡丹
reform	[rɪˈfɔːm]	vt.	改革
pavilion	[pəˈvɪliən]	n.	亭子,凉亭
sage	[seɪdʒ]	n.	圣人
proclaim	[prəˈkleɪm]	vt.	宣告,表明
recitation	[ˌresɪˈteɪʃn]	n.	背诵,详述
instrument	[ˈɪnstrʊmənt]	n.	乐器
masterpiece	[ˈmɑːstəpiːs]	n.	杰作,名作
flute	[fluːt]	n.	长笛
intangible	[ɪnˈtændʒəbl]	adj.	触摸不到的
drum	[drʌm]	n.	鼓
heritage	[ˈherɪtɪdʒ]	n.	遗产
clapper	[ˈklæpə]	n.	拍手者
humanity	[hjuːˈmænəti]	n.	人性,人类
exclusively	[ɪkˈskluːsɪvli]	adv.	专门地
inaugural	[ɪnˈɔːgjərəl]	adj.	就任的,开始的
portray	[pɔːˈtreɪ]	vt.	画,描写

batch	[bætʃ]	n.	一批
awkward	[ˈɔːkwəd]	adj.	笨拙的
verbal	[ˈvɜːbl]	adj.	言语的
stingy	[ˈstɪndʒi]	adj.	吝啬的
representative	[reprɪˈzentətɪv]	n.	代表
dialect	[ˈdaɪəlekt]	n.	方言,土话
pluck	[plʌk]	vt.	采,摘
dramatic	[drəˈmætɪk]	adj.	戏剧的
denote	[dɪˈnəʊt]	vt.	表示,代表
tune	[tjuːn]	n.	曲调,旋律
ballad	[ˈbæləd]	n.	民谣
lingering	[ˈlɪŋgərɪŋ]	adj.	逗留不去的
compose	[kəmˈpəʊz]	vt.	构图,组成
integration	[ˌɪntɪˈgreɪʃn]	n.	整合,集成
accompany	[əˈkʌmpəni]	vt.	陪同
pictorial	[pɪkˈtɔːrɪəl]	adj.	画家的,生动的
lute	[luːt]	n.	琵琶
splendor	[ˈsplendə]	n.	光辉,壮丽
zither	[ˈzɪθə]	n.	筝
aesthetics	[iːsˈθetɪks]	n.	美学
props	[prɒps]	n.	道具
repute	[rɪˈpjuːt]	n.	名气,声望
adapted	[əˈdæptɪd]	adj.	适应的
delicacy	[ˈdelɪkəsi]	n.	精美,灵敏
reunion	[riːˈjuːnɪən]	n.	团聚
string	[strɪŋ]	n.	线,弦
solo	[ˈsəʊləʊ]	n.	独奏,独唱
gauze	[gɔːz]	n.	薄纱,纱布
duet	[djuːˈet]	n.	二重唱
longevity	[lɒnˈdʒevəti]	n.	长命,长寿
trio	[ˈtriːəʊ]	n.	三重唱
tragedy	[ˈtrædʒədi]	n.	悲剧
UNESCO			联合国教科文组织

Task 3 Dialogues

Dialogue 1 Mother of All Operas—Kunqu Opera

Scene: Mr. James White and Li Lan are discussing Kunqu Opera after they watched "Peony Pavilion". (J = James White, L = Li Lan)

J: It's so beautiful. I heard that Kunqu Opera was proclaimed by UNESCO to be one of the world's nineteen "Masterpieces of Oral and Intangible Heritage of Humanity".

L: Yes. Actually, Kunqu Opera was listed as one of the 19 inaugural "Masterpieces of Oral and Intangible Heritage of Humanity" by UNESCO in 2001, May 18th. Kunqu Opera was included in the top list of the first batch "Human Beings' Verbal and Intangible Cultural Heritage Representative Work".

J: I think Kunqu is really worthy of the honor after I watched it.

L: I agree with you. And Kunqu Opera is regarded as "the mother of all operas".

J: Why? I thought that Beijing Opera was "the mother of all operas" before.

L: Regarded as "the mother of all operas", Kunqu has a long history of over 500 years and is one of China's extant oldest dramatic forms. As the current most ancient drama form, Kunqu Opera is one of the original three of the world's largest ancient dramas. Starting from the late Yuan Dynasty and early Ming Dynasty, Kunqu Opera is a performance and singing art with strict rules and forms, complete patterns, graceful and pleasant tunes, and gentle, lingering music. With an integration of literature, drama, performance, music, dance and art, Kunqu Opera is the stage art with the most poetic and pictorial splendor. Having collected all advantages of China ancient aesthetics, Kunqu Opera has always been reputed as the founder of all dramas and considered as a national treasure.

J: I see. We watched "Peony Pavilion" today. Is there any other famous play of Kunqu Opera?

L: The representative pieces of Kunqu Opera are "Peony Pavilion", which is the peak work in Chinese dramatic history and is the play that can bring the delicacy and romance of Kunqu Opera into full play. "Fifteen Strings of Coins (Shiwu Guan)", "Washing Gauze", and "Longevity Palace" are also famous plays. The famous writers are Wu Liangfu, Tang Xianzu, Hong Shen, Kong Shangren, Bai Xianyong, etc.

J: Are plots of the plays love stories like "Peony Pavilion"?

L: Yes. Plots of the plays are either romantic love stories or tragedies.

J: So Kunqu Opera must have a lot of female fans, right?

L: I think so. At least, most of the audiences are female today.

J: I heard a person named Wei Liangfu right now. By the way, who is he?

L: He was a musician, made a great reform of Kunqu in the mid-16th century, and he was considered as the Sage of Kunqu. In the Ming Dynasty, reformed by Wei Liangfu during the reign of Jiajing, Kunqu became mild, smooth and graceful, and performers attached great importance to clear recitation, correct singing and pure tunes; the composers wrote the musical scores after working out the tunes, and the songs were written in seven-character or ten-character lines. Three types of musical instruments (stringed instruments, bamboo flutes, and drums and clappers) formed the accompaniment. Kunqu had 12 roles, and all the characters other than Zhengsheng and Zhengdan could play leading roles. Moreover, the Jing and Chou roles were no longer those exclusively portraying foolish, awkward or stingy people.

J: Thank you for telling me so much about Kunqu Opera. I think I loved it already. I must watch it again if I come to Suzhou next time.

L: My pleasure. You will have a chance to watch Kunqu Opera in your hometown.

J: Really?

L: Yes. You know Kunqu Opera is attracting attention worldwide today. Thus, Suzhou Kunqu Troupe performs hundreds of times both in China and abroad every year.

J: Oh, it's exciting news for me. Thank you very much.

L: You are welcome.

Dialogue 2 Wu Dialect—Suzhou Pingtan

Scene: Li Lan is introducing Suzhou Pingtan to the Whites. And they are going to watch "The Pearl Pagoda" in a teahouse of Shiquan Street. (L = Li Lan, J = James White)

L: Good afternoon, Mr. White and Mrs. White.

J: Good afternoon, Li Lan. You know I watched TV last night. Two persons sat on the chairs, a male and a female, both of them carried a plucked instruments. But I don't know what that is. Then they played the instrument along with singing. Although I can't understand, I like it. What's that?

L: Oh, that's called Suzhou Pingtan. It is a general term denoting Suzhou Pinghua and Tanci, namely, storytelling and ballad singing in the Suzhou dialect.

J: What time did Suzhou Pingtan start from?

L: Suzhou pingtan has a long history. It is formed from the performance of storytelling in Tang and Song Dynasties. At the end of Ming Dynasty, singing was introduced into it, thus Pingtan, which performs in Suzhou dialect, formed.

J: Oh, what is the form of performance?

L: Suzhou Pingtan is a cover term for two forms of art performed in the local dialect. Pingtan performance is composed of four parts, namely "speaking, teasing, music-play and singing" (Shuo, Xue, Tan and Chang). The music is played by the actor or actress to accompany his or her Pipa (lute) and the Sanxian (three-stringed zither). Other things used as props include a piece of wood for calling special attention, a folding fan and a handkerchief. The contents are usually from traditional stories of different lengths. Popular among all classes in the society, Pingtan is celebrated as the best voice in China.

J: I agree with you. Can we watch it somewhere besides on TV?

L: We can go to the tea houses in Shiquan Street, and enjoy the performance while drinking the tea.
J: That's a good idea! Let's go. (*20 minutes later, they reach a tea house in Shiquan Street.*)
L: We are going to watch "The Pearl Pagoda", a traditional performance.
J: What story does it tell?
L: "The Pearl Pagoda" was adapted into Xi Opera, Pingtan and other art forms. It uses a pearl tower as the central clue and tells the story of the separation of a young scholar and a beauty and their final good reunion and marriage. The Pearl Tower scenic spot is also located in Tongli.
J: Yes. I remembered. We saw the Pearl Tower in Tongli.
L: Suzhou Pingtan is performed solo, in duet, or as a trio. What we are going to watch is performed in duet.
J: Right, what we watched last night was in duet, too.
L: Exactly. Oh, it's time to perform.
J: Yes. Let's enjoy.

Task 4 Useful Sentences

1. Kunqu Opera is one of the oldest extant forms of Chinese opera.
2. Kunqu was developed during the Ming Dynasty, and due to its influence on other Chinese theatre forms, it is known as the "teacher" or "mother" of a hundred operas, including Jingju (Peking Opera).
3. Kunqu Opera ranks among the most splendid and miraculous cultural art forms created by the Chinese people in their long history.
4. Kunqu Opera was honored by UNESCO as one of 19 outstanding cultural forms of expression from different regions of the "Masterpieces of the Oral and Intangible Heritage of Humanity" in May 2001.
5. Suzhou Pingtan is like a precious pearl among the treasures of Chinese stage performance.
6. Flourishing in Suzhou, Pingtan also enjoys great popularity in Jiangsu and Zhejiang provinces as well as in Shanghai, the biggest metropolis in East China.

Task 5 Listening

You will hear five sentences. Listen carefully and put down the whole sentences.
1. _____.
2. _____.

3. _____ .
4. _____ .
5. _____ .

Task 6   Dialogue-Completing

Lily: Mr. Smith, there is a music drama named "Peony Pavilion" in the theater tonight. _____?

Mr. Smith: Really? _____?

Lily: Kunqu Opera and it is a form of Chinese music drama.

Mr. Smith: Yes, I've heard of it. It is _____.

Lily: Indeed. Kunqu Opera is regarded _____.

Mr. Smith: Amazing! _____?

Lily: Yes. Kunqu Opera is _____.

Mr. Smith: I can't wait for it. _____?

Lily: "Peony Pavilion" _____. I am sure you will like it.

Mr. Smith: Great!

Lily: _____.

Mr. Smith: Thank you.

Task 7   Role-Play

Situation 1: Linda is a student major in music. Now she is visiting Suzhou with her parents. She is interested in Suzhou local music, so she wants to learn more about it from the guide Ms. Li.

Situation 2: Mr. and Mrs. Johnson are going to stay in your city for three nights. They want to see something typically Chinese.

- Recommend the show.
- Tell them what time it will start and how long it will last.
- Arrange the time they will meet the guide and go to the theatre.
- Take them to the theatre and help them find their seats.
- Discuss the history of Chinese show with them.
- Ask their opinions about the show.
- See them back to the hotel.

Task 8 Translation

Put the following passage into Chinese.

Kunqu, also known as Kunju, Kun Opera or Kunqu Opera, is one of the oldest extant forms of Chinese opera. It evolved from the Kunshan melody, and dominated Chinese theatre from the 16th to the 18th centuries. Kunqu originated in the Wu cultural area.

Today, Kunqu is performed professionally in seven Mainland Chinese cities: Beijing (Northern Kunqu Theatre), Shanghai (Shanghai Kunqu Theatre), Suzhou (Suzhou Kunqu Theatre), Nanjing (Jiangsu Province Kunqu Theatre), Zhengzhou (Hunan Kunqu Theatre), Yongjia County/Wenzhou (Yongjia Kunqu Theatre) and Hangzhou (Zhejiang Province Kunqu Theatre), as well as in Taipei. Non-professional opera societies are active in many other cities in China and abroad, and opera companies occasionally tour.

Kunqu was listed as one of the Masterpieces of the Oral and Intangible Heritage of Humanity by UNESCO in 2001. Its melody or tune is one of the Four Great Characteristic Melodies in Chinese opera.

(http://english.cctv.com/program/newfrontiers/20090915/108224.shtml)

Task 9 Supplementary Reading

Culture

The Chinese have a saying: "Firewood, rice, oil, salt, sauce, vinegar and tea are the seven necessities to begin a day." Though tea is last on the list, we still can see the importance of tea in daily life.

A simple meal in Chinese is Cu Cha Dan Fan, namely coarse tea and tasteless dinner. Even a simple meal is finished off with tea so its importance is obvious.

For the Chinese, tea drinking and tea tasting are not the same. Tea drinking is for refreshment and tonic effect.

Tea tasting has cultural meaning. Tea and tea wares should match surrounding elements such as breeze, bright moon, pines, bamboo, plums and snow. All these show the ultimate goal of Chinese culture: the harmonious unity of human beings with nature.

Tea is compared to personal character. The fragrance of tea is not aggressive; it is pleasant, low-keyed and lasting. A friendship between gentlemen is also like a cup of tea. With a cup of tea in hand, enjoying the green leaves in a white porcelain cup, you will feel peace. Fame, wealth and other earthly concerns are far away. Tea is the symbol of elegance.

Tasting tea: Emphasis is placed on the color, fragrance and flavor of tea, water quality and tea set. When taking tea, the taster should also be able to savor tea carefully.

Tea art: Attention is paid to environment, atmosphere, music, infusing techniques and interpersonal relationships.

The highest ambit—tea lore: Philosophy, ethics and morality are blended into tea activity. People cultivate their morality and mind and savor the life through tasting tea, thereby attaining enjoyment of spirit.

Clearness: It is namely cleanness, incorruptness, quietness and loneliness. The essence of tea art not only seeks the cleanness of the appearance of things, but also pursues the loneliness, tranquility, incorruptness and shame awareness of the mind. In a still ambit, only through drinking clear and pure tea soup can one appreciate the profoundness of drinking tea.

Respect: Respect is the root of everything on earth and the way of having no enemies. People should show respect for others and be cautious themselves.

Joy: The meaning of harmony lies in form and method and that of joy is in spirit and affection. Sipping bitterness and swallowing sweetness when drinking tea can enlighten the spice of life and cultivate a broad mind and a far sight so that the disputes between others and self disappear.

Truthfulness: It is namely truth and genuine knowledge. The supreme good is the whole formed by combination of truth and genuine knowledge. The ambit of supreme good is to retain nature, remove material desire without being tempted by advantages and disadvantages, study the physical world to gain knowledge and continually seek after improvements. The essence of drinking tea lies in enlightening capacity and conscience so that everyone can live a simple life to express their ambition and handle matters thriftily and virtuously in daily life, thus they can attain the ambit of truth, good and beauty.

Project 4 Folk Customs and Festivities

Learning Objectives:
- be able to illustrate some important customs and traditions in Suzhou
- be able to explain some important festivals celebrated in Suzhou
- be able to arrange an exhibition of Suzhou customs and festivals

Task 1 Warm-Up

1. Can you name some Suzhou local festivals?
2. Which is your favorite festival?

Task 2 Words and Expressions

carnival	[ˈkɑːnəvəl]	n.	嘉年华
folk	[fəʊk]	adj.	民间的
actually	[ˈæktʃuəli]	adv.	事实上
immortal	[ɪˈmɔːtl]	n.	神
lunar	[ˈluːnə]	adj.	月亮的,阴历的
disguise	[dɪsˈgaɪz]	vt.	假装,假扮
beggar	[ˈbegə]	n.	乞丐,穷人
peddler	[ˈpedlə]	n.	小贩
benefit	[ˈbenefɪt]	vt.	有益于,得益
incarnation	[ɪnkɑːˈneɪʃn]	n.	化身
fairyism	[ˈfeərɪɪzəm]	n.	仙气
dialect	[ˈdaɪəlekt]	n.	方言
variety	[vəˈraɪəti]	n.	多样化,种类
pastry	[ˈpeɪstri]	n.	糕饼
fragrant	[ˈfreɪgrənt]	adj.	芳香的
characteristic	[kærɪktəˈrɪstɪk]	n.	特点,特色
solar	[ˈsəʊlə]	adj.	太阳的
coordinate	[kəʊˈɔːdəneɪt]	v.	协调

exquisite	[ˈekskwɪzɪt]	n.	精致,讲究
ternate	[ˈtɜːnɪt]	adj.	三个的
notable	[ˈnəʊtəbl]	adj.	显著的
tranquility	[træŋˈkwɪlɪti]	n.	宁静,平静
confluence	[ˈkɒnfluəns]	n.	合流,汇合
solstice	[ˈsɒlstɪs]	n.	至,至点
osmanthus	[ɒzˈmænθəs]	n.	桂花
get rid of			摆脱,除去

Task 3　Dialogues

Dialogue 1　Carnival of Suzhounese—Ga Shenxian

Scene: Li Lan, Mr. and Mrs. White are visiting Nanhao Street. It is just the day of Suzhou folk culture festival—Ga Shenxian Festival. (J = James White, L = Li Lan)

J: Why are there so many people here?

L: Oh, we are lucky today. It's Ga Shenxian Festival in Suzhou today.

J: Ga Shenxian Festival? I have never heard of it. What festival is that?

L: Ga Shenxian is a traditional folk festival in Suzhou. Actually, It's the birthday of Lv Chunyang (Lv Dongbin), who is one of the Eight Immortals.

J: So today is his birthday, May 16th?

L: Yes. It is said the fourteenth day of the fourth lunar month. It's the May 16th this year.

J: But why so many people come to this street on his birthday?

L: On his birthday, Lv Dongbin always disguises himself as a beggar or peddler among the crowd to save the world and benefit the people. Thus on that day, everyone could be the incarnation of Lv Dongbin. If you can walk up to him, his fairyism will bring you good luck, so everyone gather together and the name Ga Shenxian comes into being.

J: Really? It's interesting. But "Ga", what does it mean?

L: The word "Ga" is a typical Suzhou dialect and it means being full of people or crowded, like the phrase "Ga Nao Meng" in Suzhou, which also means to join in the fun. It has become the carnival of Suzhounese.

J: Exactly. There are so many varieties of goods and foods here. It's exciting.

L: Yes, I hope you can enjoy it!

J: Of course. Come here, Li Lan. What's this?

L: Oh, it's called "Shenxian Pastry". Have a taste?

J: Sure. Wow, it's yummy. Soft and fragrant. But is it for Lv Dongbin?

L: No. We add the word "Shenxian" before most names of goods and foods. It means lucky!

J: Oh, that's interesting. I'll buy a pair of Shenxian shoes. I need luck everyday!

Dialogue 2   Suzhou Folk Custom

Scene: The Whites are interested in Suzhou folk customs. They are talking about it with Li Lan. (J =James White, L =Li Lan)

J: Lan, you know, we are interested in Suzhou folk customs. What's the daily life of people in Suzhou like? And what are the culture characteristics?

L: People of Suzhou pay special attention to seasonal festivals. All 24 solar coordinates with seasons. The folk customs in Suzhou are exquisite.

J: Can you tell us some festival celebration activities in Suzhou?

L: Sure. The 5th day of the first lunar month, receiving God of Wealth. The 15th day of the first lunar month, women have to walk across 3 bridges. The 14th day of the fourth lunar month, trying to find Lv Dongbin. The 5th day of the fifth lunar month, the dragon boat festival, welcoming Wu Zixu. Mid-Autumn, following moon. Winter solstice is more important than lunar New Year.

J: I knew something about Lv Dongbin and Wu Zixu. But why do women have to walk over 3 bridges on the 15th day of the first lunar month?

L: Actually, walking across three bridges is the tradition in Wujiang. The native thought, by walking across three bridges, they can get rid of bad luck. The most notable are Peace and Tranquility (Taiping) Bridge, Luck (Jili) Bridge and Lasting Celebration (Changqing) Bridge. These are known as Ternate Bridges as they cross three rivers at their confluence and form a natural ring road.

J: The three bridges have good names. And so miraculous.

L: You know, there are different meanings of walking across different bridges. Walk across Taiping Bridge, and you will be healthy forever. Walk across Jili Bridge, and you will be wealthy. Walk across Changqing Bridge and you will be young forever.

J: Oh, that's interesting. We'll walk across Ternate Bridges if we have a chance.

L: Ternate Bridges are propitious symbols in the eyes of the local residents and they walk across them for good luck.

J: And I knew that lunar New Year is the most important festival in China. But you said winter solstice is more important than lunar New Year, why?

L: Actually, winter solstice is more important than lunar New Year in Suzhou. The night of winter solstice is the longest night of the year. All the families will go back home early and have a dinner together.

J: It's similar to lunar New Year. Is there any difference?

L: Yes. We drink sweet winter solstice wine on that day.

J: Sweet winter solstice wine?

L: Yes. It has fragrance of sweet osmanthus flower.

J: I like sweet osmanthus flower fragrance. Thank you for telling us so much.

L: You are welcome.

 Task 4　Useful Sentences

1. In Suzhou, colorful festivals and cultural celebrations abound all year round.
2. There are traditional festivals, tourism official festivals, and new city-level events.
3. Ga Shenxian Festival (Crushing Gods) is a traditional public activity. It is related to Lv Dongbin who is one of the Eight Immortals in Chinese legends.
4. Nowadays, Ga Shenxian Festival has developed into an annual temple fair.
5. In the Immortal Temple, there are many food stands, fish shops, handicraft shops on that day.
6. The ancient Hanshan Temple in Suzhou is home to one of Chinese oldest and largest New Year's festivals.
7. On December 31st every year, thousands of tourists gather inside and outside the temple to listen to 108 bell tolls at the same time, praying for good luck and happiness in the coming year.

 Task 5　Listening

You will hear five sentences. Listen carefully and put down the whole sentences.

1. _____.
2. _____.
3. _____.
4. _____.
5. _____.

 Task 6　Dialogue-Completing

(J = James White, L = Li Lan)

J: Ms. Li, _____?
L: Oh, today is _____.
J: Who is he?
L: _____
J: I see, but why do people all come and celebrate his birthday?

L: _____
J: Oh, it sounds interesting!
L: _____.
   Would you like to go and see?
J: I'd love to. Let's go!

Task 7　Role-Play

Situation 1: Kate, the daughter of Mr. and Mrs. Smith is interested in Ga Shenxian. She is curious about the festival and asks to the tour leader about it.

Situation 2: Mr. and Mrs. Smith are talking to the tour leader about Suzhou local festivals. The tour leader is introducing some traditional local festivals to them.

Task 8　Translation

Put the following passage into Chinese.

Listening to Bell-Tolling at the Cold Hill Temple

A poem "Mooring Near Maple Bridge at Night" written by Zhang Ji, a famous poet of the Tang Dynasty, reads: "The moon goes down, crows cry under a frosty shy; Dimly lit fishing boats beneath maples sadly lie. Beyond the Suzhou walls the Temple of Cold Hill ring bells, which reach my boat, breaking the midnight still." This poem has been often quoted and widely loved for hundreds of years, making the Cold Hill Temple well known throughout the world. On the lunar New Year's Eve every year, thousands of people come to the temple to listen to the bell-tolling, so as to get rid of all worries in the coming year. It is the oldest and most influential tourist activity sponsored by the Cold Hill Temple in China.

The activity of listening to the bell-tolling is divided into three parts: The lunar New Year's Eve dinner, the temple fair in the Maple Bridge Scenic Zone, and listening to the bell-tolling. At about midnight, people stream into the Cold Hill Temple to burn joss sticks and pray for fortune; all monks gather at the Grand Hall for a Buddhist service; and the abbot delivers a message of congratulation to all the guests, wishing a happy and safe year for all the people. At the 10th second of 23:42, people begin to listen to the 108 rings of the bell, which symbolize an auspicious year and a good luck.

(http://www.chinafacttours.com/huangshan/suzhou-festivals-and-celebrations.html)

Task 9 Supplementary Reading

Suzhou's "Immortal Seeking" Temple Fair

The "Immortal Seeking" temple fair, which is one of Suzhou's first batch of cultural heritages that have applied for a national level heritage, opened on May 10.

The temple fair will last three days. Cartoon images of the Eight Immortals solicited from citizens were also unveiled on that day.

The "Immortal Seeking" temple fair is the largest among the public in Suzhou and was created to commemorate Lv Dongbin, one of the Eight Immortals.

According to legends, Lv would dress himself up as a beggar on the day of his birthday and go to the crowd to save people. All people in Suzhou want to burn joss sticks at the temple and take a chance. Every person one meets on that day may be disguised Lv and one will share Lv's spirit if he meets Lv. This is called "immortal seeking".

(http://english.cri.cn/974/2006/05/12/63@88156.htm)

Project 5　Food Culture

> **Learning Objectives**:
> - be able to offer an experience of tasting local food for the tour group
> - be able to introduce the development of local cuisine or snack and its features
> - be able to design a menu of local cuisine in English

Task 1　Warm-Up

1. What is your favorite food?
2. Can you name any famous dishes in your hometown?

Task 2　Words and Expressions

pine	[paɪn]	n.	松树
crane	[kreɪn]	n.	鹤
boast	[bəʊst]	vt.	拥有
stem	[stem]	n.	干
mandarin	[ˈmændərɪn]	n.	普通话
adorably	[əˈdɔːrəbli]	adv.	可爱地
squirrel	[ˈskwɪrəl]	n.	松鼠
steamy	[ˈstiːmi]	adj.	蒸汽的
fleshy	[ˈfleʃi]	adj.	多肉的
chunky	[ˈtʃʌŋki]	adj.	厚实的
tender	[ˈtendə]	adj.	嫩的
crust	[krʌst]	n.	面包皮
shelled	[ʃeld]	adj.	带壳的
humid	[ˈhjuːmɪd]	adj.	潮湿的
determine	[dɪˈtɜːmɪn]	vt.	决定
plenteous	[ˈplentiəs]	adj.	丰富的
affluent	[ˈæfluənt]	adj.	富裕的

immortal	[ɪˈmɔːtl]	n.	神
arrowhead	[ˈærəʊhed]	n.	慈姑
cress	[kres]	n.	水芹
shield	[ʃiːld]	n.	防护物
chufa	[ˈtʃuːfə]	n.	荸荠
lotus	[ˈləʊtəs]	n.	荷,莲
chestnut	[ˈtʃesnʌt]	n.	栗子
aquatic	[əˈkwætɪk]	adj.	水生的
plum	[plʌm]	n.	李子
blossom	[ˈblɒsəm]	vi.	开花
crisp	[krɪsp]	adj.	脆的
exterior	[eksˈtɪərɪə]	n.	外部

Task 3 Dialogues

Dialogue 1 Suzhou Cuisine

Scene: The Whites and Li Lan are now at Songhe Lou Restaurant (Pine and Crane Restaurant) in Taijian Long. They are talking about Suzhou cuisine while taking order. (J = James White, L = Li Lan)

J: There are so many things on the menu that look fine. I have no idea about Suzhou cuisine. What do you suggest, Ms. Li?

L: Suzhou cuisine, as an important branch of Chinese cuisine, boasts its own and unique characteristics. How about Song Shu Gui Yu? It is a representative of Suzhou cuisine.

J: Song Shu Gui Yu, I know Yu means fish.

L: Oh, Song Shu Gui Yu means Sweet and Sour Mandarin Fish in English. It is basically a whole mandarin fish adorably cut and fried in the shape of a forest squirrel. Covered in a tasty sweet and sour sauce, the steamy, fleshy chunky fish meat remains tender within the lightly breaded crust. And Song Shu Gui Yu here is the most famous in Suzhou.

J: OK, I'll take it. And what do you mean by Bi Luo Shrimp?

L: It is another representative of Suzhou dishes.

J: Biluo. Is it Bi Luo Chun Tea which we saw in Xishan Mountain several days ago?

L: Exactly. This dish is cooked by juice of green Bi Luo Chun Tea and fresh shrimps. Many Suzhou dishes are made of the shelled shrimps.

J: Shrimps are my son's favorite. We'll have it. But why so many Suzhou dishes are made of the shelled shrimps?

L: You know Suzhou is called "the Land of Fish and Rice". The unique geographical location and humid climate of Suzhou determine that it is suitable for the cultivation of rice and corn.

Suzhou has large areas of water, and it is rich in fish and shrimps, so there is an old saying, "Suzhou Shu, Tianxia Zu", which means if Suzhou has a plenteous harvest, then the whole country will be affluent. And we have Eight Immortals in Water.

J: "Eight Immortals in Water", what's that?
L: Oh, they are traditional water plants in Suzhou, arrowhead, wild rice stem, cress, water shield, chufa, lotus root, gordon euryale seed and red water chestnuts.
J: Oh, I've never heard of it. Can we have a taste here?
L: Sure. These plants are also the seasonal food on table of Suzhou people. Some are made to be dishes, some are pastries, and some are light refreshments. Stir-fried four immortals water is a good choice. We can taste chufa, lotus root, gordon euryale seed and red chestnuts.
J: That's a good idea. Is there any other traditional food in Suzhou?
L: Of course. Rice Cake, Shangdeng Dumpling, Luodi Pastry, Mandarin Fish, Green Crabs, Sweet Winter Solstice wine, Taihu Three White Aquatic Product, Duck Blood Glutinous Rice, etc.
J: Oh, thank you, Susan. I hope I can taste all of them.

Dialogue 2 Suzhou Snacks

Scene: The Whites and Li Lan are walking along the Shantang Street. They are talking about Suzhou snacks. (T = Tom, J = James White, L = Li Lan)

T: Dad, what's this? It looks yummy. Can I have a taste?
J: Sure. But what's it, Lan?
L: It's called Plum blossom-shaped pastry, a traditional Suzhou snack. This pastry looks like golden plum blossoms and tastes soft and delicious, which is suitable for both young and old.
T: (*Tom has a taste of Plum blossom-shaped pastry.*) Dad, it's yummy. Would you like to try?
J: Oh, it's delicious indeed. Ms. Li, we are hungry, but we don't want to go to restaurants. Can you take us to taste more Suzhou snacks?
L: Of course. You know Suzhou snack is one of the four famous snacks in China, and the other three are popular snacks of Nanjing, Shanghai and Changsha. Some famous and popular snacks are worth a try when you are in Suzhou.
J: Exactly. Let's go.
L: Here we are. A'er Shengjian. Shengjian and Wonton are worth trying.
J: Shengjian?
L: Yes. Shengjian means deep-fried dumplings in English. It boasts crisp exterior and juice fillings. Deep-fried dumplings are called "Shengjian Mantou" in Suzhou.
J: OK, we'll have it. And I like Wonton soup. How about Wonton here?
L: We call Wonton here as "Paopao Wonton". Paopao means bubble.
J: Wonton looks like bubbles?
L: Yes. It's delicious and filled with juice.

J: Thank you for your introduction, Ms. Li. We've learnt a lot about Suzhou snacks.

Task 4　Useful Sentences

1. Suzhou locates near Taihu Lake, so it teems with plum, apricot, loquat, waxberry, peach, golden orange, etc.
2. Ao Zao Noodle: The quick-fried fish noodle and bittern duck noodle are the most famous noodle. Except for good materials and delicious taste, there are three features of the noodle. First, the noodle is very hot. Second, the soup is very hot. Third, the bowls are very hot. Even in winter, after eating a bowl of this kind of noodle, you may sweat.
3. Pine Nut and Date Cake: It is a famous traditional snack in Suzhou. It chooses sugar, eggs, food oil, and wheat powder as the raw materials to make the skin. The nutlets, fruit flesh, and pine nuts are the stuffing. Then, the cake is baked over a slow fire. This snack is sweet but not greasy. It is very delicious. It is exactly a good choice to give to friends and relatives as gifts.
4. First Dish on Earth: As a well-known traditional dish of Songhe Lou Restaurant, the First Dish on Earth is highly appreciated by guests from home and abroad.
5. White Bait Soup: It is a specialty of Suzhou. The fish characterized by its tender flesh, appears on the market every fall. The light delicious soup is made up of liver and flesh. Seasoned with ham, bamboo slice and green vegetable leaves, the fleshy liver tastes savory and attracts countless guests.
6. Cracking Eel Paste: Ricefield eel is nutritious and can be prepared broiled, stir-fried or quick-boiled. Quick-boiled eel slivers, stir-fried eel slices and cracking eel paste are all Suzhou cuisines enjoying great popularity.

Task 5　Listening

You will hear five sentences. Listen carefully and put down the whole sentences.

1. _____.
2. _____.
3. _____.
4. _____.
5. _____.

Task 6 Dialogue-Completing

Mike: Waiter!
Waiter: Yes, sir and madam. _____?
Mike: Yes. It's our first time to Suzhou, _____. Would you recommend some to me?
Waiter: _____. Our restaurant is very famous for Song Shu Gui Yu.
Mike: Excuse me, _____?
Waiter: Well, _____
_____.
Mike: Interesting! We'll have one. _____?
Waiter: _____, sir and madam?
Mike: A bottle of beer, thanks.

Task 7 Role-Play

Situation 1: Lily is a girl born in Suzhou. Her pen friend Susan is an American girl. Now Susan is on her holiday in China. Lily is showing her around Suzhou and introduces some famous Suzhou snacks to her.

Situation 2: Mr. Chen has been living abroad for many years. Today, he is back to his hometown Suzhou and visiting his old friends. They are having lunch in Song He Lou.

Task 8 Translation

Put the following sentences into Chinese.
1. Arrowhead, wild rice stem, cress, water shield, chufa, lotus root, gordon euryale seed and red water chestnuts are known as the "Eight Immortals in Water", which are traditional water plants in Wuzhong, Wujiang, Kunshan, Changshu and Zhangjiagang of Suzhou. These plants are also the seasonal food on tables of Suzhou people. Some are made to be dishes, some are pastries, and some are light refreshments.
2. Suzhou dishes are praised highly by food connoisseurs from both home and abroad.
3. Suzhou cuisine attains its unique sweet flavor from strictly selected materials.
4. Nearby Taihu Lake supplies abundant fresh sea food that adds more color to the table culture of Suzhou.
5. It is an important custom for locals to eat specific dishes according to the changing seasons.

6. Suzhou snacks are also worth trying since they are no less famous than Suzhou cuisine.

Task 9　Supplementary Reading

The Squirrel-Shaped Mandarin Fish

The Squirrel-Shaped Mandarin Fish, a typical traditional dish in Suzhou, is highly appreciated by guests from home and abroad. Not only does it feature in the color and flavor, but also in the taste and shape. What is more, when the fried Squirrel-Shaped Mandarin Fish is ready and pored with steaming hot bittern, there will be a noise as if the squirrel is cheeping.

As a well-known traditional dish in Suzhou, it is regarded as the required dish in the banquets and feasts in the south area of the Yangtze River. It is recorded that when the Emperor Qianlong of Qing Dynasty visited the south area of Yangtze River, the chef in the Song He Lou Restaurant well satisfied him with the Squirrel-shaped Mandarin Fish. He carved on the boneless carp, covered yolk paste on it and fried it, then scattered some sweet and sour sauce on it. The dish shaped as a squirrel, tasted crisp and soft, sour and sweet. The emperor felt very content to the dish. From then on it was widely spread and named as the Squirrel-Shaped Mandarin Fish.

There are some notes we should take in the making of Squirrel-Shaped Mandarin Fish. Firstly, fresh and alive mandarin fish should be chosen so that the meat can well retain fresh and tender. Secondly, the cutting should be very good and delicate and make it shape as a squirrel. Thirdly, the sauce should be tasted both sweet and sour, making the fish tasty.

Steamed Crab

Autumn is the best time to eat crabs. During that time, the best-quality Yangcheng Lake hairy crabs with green shells and white bottoms, rich in fat, are shipped to restaurants. When the crabs are properly cooked, the fragrance appeals to diners' palate.

There are such famous dishes like the crab meat bean curd, lily fruit in crab fat, rice cake in crab meat, delicacies much appreciated by diners. The most popular one is the steamed crab which maintains the original flavor of the crab. It focuses on bringing out the natural crab flavor. The meat is tender, juicy and delicious.

Beggar's Chicken

This is a wonderful story. A homeless, starving beggar is wandering along a road when he catches sight of a chicken. Desperate for food, he kills the chicken by wringing its neck. Lacking a stove, he covers the chicken in mud, makes a fire and bakes it.

At this point an Emperor passes by with his entourage. Attracted by the aroma of the baked chicken, he stops and dines with the beggar, demanding to know how he created such a delicious meal. "Beggar's Chicken" is subsequently added to the list of dishes served at the imperial court.

While the chicken is marinating, prepare the vegetables and pork. Reconstitute dried mushrooms by soaking them in warm water until softened. Squeeze dry and cut into thin slices. For fresh, wipe with a damp cloth and slice. Cut the pork into thin matchstick pieces. Finely chop the remaining vegetables.

Stuff the chicken loosely with the stuffing and close with skewers or strong toothpicks. Wrap the chicken tightly in the aluminum foil. Place the wrapped chicken in a roasting pan.

(http://www.chinahighlights.com/suzhou/food/the-squirrel-shaped-mandarin-fish.htm)

Project 6　Tea Culture

Learning Objectives:
- be able to explain tea culture and its importance in China
- be able to demonstrate the customs of drinking tea
- be able to arrange a tour to enjoy Bi Luo Chun Tea in Suzhou

Task 1　Warm-Up

1. How many varieties of Chinese tea do you know?
2. Do you know how Bi Luo Chun got its name?

Task 2　Words and Expressions

variety	[vəˈraɪəti]	n.	种类
miracle	[ˈmɪrəkl]	n.	奇迹
mellow	[ˈmeləʊ]	adj.	成熟的,醇的
presentation	[ˌprezenˈteɪʃn]	n.	介绍,陈述
classify	[ˈklæsɪfaɪ]	vt.	分类,归类
souvenir	[ˌsuːvəˈnɪə]	n.	纪念品
category	[ˈkætɪɡəri]	n.	种类,类别
bud	[bʌd]	n.	芽,花蕾
shoot	[ʃuːt]	n.	嫩枝,发射
fearful	[ˈfɪəfl]	adj.	可怕的,非常的
ferment	[ˈfɜːment]	v.	发酵,动乱
		n.	发酵,酵素
submerge	[səbˈmɜːdʒ]	vt.	浸没,覆盖
		vi.	浸没
ceremony	[ˈserɪməni]	n.	仪式,典礼
aroma	[əˈrəʊmə]	n.	浓香,香气
entertain	[ˌentəˈteɪn]	v.	娱乐,招待

brew	[bruː]	n.	酿造
		vt.	泡茶
brick	[brɪk]	n.	砖,砖块
emperor	[ˈempərə]	n.	皇帝
steamed	[stiːmd]	adj.	蒸熟的
snail	[sneɪl]	n.	蜗牛
compressed	[kəmˈprest]	adj.	压缩的
spiral	[ˈspaɪrəl]	adj.	螺旋形的
resemble	[rɪˈzembl]	vt.	相似,类似
resembling	[rɪˈzemblɪŋ]	adj.	类似的
blooming	[ˈbluːmɪŋ]	adj.	正开花的
crop	[krɒp]	v.	收获,出现
initially	[ɪˈnɪʃəli]	adv.	最初
sample	[ˈsæmpl]	vt.	采样,取样
bulb	[blʌb]	n.	电灯泡,球状物
refreshing	[rɪˈfreʃɪŋ]	adj.	有精神的,使清爽的
incense	[ˈɪnsens]	n.	香
Oolong tea	[ˈuːlɒŋ]		乌龙茶
scented tea	[ˈsentɪd]		花茶
give off			发出,散发

Task 3   Dialogues

Dialogue 1   Varieties of Tea

Scene: The tour guide Li Lan and her guests are drinking tea in a tea house, and the guests are interested in Chinese tea. Li Lan is introducing Chinese tea to them. (L = Li Lan, J = James White)

L: What do you think about the Bi Luo Chun Tea?
J: Oh, it's good! So fresh!
L: Yes, it's the best green tea in China.
J: But you know we Westerners drink black tea rather than green tea.
L: Yes. You add milk and sugar in black tea.
J: Oh, they can make the taste mellower.
L: We drink the same, only without milk and sugar.
J: Black tea, green tea. Is there any other tea in China?
L: Of course. Although there are a variety of Chinese tea, they can be mainly classified into six categories: green tea, black tea, Oolong tea, scented tea, white tea and brick tea.

J: What's the Oolong tea?

L: It's a kind of semi-fermented tea. It is often used for "Gongfu Tea". The Gongfu Tea Ceremony here can not only entertain us but also get better understanding about Chinese tea culture.

J: Never heard about it before. What about brick tea? Is it like a brick?

L: Yes, fresh tea leaves are steamed first, and then compressed tightly into the shape of a brick.

J: I see. What's scented tea? Do you add something special to the tea to make it fragrant?

L: Well, yes. Fresh or dried flowers are added to the tea leaves. So it can give off a nice smell of both the tea and the flowers. And it's a favorite for ladies.

J: Yes, I like the smell. Oh, I see a little blooming flower in the glass. What is this going on there, please?

L: Yes, it's called blooming tea, a very new kind of scented tea.

J: How interesting! Can you explain more about it for us?

L: Sure. Actually, they handmade each of this, so called "bloom". Initially, it's all into a bulb. But once it submerges in hot water, it opens up, almost like a bloom coming to a full flower.

J: It's a miracle.

L: It's not only for drink but also for presentation.

J: Really? How long can it keep in the water?

L: Usually, more than one month.

J: Oh, that's good. I'll buy some to take home as a souvenir.

Dialogue 2 Famous Green Tea—Bi Luo Chun

Scene: A couple is traveling at West Mountains of Suzhou. Li Lan, their tour guide is introducing Bi Luo Chun Tea to them. (J =James White, L =Li Lan)

J: What are they doing, Li Lan?

L: Oh, they are picking Bi Luo Chun tea leaves.

J: Picking tea leaves?

L: Yes. April is a good season to pick Bi Luo Chun tea leaves. Bi Luo Chun picked before Qing Ming Festival is the best.

J: Can you teach us to pick tea leaves?

L: Sure. Take the basket first, please.

J: OK, it's interesting. We are ready!

L: You see, pick the top two leaves and bud from new shoots. Others are old.

J: (*20 minutes later*) Hi, Li Lan, you see the tea leaves we picked. Is it OK?

L: Yes, it's good.

J: You said it is called Bi Luo Chun. What does it mean?

L: Actually, it is locally known as "Fearful Incense" due to the strong aroma of the brew in ancient! It was not until the Qing Dynasty that Emperor Kangxi visited Suzhou and changed the name. Bi Luo Chun can be translated to Green Snail Spring, because it is a green tea, and it is rolled into a tight spiral resembling snail meat. Finally it is cropped in early spring.

J: It's a nice name now.

L: And now, Bi Luo Chun Tea is one of the ten most famous teas in China.

J: That's great. I'll have a drink.

L: If you have never sampled Chinese green tea, Bi Luo Chun is a good one to start with. It's very light.

J: We drank black tea before.

L: And it is much healthier and more refreshing than black tea.

J: Oh, I am thirsty. Can you take us to have a cup of Bi Luo Chun Tea?

L: Of course. Let's go.

Task 4 Useful Sentences

1. Chinese tea can be divided into ten main categories. Among them, green tea has the longest history and rank the first in varieties and consumption.
2. Originally grown in the Dongting Hills of Taihu Lake, Bi Luo Chun Tea is a famous green tea in history, which was first produced in the early Qing Dynasty.
3. China ranks the number one in the world in green tea output and exportation.
4. Black tea is the complete fermented tea. China is the birth country of black tea.
5. First grown in China, black tea has the greatest consumption in the world now.
6. Black tea can be drunk alone, and also can be mixed with milk, cubic sugar, fruit juice or alcohol, to be served as appetizing romantic beverage.
7. Oolong Tea is semi-fermented tea.
8. Oolong Tea is mainly grown in Fujian Province, Guangdong Province and Taiwan.
9. Oolong Tea has big varieties, including Da Hong Pao Tea, Tie Guan Yin Tea, Phoenix Dancong Tea, and Taiwan High Mountain Tea.
10. Tie Guan Yin Tea (Iron Mercy Goddess) is the most famous Oolong Tea, which is grown in Anxi, Fujian Province.

Task 5   Listening

You will hear five sentences. Listen carefully and put down the whole sentences.

1. _____.
2. _____.
3. _____.
4. _____.
5. _____.

Task 6   Dialogue-Completing

Dialogue 1

Mr. Smith: _____. Is it green tea?
Lily: Yes, it is _____, we call it Bi Luo Chun.
Mr. Smith: Bi Luo Chun? What does it mean?
Lily: Well, _____
_____

Mr. Smith: Amazing!
Lily: _____?
Mr. Smith: _____, I'd like to.

Dialogue 2

Mr. Smith: _____. What is Oolong Tea?
Lily: It is _____ tea.
Mr. Smith: What varieties does Oolong Tea have?
Lily: The most famous ones are _____
_____.

Mr. Smith: Thanks for your introduction.

Task 7   Role-Play

Situation 1: Mr. and Mrs. Black are from America, and they would like to buy some green tea before they leave Suzhou. The local guide from China Youth Travel Service, Wang Yan is talking with them in the hotel lobby.

Situation 2: Anna, a British girl, is interested in tea ceremony. Now she is talking with her tour guide, Ms. Li about it.

Task 8   Translation

Put the following sentences into Chinese.
1. We have various kinds of high-quality Oolong Tea for you to choose.
2. Pu'er Tea is post-fermented tea.
3. Pu'er Tea has effectiveness in reducing body weight and blood fat.
4. Scented Tea is considered to be the most poetic tea.
5. Jasmine Tea has a strong and rich fragrance and it is very popular.
6. The quantity of tea, the temperature of water, and the timing of serving tea are three variable keys for making good tea.
7. Oolong Tea reminds tea gourmets of Gongfu Tea, which features a whole set of tea wares from a small oven to a tea pot and tiny tea cups. Gongfu means skill. Tea is poured into tiny tea cups one by one. The mellowness of Oolong Tea as well as that of friendship is strengthened as time passes by. The three major Oolong growth areas are Fujian, Guangdong, and Taiwan. Tieguanyin has become the representative of Oolong Tea although the most precious is Da Hong Pao (Big Red Robe), which was once used as a tribute.

Task 9   Supplementary Reading

Green Tea

Green tea is the most popular in most places in China. It is the best drink for sultry summers as it is cool and fights off inflammation, or relieves fever.

Green tea is withered and rolled but not fermented during processing. Thus the original color of the leaves is retained. The result is a fresh tasting tea that produces a pale green-yellow liquid that has a grassy flavor. Quality green tea is picked around Pure Brightness (around April 4-6) and Grain Rain (around April 19-21). The water is clear and the leaves remain green.

The temperature of water should be varied according to the type of green tea. Generally, water temperature of 85℃ is the best.

Well known green teas include Long Jing from the West Lake, Bi Lou Chun from Suzhou, Jiangsu Province, Huangshan Mao Feng from Mt. Huangshan in Anhui, and Junshan Silver from the Hills of Junshan, Dongting Lake, Hunan Province.

The tonic effect of green tea has long been known. Its radiation-resistance effect makes it a top choice for people who sit before computers for long hours. Since it reportedly helps keep one fit and has a whitening effect on skin color, women prefer it.

Black Tea

Black tea is fermented tea. Unlike green tea, black tea does not lose its fragrance easily so it is suitable for long-distance transportation. This may explain why it was exported to the West. Black tea is believed to warm the stomach and is good in autumn and winter.

The most famous black teas include Qi Hong, Dian Hong and Ying Hong. Hong means red; black tea is called Hong Cha, red tea, in Chinese.

Qi Hong originates from Qimen, Anhui Province. It has been the favorite black tea among Chinese black tea connoisseurs since it was developed in 1876. By 1939 this type of tea accounted for one-third of black tea consumed in China. Qi Hong, Darjiling from India and Uva from Sri Lanka are the world's three major types of black tea.

Dian Hong is from Yunnan as Dian is the short name for Yunnan. The area's favorable climate ensures the widespread production of black tea, especially in southern and western areas.

Oolong Tea

Oolong Tea lies somewhere in the middle between green and black tea. It is fermented like black tea, but the process is stopped part way through. The crucial stage in the process is to stop the fermentation process at exactly the right time, and the best time to stop the fermentation is when the leaves are 30% red and 70% green.

Oolong Tea reminds tea gourmets of gongfu tea, which features a whole set of tea wares from a small oven to a tea pot and tiny tea cups. Gongfu means skill. Tea is poured into tiny teacups one by one. The mellowness of Oolong Tea as well as that of friendship is strengthened as time passes by. The three major oolong growth areas are Fujian, Guangdong, and Taiwan. Tie Guan Yin has become the representative of Oolong Tea although the most precious is Da Hong Pao (Big Red Robe), which was once used as a tribute.

Tea compressed into the shape of brick is called brick tea. It is very popular among the Tibetan, Mongolian and Uigur for making yak butter tea or milk tea. For nomads, this kind of tea is easy to transport. There are many places in China producing brick tea, including Hunan, Hubei, Sichuan and Yunnan. Sichuan is the largest producer, while Pu'er Tea is grown in Yunnan Province. Pu'er has come into vogue among white-collar workers in major cities owing to its unique earthy mellowness.

(http://en.wikipedia.org/wiki/Suzhou)

Module III Main Tourist Attractions in Suzhou

Project 1   The Tiger Hill

Part I

Task 1   Warm-Up

1. What is the altitude of the Tiger Hill? How big is this scenic area (in acres or hectares)? Why was it called firstly as the Hill of Emergence from the Sea, and later the Tiger Hill?
2. Why is the Tiger Hill also called the Premier Scene in Wu Area? Or Hidden Mountain in the Temple?

Task 2   Words and Expressions

regret	[rɪˈgret]	n.	遗憾
remote	[rɪˈməʊt]	adj.	遥远的
ebb	[eb]	n.	退潮
tide	[taɪd]	n.	潮汐
funeral	[ˈfjuːnərəl]	n.	葬礼
tomb	[tuːm]	n.	坟墓
pagoda	[pəˈgəʊdə]	n.	塔
rail	[reɪl]	n.	栏杆
architecture	[ˈɑːkɪtektʃə]	n.	建筑
oval	[ˈəʊvəl]	adj.	椭圆的
grant	[grɑːnt]	v.	授予,承认
mud	[mʌd]	n.	泥
preach	[priːtʃ]	v.	讲道
form	[fɔːm]	v.	形成

islet	[ˈaɪlɪt]	n.	小岛
flow	[fləʊ]	v.	流动
burial	[ˈberɪəl]	n.	埋葬
crouch	[ˈkraʊtʃ]	v.	蹲伏
slope	[sləʊp]	n.	斜坡
tail	[teɪl]	n.	尾巴
paw	[pɔː]	n.	爪子
nail	[neɪl]	n.	钉子
chop	[tʃɒp]	v.	砍
forge	[fɔːdʒ]	v.	锻造
monk	[mʌŋk]	n.	僧侣
log	[lɒg]	n.	木头
Broken Beam Hall			断梁殿
Pillow Stone			枕石
a variety of			许多
Yangtze River Delta			长江三角洲
Sea Emergence Bridge			海涌桥
Sword-Testing Rock			试剑石
scenic spot			景点
historical interest			历史名胜
Jiangsu Provincial Government			江苏省政府

Task 3　Dialogues

Scene：Now, it is one o'clock in the afternoon. The guide is leading the group at the entrance gate of the Tiger Hill. (V＝Visitor, G＝Guide)

Travel Route：Entrance—Sea Emergence Bridge—Broken Beam Hall—Sword-Testing Rock—Pillow Stone

Entrance：

G： Hello, everyone. Now, we are here at the No. 1 scenic spot of Wu Area, the Tiger Hill. Among a variety of historical interests in Suzhou, the Tiger Hill is the most famous with great natural beauty and long history.

V： Great!

G： The famous poet Su Dongpo in Song Dynasty once remarked, "To visit Suzhou without seeing the Tiger Hill would be a thing for regret."

V: I can't wait to visit it. Why do you give it such a name?
G: The original name of the Tiger Hill is Sea Emergence Hill, which formed in the remote time. At first it was a small islet in the ocean, emerged and disappeared with the ebb and flow of the tides, hence the name. Later the Yangtze River Delta came into being with the change of time (nature), the original island in the sea turned into the hill today. Here is the burial place of Helv, King of State Wu, who was the founder of Suzhou. A legend says that three days after the funeral, a white tiger was seen crouching on the tomb, which is the reason why we call it the Tiger Hill.
V: I see. What an interesting name!
G: This is the whole view of the Tiger Hill Spot. Attention please, we will stay here for about 2 hours. This is our travelling route. At about 3 o'clock, let's gather here, the main entrance. OK?
V: No problem.

Sea Emergence Bridge

G: Now we are on the Sea Emergence Bridge.
V: I guess the name is connected with the name of this scenic spot.
G: Yes! From this position we can command a nice view. In front of us the Second Entrance Hall over there looks like the head of a tiger, the slope of the hill, the back of the tiger, of course the pagoda, the tail. That is another reason why we call it the Tiger Hill.
V: Yeah. That really is.
G: Have you noticed the rails of both sides of the bridge?
V: Oh, some beautiful stone lions.
G: The bridge is made of granite, produced in Suzhou. 6 male lions with their paws engraved balls which symbolize the power while other 6 females with baby lions under their paws, which mean the endless offspring one generation after another.
V: Very interesting!
G: Here is a nice view point. Would you like to take a photo?
V: Of course. We would not miss such a good chance!

Broken Beam Hall

G: Here is the second entrance hall, which is also called the Broken Beam Hall.
V: Why? Is its main beam broken?
G: Yes, you are right! The main beam of the hall is made of two logs not joined in the middle to support the whole weight of the roof. Unlike other architectures, it has only one piece of beam to support the roof.
V: It is amazing that there is no single nail in the whole hall

but it is fastened.
G: Yes, this hall was firstly built in Yuan Dynasty, about 700 years ago.
V: Wow! But it is still in very good condition!
G: This hall is now listed as a historical site under the protection of Jiangsu Provincial Government. OK! Let's move on!

Sword-Testing Rock

V: This piece of stone is so interesting! A big oval rock burst in the middle as though it was chopped by a sword.
G: Yes! This is the famous Sword-Testing Rock.
V: Can you tell me whether it is natural or man-made?
G: A legend says that King Helv loved swords very much, he granted the famous sword-couple Ganjiang and Moye to forge sharp swords for him. When swords were finished, he came here to test. Down came the sword, burst the rock like mud. The rock is said to be today's Sword-Testing Rock.

V: But I still doubt that story.
G: Yes, it's just a story.

Pillow Stone

G: This big stone is the Pillow Stone.
V: I have found that it shapes like a big pillow.
G: Yes, it is said that Shenggong, a famous monk, came here to preach; when he felt tired he would climb onto the stone to rest, taking the stone as a pillow, so later we called it Pillow Stone.

Task 4　Useful Sentences

1. Now, we are here at the No. 1 scenic spot of Wu Area, the Tiger Hill.
2. The original name of the Tiger Hill is Sea Emergence Hill, which formed in the remote time.
3. I guess the name is connected with the name of this scenic spot.
4. Unlike the other architectures, it has only one piece of beam to support the roof.
5. A legend says that King Helv loved swords very much, he granted the famous sword-couple Ganjiang and Moye to forge sharp swords for him.

Task 5　Listening

You will hear five sentences. Listen carefully and put down the whole sentences.

1. _____.
2. _____.
3. _____.
4. _____.
5. _____.

Task 6　Role-Play

Situation 1: Arrange a travel route of Entrance—Sea Emergence Bridge—Broken Beam Hall—Sword-Testing Rock—Pillow Stone for the James.

Situation 2: You are at the airport to meet a tour group of 20 people by the name of "China Experience". Its tour escort is Mark Lee. Several groups get off the plane. You don't know which is your group.
- ◆ Find Mr. Lee and the tour group.
- ◆ Introduce yourself.
- ◆ Welcome the group.
- ◆ Ask Mr. Lee for their luggage claim checks and help them get their luggage, then show them to the bus.

Task 7　Translation

1. 在苏州各景点中,虎丘,有着美丽的自然风光和悠久的历史,是最负盛名的一个景点。
2. 到苏州不游虎丘乃憾事也。
3. At first it was a small islet in the ocean, emerged and disappeared with the ebb and flow of the tides.
4. In front of us the Second Entrance Hall over there looks like the head of a tiger, the slope of the hill, the back of the tiger, of course the pagoda, the tail.
5. It is said that Shenggong, a famous monk, came here to preach; when he felt tired he would climb onto the stone to rest, taking the stone as a pillow, so later we called it Pillow Stone.

Task 8 Supplementary Reading

Mansion, Temple and Cemetery of Confucius

The Mansion, Temple and Cemetery of Confucius in Qufu, Shandong Province, are cultural sites and attract tourists from both China and abroad. In 1994, they were listed as world cultural heritage sites.

The Mansion of Confucius is the living quarters of the first grandson of Confucius, a great philosopher, educator and a founder of Confucianism. It is also known as Master Yansheng's Mansion because in 1055, or the second year of the reign of Song Emperor Zhaozhen, Kong Zongyuan, the 46th generation male descendant of Confucius was given the title "Master Yansheng". The title was passed down to Kong Decheng, the 77th generation male descendant of Confucius. Built on an area of 160,000 square meters, the mansion has nine courtyards with 463 rooms along the east, west and middle routes. The houses along the middle route are the main part of the mansion. The first four yards contain offices and the other five serve as residences. At the rear is a garden. The mansion stores more than 9,000 volumes of files from 1534 (the 13th year of the reign of Ming Emperor Jiaqing) to 1948 and great quantities of rare and precious cultural and historical relics.

The Temple of Confucius was, in various dynasties, a place for worshipping Confucius. In 478 B.C., the second year after Confucius' death, the ruler of the State of Lu converted the three-room Confucius' former mansion into a temple and this became a place for worshipping Confucius. The temple was constantly renovated and expanded to its present size by emperors of the Western Han Dynasty and following historical periods. It covers an area of 218,000 square meters and is 1,120 meters in length from south to north. There are nine courtyards and 466 rooms along three routes in the left, right and middle. The temple has an outer wall, with four corner towers, which shelters ancient pines. The main buildings along the middle route are Kuiwen Pavilion, Thirteen Stele Pavilion, Xingtan Pavilion, Dacheng Hall, Hall of Confucius wife and Shengji Hall. Dacheng hall stands out and is the main hall where Confucius was worshipped. The temple houses some 2,000 tablets dating from the Western Han Dynasty right up to the founding of New China; they are one of the largest collections of tablets in the country. There are now three exhibition halls displaying tablets from the Han Dynasty and Six Kingdoms of Wei, stone statues from the Han Dynasty and calligraphic carvings on Yuhonglou tablets. The 17 tablets of Han Dynasty are the largest collection in the country by the quantity reserved in one place. The Cemetery of Confucius is about 1.5 kilometers north of Qufu and is the Confucius family cemetery. It takes up 1,998 million square meters and around it there is a seven-kilometer-long hedge. The pavilions, towers, halls and archways built in various historical periods are set in a forest. Behind the Zhushui Bridge is the graveyard, dating from the Eastern Zhou, which houses the tomb of Confucius, the tombs of his son Kong Li and grandson Kong Ji. The tomb of Confucius is 6.2 meters high and has a circumference of 88 meters.

(Source: http://travel.chinavista.com/destination-sight-17.html)

> Questions:
> 1. What is the significance of the Mansion, Temple and Cemetery of Confucius in Qufu?
> 2. Why is it also known as Master Yansheng's Mansion?
> 3. When was this place converted into a temple?
> 4. Who do people worship here?
> 5. Use some words to describe Confucius.

Part Ⅱ

Task 1　　Warm-Up

1. When was the Broken Beam Hall constructed? Under which level of Heritage Protection was it endorsed? How come that it hasn't collapsed? There are two plaques in the hall, can you explain them?
2. In which dynasty did the legend of Han-Han Spring's excavation take place? How many years does it date back to? What relevance does it have with Hong Jun, the No. 1 scholar?

Task 2　　Words and Expressions

rare	[reə]	adj.	罕见的
banquet	[ˈbæŋkwɪt]	n.	宴会
oppose	[əˈpəʊz]	v.	反对
learned	[ˈlɜːnd]	adj.	博学的
temple	[ˈtempl]	n.	寺庙
prosperous	[ˈprɒspərəs]	adj.	繁荣的
Taoism	[ˈtaʊɪzəm]	n.	道教
portrait	[ˈpɔːtrɪt]	n.	画像
fade	[feɪd]	v.	逐渐消失
dredge	[dredʒ]	v.	挖泥
rashly	[ˈræʃli]	adv.	急躁地,草率地

smooth	[smuːð]	adj.	光滑的
pretend	[prɪˈtend]	v.	假装
stain	[steɪn]	v.	着色
plain	[pleɪn]	adj.	简单的
omen	[ˈəʊmən]	n.	预兆
festival	[ˈfestəvəl]	n.	节日
founder	[ˈfaʊndə]	n.	建立者
couplet	[ˈkʌplɪt]	n.	对联
elegant	[ˈelɪgənt]	adj.	优雅的
fake	[feɪk]	adj.	假的
tunnel	[ˈtʌnəl]	n.	隧道
Thousand-Man Rock			千人石
Two Immortals' Pavilion			二仙亭
Nodding Stone			点头石
keep in good condition			保存完好
settle down			定居
Sheng Gong's Rostrum			生公讲台
Sword Pond			剑池
White Lotus Pond			白莲池
Chinese characters			汉字

Task 3　Dialogues

Scene: Now the guide is standing beside Thousand-Man Rock. (V-Visitor, G = Guide)
Travel Route: Thousand-Man Rock—Sheng Gong's Rostrum—Two Immortals Pavilion—Sword Pond

Thousand-Man Rock

G: Here is a huge plain smooth rock. We called it the Thousand-Man Rock.
V: Is there something special about it?
G: There are two stories about it.
V: OK, I would like to listen.
G: As we have already known Helv was buried in the Tiger Hill. There are many rare funerary objects inside this tomb, especially 3,000 sharp swords, including Ganjiang and Moye, which we have just mentioned. In order to keep this secret, his son Fuchai pretended to invite all the builders to a banquet. After they had been drunk,

Fuchai ordered his army to kill all the builders, altogether more than a thousand men. It's said that their blood stained this big rock. That's the reason why this rock is red.

V: It is so terrible. How about the other one?

G: The other story is about Sheng Gong that we have just mentioned. Sheng Gong preached Buddhism and gathered a thousand listeners sitting here. So the other name of this rock is the Thousand-Man Seat.

V: I see. I hope the second one is a true one.

G: Yes, here is a nice view point, would you like to take a photo here?

V: Of course, I would not miss such a good chance!

Sheng Gong's Rostrum

G: Here is the Sheng Gong Rostrum.

V: You have mentioned him many times. What kind of person was he?

G: He was a learned Buddhist monk in Jin Dynasty around 3rd and 4th centuries. He put the new theory "those who have the sense of Buddhism can all become Buddha". His theory was opposed by the old schools. And then he travelled in China. Finally he settled down in the temple on Shantang Street, and he came to the Tiger Hill to preach.

V: I see here is a place for him to give lectures.

G: Yes. Over there is the White Lotus Pond, and a big square stone is in the centre, which is called the Nodding Stone. Sheng Gong's preaching was so wonderful that even the stones nodded in agreement and flowers rained from sky. Local people thought it was a good omen. So many came here to pick small ones home, hoping these could bring good luck to them. The last one was too big and too heavy to carry, so it was left here, which is the Nodding Stone of today.

V: So amazing!

G: OK, let's move on!

Two Immortals' Pavilion

G: We call this pavilion the Two Immortals' Pavilion.

V: I guess there are two immortals about it.

G: Yes. It's said that two immortals, Lv Chunyang and Chen Tuan once played chess here, so it has the name. Lv is one of the Eight Immortals of legend. He is closely connected with Suzhou, where there is a traditional temple festival about him. On the 14th day of the fourth lunar

month, he would disguise himself as a beggar or peddler among the crowd. All locals hope to touch him to have good luck, so it is very busy and prosperous that day. Until now, we still have that custom. Chen was the founder of Taoism. There are two couplets and two portraits inside the pavilion.

V: Very interesting! I found this pavilion is very beautiful.

G: Yes. What is worth mentioning is that the roof of the pavilion is carved out of a whole piece of stone in Qing Dynasty about 200 years ago, very elegant.

Sword Pond

G: Here are four big Chinese characters.

V: What do they mean?

G: They mean the Tiger Hill and the Sword Pond, the name of this spot and the scenic spot inside.

V: Are these words very famous?

G: These four words were all written by Yan Zhenqing, who is a famous calligrapher in Tang Dynasty about 1,300 years ago. With the time went on, the Tiger Hill faded. In Qing Dynasty, it was re-written by Zhang Zhongyu, another calligrapher about 200 years ago. A local saying was that "fake Tiger Hill and real Sword Pond".

V: A very interesting saying.

G: People have been regarding them as the symbol of the Tiger Hill. So visitors like taking photos here.

V: OK, I would like to take one too.

G: Behind the moon gate is the famous Sword Pond.

V: Is there a sword inside?

G: It is said that Helv, King of Wu State, was buried under the water, together with 3,000 sharp swords. Many people want to know whether there really is the tomb of Helv inside here, but no one can answer that. From Qin Dynasty more than 2,000 years ago, many emperors came here to explore but found nothing. In 1955 the local government had Sword Pond dredged. They found a cave and a tunnel, which was clearly man-made. Together with historical records and other evidences, researchers believed that there is a tomb inside, which may be the tomb of Helv.

V: Has the tomb been open yet?

G: No, the pond is just under the base of the pagoda. If we open the tomb rashly, the pagoda would be in danger. We all hope that with the development of science and technique, one day we could open it and find out whether it really is the tomb of Helv and whether there are 3,000 sharp swords inside it. At the same time the pagoda is kept in good condition.

V: I am longing for that day.

Task 4   Useful Sentences

1. It's said that two immortals, Lv Chunyang and Chen Tuan once played chess here, so it has the name.
2. If we open the tomb rashly, the pagoda would be in danger.
3. They found a cave and a tunnel, which was clearly man-made.
4. Over there is the White Lotus Pond, and a big square stone is in the centre, which is called the Nodding Stone.
5. There are many rare funerary objects inside this tomb, especially 3,000 sharp swords, including Ganjiang and Moye, which we have just mentioned.

Task 5   Listening

You will hear five sentences. Listen carefully and put down the whole sentences.

1. _____.
2. _____.
3. _____.
4. _____.
5. _____.

Task 6   Role-Play

Situation 1: Arrange a half-day tour for the James including the sites: Thousand-Man Rock, Sheng Gong's Rostrum, Two Immortals Pavilion, Sword Pond.

Situation 2: You are at the airport with General Manager Zhang of your travel service to meet Mr. White, who is coming with his wife. Mr. White is the general manager of the Orient Travel Company in the U. S. They come to China to hold some business talks with their Chinese counterparts.
- ◆ Find Mr. White and introduce yourself.
- ◆ Mr. White introduces his wife to you and expresses their pleasure to see you.
- ◆ Make introductions between Mr. and Mrs. White and General Manager Zhang.
- ◆ General Manager Zhang welcomes the Whites; you help them claim their luggage.
- ◆ The Whites are eager to know where they are going to stay; tell them something about the

hotel.

- General Manager Zhang wants to invite the Whites to dinner, try to find out the most convenient time for them.

Task 7   Translation

1. 这就是石头为什么会是红色的原因。
2. 池塘位于塔的下方。
3. We all hope that with the development of science and technique, one day we could open it and find whether it really is the tomb of Helv and whether there are 3,000 sharp swords inside it.
4. There are two couplets and two portraits inside of the two immortals.
5. Sheng Gong's preaching was so wonderful that even the stones nodded in agreement and flower rained from sky.

Task 8   Supplementary Reading

Sceneries in Yangshuo

About Yangshuo

Yangshuo, located in northeastern part of Guangxi Zhuang Autonomous Region, lies south of Guilin and is under the jurisdiction of the city of Guilin. Yangshuo County covers an area of 1,428 square km and has 20,000 hectares of land used for agricultural cultivation. It has a population about 300,000, making up of different ethnic groups such as Han, Zhuang, Yao, Hui, etc. The weather in Yangshuo is subtropical, with sufficient rainfall, sunlight, and heat around the whole year. On average each year the temperature is 19 centigrade, the amount of sunlight is 1,465 hours, the rainfall is 1,640 mm. There are about 300 days per year without frost. In general, the weather is neither too hot in summer nor too cold in winter.

Yang shuo has a long history of 1,400 year in which the people there have created their own culture, such as long drum dance, song gathering Cai Diao opera, dragon and lion dance. The natural scenery there are gardens, relics and sites in the history, ancient bridge and other architectures and stone carvings.

As the old saying goes, "Guilin's scenery is the most beautiful in the world, Yangshuo's scenery is far more superior to that of Guilin's." From this, one can know that the natural scenery of Yangshuo is unique and like none other in the world. In Yangshuo County alone, there are over 20,000 hills and over 250 scenic spots. The clean and clear Li River winds through Yangshuo for 56 km. On both sides of the river, magical peaks and push green bamboo trees reflect off the mirror like surface of the water to paint beautiful mountain and water murals. The most notable scenic spots of Guilin are in Yangshuo, i. e. Nine-Horse Painted Hill, Yellow Reflection Point, Xingping Village, Lotus Cave, Young Scholar Hill, Snow Lion Ridge, the Big Banyan Tree, Moon Hill, and Dragon River. Moreover, many consider the landscape of the plains and the villages to be like a beautiful picturesque poem. Amongst the mountains and waters are old buildings and old bridges that reflect the rich cultural heritage of Yangshuo. Just by observing these, one can learn much about Yangshuo's history. Yangshuo was one of the first counties to be appointed as a national tourism area. Each year 1.5 million visitors come to Yangshuo.

Baisha Town: Bridge the Centuries on the Yulong River

The "Meet the Dragon" or Yulong River, which begins in Zouzai Village, is the largest tributary running into the Li River. The excellent composition of water, ancient bridges and mountains along this waterway is one of the favorite choices of photographers and artists coming to the area. For those who are looking for a fabulous hike, start at Baisha's Yulong Bridge and stay on the path down river to Gao Tian. You'll pass six unforgettable ancient bridges during the 5-hour walk.

Fuli: Home to the "Third Sister"

Those who know Chinese cinema will immediately recognize Fuli's distinctive wharf as the backdrop for shooting parts of the now famous film, "The Liu Family's Third Sister". Like Xingping, travelers can experience the lovely "mountain-water" scenery of the area by taking the 50-minute boat ride on the lower reaches of the Li River down to this quaint spot. In the town, visit some of the best local artists and their shops or just sip some tea on the wharf at "Three-Sister's" Restaurant.

Gaotian: Retreat to the Country

The most popular route for 1-2 day biking trips is the road to Gaotian. Gaotian, a predominantly Zhuang minority area, offers some of the most memorable sights and experiences for those who want to encounter China "off the road" Moon Hill, a large mountain with a cavity that appears to "change phases" as travelers pass by, is the centerpiece of the area. On a day trip, bikers will usually go first to the Big Banyan Tree, and perhaps do some caving. Many then opt to stay overnight in the county at a farmer's home or better yet, rent a room at the "Riverside Retreat", a very welcoming bed and breakfast run in a renovated mill house beside the "Meet the Dragon".

Xingping: Take me home country roads

The cruise from Yangshuo to Xingping is a "must do" for many adventurous travelers who want to see the mountains and Li River from another vantage point. The fascinating shapes and coloration of the Limestone Mountains sometimes tell a story. River men eagerly point out such sights as "Nine Horses Painted Cliff", "Monk and Nun's Peak", and "Snail Hill". With bikes loaded onto small riverboats, energetic tourists travel up, enjoy the serenity of the magnificent hills surrounding the town, and then bike back by way of winding country roads.

The "Fish Village" of Yangshuo County—a "Time Capsule" You Shouldn't Miss

During the boat cruise from Guilin to Yangshuo, travelers often stop near the halfway point to visit the famous "Fish Village". From the start, visitors notice the authentic and well-preserved structures, which reflect a way of life that has continued for nearly 500 years. What is striking as well is that this is not a museum; locals still eat, sleep, and work out their lives there.

Historically, the village has enjoyed its moments. Kang Youwei, a Qing Dynasty reformist, publicized his progressive ideas of reform there. Sun Yat Sun visited Fish Village when he made preparations for the war against the warlords of the north.

Elegant, sloping rooftops, ornamental eaves, and narrow lanes set among the famous mountains of Yangshuo, have attracted scholars and notable persons for years. On July 2, 1998, American President Clinton and his delegation visited Fish Village to enjoy its history and architecture.

(Source: http://travel.chinavista.com/destination - sight.php? id = 167)

Questions:
1. Where is Yangshuo located?
2. How many ethnic groups are living in Yangshuo? What are they?
3. What's the weather like in Yangshuo?
4. Which part of the cruise is a "must do"?
5. If one wants to express that the natural scenery of Yangshuo is unique and like none other in the world, which saying is appropriate?

Part III

Task 1 Warm-Up

1. Can you explain the legend of Sword-Testing Rock on the Tiger Hill? Can you also elaborate on the engraved poem on the cliff?
2. To which dynasty and which Buddhist monk is the Pillow Stone relevant? When did the Buddhist temples start to be built on the hill? Why is the Pillow Stone also known as the Worm Stone?

Task 2 Words and Expressions

attendant	[ə'tendənt]	n.	侍从
magnificent	[mæg'nɪfɪsnt]	adj.	壮丽的,伟大的
storey	['stɔːri]	n.	层
lean	[liːn]	v.	倾斜
ton	[tʌn]	n.	吨
collapse	[kə'læps]	v.	倒塌
worship	['wɜːʃɪp]	v.	景仰,敬奉
deviate	['diːvɪeɪt]	v.	偏离
vertical	['vɜːtɪkəl]	adj.	垂直的
direction	[dɪ'rekʃən]	n.	方向
native	['neɪtɪv]	n.	本地人
landmark	['lændmɑːk]	n.	地标
Fifty-three Steps = Fifty-three Salute			五十三级台阶,五十三参
Boy of Treasures			善财童子
pay tribute to			供奉
Cloud Rock Temple Pagoda			云岩寺塔
Bodhisattva [ˌbɔdi'sɑːtvɑː] of Compassion			观音菩萨
suffer from			忍受

Task 3 Dialogues

Scene: Now the guide is standing beside the 53 steps. (V = Visitor, G = Guide)
Travel Route: Fifty-three Steps—Cloud Rock Temple Pagoda

Fifty-Three Steps

G: Here are 53 stone steps.
V: There are exactly 53 steps here?
G: Yes.
V: Why does it get such a special name?
G: The reason why 53 steps are built should be started from a Buddhist story. It goes like that, the Boy of Treasures, who was the attendant of Bodhisattva of Compassion, worshipped 53 Bodhisattvas as his teachers

early and later. The last one was Guan Yin, and then he finished his practice on Buddhism and became an immortal. In Buddhism it is said that people should climb 53 steps to pay tribute to Buddha, which is called Fifty-three Salute. So in China in some hilly areas 53 steps can be seen as a temple.

V: OK. Let us climb on and check.

Cloud Rock Temple Pagoda

G: The last, the best. Now we are in front of the world famous Cloud Rock Temple Pagoda. We also call it the Tiger Hill pagoda.

V: So magnificent!

G: It is 47.7 meters with 7 stories and 8 sides.

V: How old is this pagoda?

G: Its history can be traced back to Song Dynasty, 1,000 years ago. The exact building year is 959-961 AD. At first, it was brick-wood structure; in the long history it suffered from 7 times fire-catching, so only the brick central part is left.

V: I found this is a leaning pagoda.

G: Yes. Obviously we can see that it is a leaning pagoda. Now the central line of the pagoda already deviates 2.34 meters from its vertical line.

V: Why?

G: Because of its foundation, one side of its base is hard rock but the other side is soft and the pagoda itself is very heavy about 6,000 tons, so step by step it leans to north-east direction.

V: I wonder whether it would collapse.

G: It won't happen. Since the founding of new China, the government has taken many ways to save this pagoda. The main method is to change the condition of its foundation. Now both sides are balanced. Attention please. From the first storey to the sixth one, the pagoda leans to one direction. But the top storey (the seventh storey) is a little higher than the sixth one. From there, the pagoda leans to the opposite direction. Because the top storey was rebuilt in 1638, which helps correct the slant. Until now, this pagoda is in a good condition despite of its leaning. Suzhou natives regard it as the landmark.

V: Amazing! I would like to take a photo here!

G: Enjoy yourself. We have visited the Tiger Hill Spot. You will have 50 minutes' free time. Please follow the time table. Let's gather at the main entrance at about 3 o'clock. OK?

V: No problem. Thank you for your explanation.

G: My pleasure.

Task 4 Useful Sentences

1. Its history can be traced back to Song Dynasty, 1,000 years ago.
2. At first, it was brick-wood structure; in the long history it suffered from 7 times fire-catching, so only brick central part left.
3. The reason why 53 steps are built should be started from a Buddhist story.
4. Please follow the time table. Let's gather at the main entrance at about 3 o'clock. OK?
5. Obviously we can see that it is a leaning pagoda, now the central line of the pagoda already deviates 2.34 meters from its vertical line.

Task 5 Listening

You will hear five sentences. Listen carefully and put down the whole sentences.

1. _____.
2. _____.
3. _____.
4. _____.
5. _____.

Task 6 Role-Play

Situation 1: Introduce the Cloud Rock Temple Pagoda to the James.

Situation 2: You are meeting an independent traveler at the railway station. Find out his travel plans and what you can do for him.

Task 7 Translation

1. 苏州人认为虎丘是当地的标志。
2. 大家还有50分钟自由活动的时间。
3. In Buddhism it is said that people should climb 53 steps to pay tribute to Buddha.
4. Because of its foundation, one side of its base is hard rock but the other side is soft and the pagoda itself is very heavy about 6,000 tons, so step by step it leans to northeast direction.
5. It goes like that, the Boy of Treasures, who is the attendant of Bodhisattva of Compassion,

worshipped 53 Bodhisattvas as his teachers early and later.

Task 8　Supplementary Reading

English Name: Xi'an, Hsian, Sian
Chinese Name: 西安(xī ān)
Alias: Chang'an
Location: Guanzhong Plain, Shaanxi Province, Northwest China (34°16′N,108°54′E)
Postal Code: 710000-710090
Area Code: 029

Were China a tree, Beijing would be the crown while Xi'an would be its deep roots. As a saying goes: "Go to Shanghai and you will find a 100-year-old China; go to Beijing and you will find a 1,000-year-old China; go to Xi'an and then you will find a 3,000-year-old China." Xi'an, the cradle of China, is, by any means, on your China travel list.

Historically known as Chang'an, it was home to the ruling house of 13 dynasties, notably, the Qin (221 BC-206 BC), Han (206 BC-220 AD), Sui (581 AD-618 AD) and Tang (618AD-907AD) Dynasties. The Emperor Qin Shihuang united China for the first time and left Xi'an and the world one of the most extraordinary archeological finds in history—the Terracotta Warriors, which attracts hundreds of thousands of visitors every year. The city reached its peak in the Tang Dynasty, boasting 2 million taxable inhabitants and the largest, most cosmopolitan, settlement in the world during the reign of Xuanzong (712 AD-756 AD).

Together with Athens, Cairo and Rome, Xi'an is among the four major ancient civilization capitals of the world. Xi'an is on the natural westward land route out of China into Central Asia, the starting point and terminus of the Silk Road, which brought the city material wealth as well as religious and cultural melting for over a thousand years.

Surviving monuments open a window to this ancient city. The short-lived totalitarian state of Qin Shihuang is mirrored in the awe-inspiring massed terra-cotta armies of the Terracotta Warriors. The influence of Buddhism is clear from the Wild Goose Pagoda, a chamber for the translation of the Buddhist scriptures by then widely renowned Master Xuan Zang, who returned to China in 645 after 15 years of travel across India and central Asia. Evidence of the flourishing trade along the Silk Routes may be found in the Shaanxi History Museum and Famen Temple. Another reminder of the enduring legacy of the Silk Road is the Great Mosque of Xi'an, presenting a strong Muslim minority, whose faith remains unchanged although their architecture is a mixture of Chinese design and western Islamic tradition.

Today, despite the searing summer heat and freezing winters, Xi'an is a joy to visit. The central city is pleasantly compact and its grid layout within the city wall makes it easy to navigate. The Bell Tower is the geographical center of Xi'an, from which four main business streets radiating,

North Avenue, South Avenue, West Avenue and East Avenue. With many universities around, Xiao Zhai is popular with youth and students and thus is one of the busiest commercial areas. The ancient streets of Shuyuanmen and Luomashi commercial area are two must-visit places. Actually, sightseeing in and around Xi'an can keep even the most energetic visitors busy for a week or two.

The cuisine of Xi'an is not among the eight great cuisines of China, but it enjoys enormous popularity. If you visit one of the local cuisine restaurants and taste local favorites like Yang Rou Pao mo, you will find out why. After dinner, you can either enjoy a traditional form of entertainment, like the Qin Opera and the Tang Dynasty Music and Dance Show, or indulge in modern bars and karaoke places.

Feel like shopping? Just go for traditional arts and crafts, folk handicrafts or replicas of antiquities. Xi'an is famous for good imitations of arts and crafts of the Qin and Tang Dynasties, such as tri-colored glazed pottery and imitations of ancient bronze ware. Beyond that, tourists can also find replica of the Qin Dynasty embroidery, artistic porcelain ware, jade, carvings, paper cuttings, and paintings by the farmers of Huxian County which features strong Chinese traditions and local characteristics.

Locals are easygoing, yet shake their heads in regret that their ancestors "fell behind" their richer cousins in Beijing. However, tens of thousands of worldwide visitors, together with plenty of upscale new malls full of well-dressed shoppers, tell you that Xi'an is not that far behind.

Questions:
1. What is the role of Xi'an in Chinese history?
2. What was the old name of Xi'an?
3. In which dynasty was the city in its peak?
4. What are the four major ancient civilization capitals in the world?
5. Introduce some museums in Xi'an.

Project 2　The Humble Administrator's Garden

Part Ⅰ

Task 1　Warm-Up

1. Which part is the most distinctive part of the corridor in the Humble Administrator's Garden? Try to introduce the main features of it.
2. Plants are the most important factor in the garden. The plants in the Humble Administrator's Garden are the best among all. List more than four places whose names are related to plants.

Task 2　Words and Expressions

elegant	[ˈelɪgənt]	adj.	优雅的
imperial	[ɪmˈpɪərɪəl]	adj.	皇帝的
masterpiece	[ˈmɑːstəpiːs]	n.	杰作
preservation	[ˌprezəˈveɪʃn]	v.	保存
principal	[ˈprɪnsəpəl]	adj.	主要的
layout	[ˈleɪaʊt]	n.	布局,安排
censor	[ˈsensə]	n.	审查官
envoy	[ˈenvɔɪ]	n.	特使
corruption	[kəˈrʌpʃn]	n.	贪污,腐败
corrupt	[kəˈrʌpt]	adj.	腐败的
remove	[rɪˈmuːv]	v.	免除
offend	[əˈfend]	v.	冒犯
resign	[rɪˈzaɪn]	v.	辞职
extol	[ɪkˈstəʊl]	v.	颂扬
officialdom	[əˈfɪʃəldəm]	n.	官场
gamble	[ˈgæmbl]	v.	赌博
pursuit	[pəˈsjuːt]	n.	追求
proportion	[prəˈpɔːʃn]	n.	部分,比例
construction	[kənˈstrʌkʃn]	n.	建设,构造
festival	[ˈfestəvəl]	n.	节日
well	[wel]	n.	井

separate	['sepəreɪt]	v.	分开
visible	['vɪzəbl]	adj.	看得见的
tempting	['temptɪŋ]	adj.	诱惑人的
locate	[ləʊ'keɪt]	v.	使坐落于
classical	['klæsɪkəl]	adj.	古典的
representative	[reprɪ'zentətɪv]	n.	代表
represent	[ˌreprɪ'zent]	v.	表现，代表
appraise	[ə'preɪz]	v.	评价，评估
procurator	['prɒkjʊəreɪtə]	n.	检察官
mandate	['mændeɪt]	v.	命令，授权
supervise	['sjuːpəvaɪz]	v.	监督
abuse	[ə'bjuːs]	n.	滥用
prosecute	['prɒsɪkjuːt]	v.	起诉
profitable	['prɒfɪtəbl]	adj.	有利可图的
essay	['eseɪ]	n.	散文
seclusion	[sɪ'kluːʒn]	n.	隐居
specimen	['spesɪmən]	n.	样本
celebrity	[sɪ'lebrɪti]	n.	名人
lacquer	['lækə]	n.	漆
common	['kɒmən]	adj.	普通的
partially	['pɑːʃəli]	adv.	部分地
lattice	['lætɪs]	n.	格子
reveal	[rɪ'viːl]	v.	显示，透露
eager	['iːgə]	adj.	热切的
Summer Resort			避暑山庄
Lotus Pavilion			芙蓉榭
Millet Fragrance Hall			秫香馆
trace back to			追溯到
aloof from			远离
Summer Palace			颐和园
Orchid Snow Parlor			兰雪堂
Heavenly Spring Pavilion			天泉阁
Double Corridor			复廊
account for			解释
high-ranking			高级的

Task 3　Dialogues

Scene: Now, it is one o'clock in the afternoon. The guide is leading the group at the entrance gate of the Humble Administrator's Garden. (V = Visitor, G = Guide)

Travel Route: Main Gate—Orchid Snow Parlor—Lotus Pavilion—Heavenly Spring Pavilion—Millet Fragrance Hall—Double Corridor

Main Gate

G: Hello everyone, now we are at the famous Humble Administrator's Garden. I will introduce something about it for you.

V: OK!

G: The Humble Administrator's Garden is located in northeast of the old Suzhou city, Jiangsu Province. It's an elegant, typical and classical private garden. The Humble Administrator's Garden is one of the four most famous classical gardens in China.

V: How about the other three?

G: They are the Summer Palace in Beijing, the Summer Resort in Chengde, Heibei Province, and the Lingering Garden in Suzhou too. The Summer Palace and the Summer Resort are the representatives of imperial gardens in China, while the Humble Administrator's Garden and the Lingering Garden are the representatives of private gardens in China.

V: It is really famous!

G: Yes. It is regarded as the best classical garden in the southern Yangtze River area, a masterpiece representing all private gardens. Since 1961, it has been the national key cultural preservation centre. In 1997 it was listed as the world heritage of UNESCO and in 2006 it was appraised the 5A level national tourism site.

V: How old is this garden?

G: About 400 years. Its history can be traced back to Ming Dynasty, about 16 century. It took sixteen years to complete the garden, from 1513 to 1528.

V: How about the area of it?

G: It takes an area of about 5 hectares, which is separated into 3 parts: eastern part, central part and western part. Each part has its distinctive feature. Central part is the cream. The principal element of its layout is water, which accounts for one fifth of its total area. And in its central part, water occupies one third of the area. Most of the major buildings are constructed beside the water.

V: That sounds great. Who built this garden?

G: This garden was first built by a high-ranking official. This official, by the name of Wang

Xianchen, held the position of a censor, which is something like today's chief procurator.

V: So he was very rich.

G: Yes, the position gave him a lot of power, because by the emperor's mandate, a censor was authorized to act like the imperial envoy, whose job was to inspect the work of local governments. This censor had the responsibility to supervise the corruption of local officials. If he found someone was abusing his official post, he would exercise his authority to prosecute him or remove him from the office.

V: I guess this garden must be very beautiful but the name is so strange, what's the meaning?

G: The post made him offend many other officials. It was very profitable, so many officials, especially the corrupt ones, wanted to kick the censor out of the office and have another one to replace him. The censor was upset and disappointed. He resigned from his post and returned to his hometown and built this garden on the site of Dahong Monastery. The name of the garden comes from the essay of a famous poet. It extols the idea of "returning to nature". By calling himself humble administrator, the owner of the garden imagined himself leading a poetic and rustic life in seclusion. And by this name he also wanted to imply that he had been tired of politics and disgusted with the officialdom of the time, and that he was only interested in his garden where he found true pleasure and peace of mind.

V: I see. But I still wonder why this one is so famous since there are so many gardens in Suzhou.

G: There are two reasons. First, the Humble Administrator's Garden is the best classical garden in south Yangtze River area. It's the specimen of all Chinese private gardens. All elements of the garden and many gardening art skills can be found here. Second, there is a saying in China "the rich never lasts 3 generations". After Wang Xianchen's death, his son lost this garden by gambling. From then on, the garden was sold from time to time. Many celebrities in China once lived here. Each owner improved the garden a bit. Gradually, this garden became more and more beautiful and perfect.

V: I can not wait to see it.

G: OK. Follow me and let us enjoy this wonderful garden.

Orchid Snow Parlor

G: Here is the Orchid Snow Parlor. It's the first classical building of this garden.

V: What is the meaning of the parlor's name?

G: The name of the parlor comes from an ancient poem, meaning that the owner was aloof from politics, material pursuits and worldly considerations.

V: I see. How beautiful this painting is!

G: In front of us is a large lacquer screen, on which a carved picture shows the general layout of the garden. We can see the general layout of garden. The whole garden is divided into 3 parts: the eastern, central and western part. Openness is its distinctive feature. The black part stands for water, so you can see a large proportion of the area is devoted to water.

V: Where are we now?

G: Here! This is our travel route; we'll stay in this garden for about one and a half hour.

V: OK!

G: Let's move on!

Lotus Pavilion

G: Now we are at the Lotus Pavilion. It's a common traditional Chinese construction, built partially on water and partially on land.

V: Yes, I find that in front of us, there is a big pond full of lotus. Maybe it is the reason why it got such a name.

G: Exactly. We can enjoy the beautiful lotus here every summer. Hence is the name. From the 1990's, the garden has held the lotus festivals every summer. Shown in the garden are over 100 kinds of lotus, such as the king lotus, the lotus grown in blows and so on.

V: That's great!

G: Have you ever noticed the frame over there?

V: Yes!

G: From the frame, we can get a very good point and find the whole view in front of us just like a piece of huge Suzhou embroidery.

V: Yes, that is so elegant. I would like to take a photo here.

G: Enjoy yourself!

Heavenly Spring Pavilion

G: Now we are in the Heavenly Spring Pavilion.

V: It is a very big pavilion.

G: Looked from outside, it seems to have 2 storeys, but actually only one.

V: So special design! Why does it get such a name? Is there a spring inside?

G: Yes, there is an old well inside, which was dug in the Yuan Dynasty in about 13 the century, hence comes the name. Speaking of the well, we must mention that Suzhou is a water city, so there are over 10,000 wells inside the city. The well is very important for people in the past.

V: I see.

G: OK, let us move on!

Millet Fragrance Hall

G: Now here we are at the Millet Fragrance Hall.
V: A very interesting name.
G: In the past, when people were farming outside, to the north of here, we can smell rice fragrance inside, and then it gets the name.
V: How old is this architecture? It looks very new.
G: This building was moved here from the West Hill in 1960s.
V: I find that the long window over there is very beautiful.
G: Yes, 8 long windows above with good wood carvings tell us a moving love story.
V: Is it now a souvenir shop?
G: Yes. Once it was used as a tea house for many years. Now the house is a souvenir shop. You can buy some local products for your friends and relatives.
V: That is a good idea.

Double-Corridors

G: Now, in front of us is one of the few double corridors of Suzhou classical gardens. It separates the east and central section of the garden.
V: That is to say we have already visited the east part of the garden?
G: Yes. Attention please. Through the 25 lattice windows the scene in the other section become visible, but not fully revealed, so the windows produce a tempting effect upon the visitors, who are eager to go in and find out what's inside. This enflamed scenery gardening method is commonly used.
V: What an ingenious way of the design!

Task 4   Useful Sentences

1. It's an elegant, typical and classical private garden.
2. It is regarded as the best classical garden in the southern Yangtze River area, a masterpiece representing all private gardens.
3. In front of us is a large lacquer screen, on which a carved picture shows the general layout of the garden.
4. Looked from outside, it seems to have 2 stories, but actually only one.
5. What an ingenious way of the design!

Task 5　Listening

You will hear five sentences. Listen carefully and put down the whole sentences.

1. _____.
2. _____.
3. _____.
4. _____.
5. _____.

Task 6　Role-Play

Situation 1: Arrange for the James a half day visit of the Eastern Part of the Garden.

Situation 2: Two individual travelers want to see something typically Chinese in the evening. They ask for recommendations.
- Recommend a certain Kunqu Opera show.
- Tell them what time it will start and how long it will last.
- The two travelers want a guide to go with them. Arrange the time they will meet the guide and go to the theatre.
- Take them to the theatre and help them find their seats.
- Discuss the history of Kunqu Opera with them.
- Ask their opinions about the show.
- See them back to the hotel.

Task 7　Translation

1. 拙政园坐落于苏州古城东北角。
2. 拙政园是中国四大园林之一。
3. It's a common traditional Chinese construction, built partially on water and partially on land.
4. Through the 25 lattice windows the scene in the other section become visible, but not fully revealed, so the windows produce a tempting effect upon the visitors, who are eager to go in and find out what's inside.
5. Shown in the garden are over 100 kinds of lotus, such as the king lotus, the lotus grown in blows and so on.

Task 8 Supplementary Reading

Ancient Pingyao City

Pingyao, a state historical and cultural city, has been named on the World Cultural Heritage list. It sits in the central part of Shanxi Province, 90 km southward from Taiyuan, the capital city of Shanxi. The Fenhe River runs from north to south across the city. Pingyao has a history of more than 1,700 years. It was prosperous and well developed in both Ming and Qing Dynasties. People in those times who knew little about Pingyao were as incredible as people today knowing nothing about Shenzhen. Nicknamed "little Beijing", Pingyao was too big to be completely crowed.

Although Pingyao's glory has long since gone, we can still sense its past prosperity from its completely preserved city walls, its downtown layout of the Ming and Qing Dynasties, its banks, shops, its groceries and its residential quarters.

The first must-see in Pingyao is its city wall. The rammed clay wall was begun in 828 BC, when general Yin Jifu of the West Zhou Dynasty was stationed here. It was designed as a military strong-hold. In the third year (1370) of Hongwu Reigh in the Ming Dynasty, the city wall was enhanced, by using bricks and stones, to a circumference of 6.4 km and a height of 10 meters. The moat is three meters both in width and in depth. During the Ming and Qing Dynasties, the city wall was renovated 25 times. After this the inner and outer city walls were strongly fortified. It has long been called "tortoise city", symbolizing its longevity. The southern and northern gates are the tortoise's head and tail, the other four gates, two on the east side and two on the west are the tortoise's legs. With its avenues, streets and lanes, the pattern of the whole town resembles a bagua (a combination of eight of the 64 Trigrams of the "Book of Changes" traditionally used in divination), which is similar to the pattern on a tortoise shell.

Its ancient architecture fully reflects the historical flavor of both the Ming and Qing Dynasties. The ancient city covers an area of 2.25sq km and its streets and avenues form a " + " shape. The 750-meter long street running north-south has attracted 78 shops and firms. The buildings in the town are built symmetrically along this street as an axis and the Market Tower as its central point.

Along this street of typical Ming and Qing style are banks, pawnshops, Chinese herb shops, silk shops and groceries, through a study of which visitors can revisit one-glorious days. During the last century, countless Shanxi traders did business here. The most famous was Rishengchang, the first private banking unit in China to handle money exchanges and deposits. Following this it had many branch shops throughout China.

The residential houses are distributed along the lanes and paths, set off against the ancient streets and shops. The courtyards feature grey tiles, formal design, clear axes and enclosed walls. The houses are all decorated inside and outside with exquisite wood, brick and stone carvings on the gates, doors, windows, eaves, poles and corridors. They are a combination of artistry and practicability.

There are many other historical attractions inside and around Pingyao. Shuangling Temple, 6 km southwest from Pingyao is famous for its colorful sculpture. The Zhengguo Temple, 12 km to the northeast features unique wooden structural architecture.

The UNESCO World Heritage Committee remarks, "The ancient city of Pingyao is an outstanding example of Chinese Han Nationality cities in the Ming and Qing Dynasties, displaying all the features of those periods. Pingya, in particular, reveals a picture of unexpected cultural, social, economic and religious development in Chinese history."

(Source: http://travel.chinavista.com/destination-sight.php? id = 19)

Questions:
1. Which river runs through the city?
2. What is the significance of the ancient Pingyao City?
3. List some historical attractions inside and around Pingyao.
4. Where is the city located?
5. What is the feature of the courtyard in Pingyao?

Part Ⅱ

Task 1　Warm-Up

1. List at least four buildings that are named after lotus in the Humble Administrator's Garden.
2. What are the characteristics of the region composed of little surging wave and little flying rainbow?

Task 2　Words and Expressions

flank	[flæŋk]	v.	位于……侧面
touch	[tʌtʃ]	n.	修饰
remind	[rɪˈmaɪnd]	v.	使想起
flourishing	[ˈflʌrɪʃɪŋ]	adj.	繁荣的
refreshing	[rɪˈfreʃɪŋ]	adj.	新鲜宜人的
hillock	[ˈhɪlək]	n.	小丘
tranquility	[træŋˈkwɪləti]	n.	宁静

frost	[frɒst]	n.	霜
charming	[ˈtʃɑːmɪŋ]	adj.	迷人的
amidst	[əˈmɪdst]	prep.	在……当中
quote	[kwəʊt]	v.	引述
appreciation	[əˌpriːʃiˈeɪʃn]	n.	欣赏
shrill	[ʃrɪl]	n.	尖锐的声音
quietude	[ˈkwaɪətjuːd]	n.	安静
pillar	[ˈpɪlə]	n.	柱子
reflection	[rɪˈflekʃn]	n.	折射
expanse	[ɪkˈspæns]	n.	宽阔的区域
economical	[ˌiːkəˈnɒmɪkl]	adj.	节俭的
penny	[ˈpeni]	n.	便士
attractive	[əˈtræktɪv]	adj.	有吸引力的
breeze	[briːz]	n.	微风
stillness	[ˈstɪlnəs]	n.	静止
tangerine	[ˌtændʒəˈriːn]	n.	橘子,橘子树
thriving	[ˈθraɪvɪŋ]	adj.	繁荣的
overlook	[ˌəʊvəˈlʊk]	v.	俯瞰
willow	[ˈwɪləʊ]	n.	柳树
poetic	[pəʊˈetik]	adj.	诗的
literal	[ˈlɪtərəl]	adj.	字面上的
cicada	[sɪˈkɑːdə]	n.	蝉
twittering	[ˈtwɪtərɪŋ]	n.	唧啾
Snow Fragrance Abundant Clouds Pavilion			雪香云蔚亭
Secluded Pavilion of Phoenix Tree and Bamboo			梧竹幽居
Lotus Breeze on Four Sides Pavilion			荷风四面亭
Rainbow-Embraced Pavilion			倚虹亭
Frost-Awaiting Pavilion			待霜亭

Task 3　Dialogues

Scene: Now the group is standing in front of the Rainbow-Embraced Pavilion. (V =Visitor, G =Guide)

Travel Route: Rainbow-Embraced Pavilion—Secluded Pavilion of Phoenix Tree and Bamboo—Frost-Awaiting Pavilion—Snow Fragrance Abundant Clouds Pavilion—Lotus Breeze on Four Sides Pavilion

Rainbow-Embraced Pavilion

G: Entering this gate we come to the central section, the most successfully designed part in the garden.

V: So beautiful!

G: Here you can see the expanse of water running through the entire length of the section, up to the other end, flanked by elegant buildings on one side, and an artificial hill on the other.

For hundreds of years there is a saying in China which goes like this, "Chinese gardens in Southern Yangtze area are the most elegant, yet those in Suzhou beat all the others."

V: Yes! I have already heard about that saying!

G: Please look at the opposite direction, there is a moon gate over there, and behind it is the western section. Above it you can see a pagoda.

V: Yes. Is it in the western part of the garden?

G: It looks as if the pagoda is right inside the western section. But actually the pagoda is located about a mile away. Here we can see the designer of this garden is very clever and very economical when building the garden. He didn't spend a single penny with some outside object being borrowed into the garden to add a touch to the scenery.

V: I see!

G: This common technique is known as "to borrow a view".

V: That is very unique. I would like to take a photo here.

Secluded Pavilion of Phoenix Tree and Bamboo

G: We call this special pavilion the Secluded Pavilion of Phoenix Tree and Bamboo.

V: I see. The four sides of this pavilion all have got round gates.

G: If you stop inside and look through the moon gates, you will be given four different views. When you move around, you will find the pictures change with every step. Like a view-finder,

the gates frame particular attractive pictures. Probably, this will remind you of the traditional Chinese paintings.

V: Really! It is!

G: What is more, all 4 seasons' views of the garden can be enjoyed through these gates. In spring, looking from the north side, one can enjoy the beautiful flowers and willows. In summer, looking from this way, one can appreciate the flourishing lotus. In autumn, one can see the phoenix trees and bamboos.

V: How about winter?

G: East side, snow and ice on roof, which looks like a piece of Shanshui Painting of China.

V: Here I can also see a couplet. What does it mean?

G: It reads the gentle breeze brings refreshing cool and moonlight, illustration. The flowing water expressed movement and hillock, stillness. This couplet describes the tranquility of the garden.

Frost-Awaiting Pavilion

G: Here we are in the Frost-Awaiting Pavilion.

V: What kind of tree is it?

G: Around this pavilion, we can find many tangerine trees, which are richly produced in Suzhou, deep green in autumn and change to red after frost bitten. Hence the name.

V: I've found there are so many pavilions in different gardens!

G: We know that pavilions can provide us with a good view point in garden. Indeed, in the central part of this garden, we can get 4 seasons' views in 4 different pavilions. In spring, we stay in Xiuyi Pavilion opposite from here; there is a good place to enjoy beautiful flowers and thriving willows. In summer, we can view lotus flowers and smell the fragrance in Lotus Breeze on Four Sides Pavilion. In autumn, it shows the charming view of tangerine here. In winter, we will choose the Snow Fragrance Abundant Clouds Pavilion. Let's go there right now.

Snow Fragrance Abundant Clouds Pavilion

G: Here is the highest point of the garden, overlooking the entire view of the central section. The hill itself is not very high, but because the lake is dug below it, and the front part of the hill rises sharply above the water, the hill looks much higher than it really is.

V: Yes, so amazing!

G: From this brick-laid terrace a group of buildings in the opposite direction are in view, the major hall in the middle a pavilion on a hill and a water-side pavilion on the other side.

V: That is very beautiful!

G: The inscription on the wooden tablets describes the atmosphere that the pavilion is located amidst mountain flowers and wild birds. The Ming Dynasty artist Wen Zhenming also expressed his poetic appreciation of the scenery by quoting two lines from an ancient poem, which was placed here in his handwriting.

V: What are those words?

G: A literal translation reads like this: "The shrill of cicadas' brings more quietude to the forest and the twittering of birds' lends more tranquility to the hill."

V: Very nice atmosphere!

Lotus Breeze on Four Sides Pavilion

G: This pavilion is designed for viewing lotus flowers in summer. When you sit here, no matter which way you face, you will see the graceful flowers and smell the lotus fragrance.

V: I see!

G: What's worth mentioning here is the couplet on the wooden pillars! Four sides of lotus flowers, three sides of willow, half pool of water, one house of hill. Only 14 words described 4 seasons' nice view of the garden. In spring we can enjoy luxuriant willows, in summer blooming lotus in the pond, in autumn, clear water, and in winter, reflection of building on the water.

V: It's so nice. I would have a rest here and take some photos.

Task 4 Useful Sentences

1. Entering this gate we come to the central section, the most successfully designed part in the garden.
2. What's worth mentioning here is the couplet on the wooden pillars!
3. This pavilion is designed for viewing lotus flowers in summer.
4. A literal translation reads like this: "The shrill of cicadas' brings more quietude to the forest and the twittering of birds' lends more tranquility to the hill."
5. We know that pavilion can provide us a good view point in the garden.

Task 5 Listening

You will hear five sentences. Listen carefully and put down the whole sentences.

1. _____.
2. _____.
3. _____.
4. _____.
5. _____.

Task 6 Role-Play

Situation 1: Suppose the James are not interested in the route of Rainbow-Embraced Pavilion—Secluded Pavilion of Phoenix Tree and Bamboo—Frost-Awaiting Pavilion—Snow Fragrance Abundant Clouds Pavilion—Lotus Breeze on Four Sides Pavilion, discuss with the family to reach an agreement of the spots.

Situation 2: You would like to travel around a city you are interested in during the summer vacation. You need to get some information in order to plan your trip, so you go to a travel agency for help. There you ask the staff on duty various questions, such as how far away the city is, whether the bus or train goes there, the details of the scenic spots there, etc.

Task 7 Translation

1. 亭子的四面都是圆门。
2. 这种技术叫借景。
3. Here you can see the expanse of water running through the entire length of the section, up to the other end, flanked by elegant buildings on one side, and an artificial hill on the other.
4. Around this pavilion, we can find many tangerine trees, which are richly produced in Suzhou, deep green in autumn and change to red after frost bitten.
5. When you sit here, no matter which way you face, you will be seeing the graceful flowers and smell the lotus fragrance.

Task 8 Supplementary Reading

Tibetan Folklore

Snowcapped mountains, white clouds, blue sky, grassland and unique Tibetan folklore are wonderful charms of Tibet. The Tibetan Folklore Festival held on Mount Lingshan, 120 kilometers from Beijing proper, provides a special chance for people to learn about the far-away region.

The main peak of Lingshan Mountain is 2,300 meters above sea level, the highest in the Beijing area. It has a typical landform of plateau and gentle slopes. In summer, green meadows with wild flowers cover the mountain. It seems as if low-flying clouds could be touched by hand.

It is surprising to see mountain yaks known as the "boat of the plateau" there. They have been raised in a wild state since the 1970s.

You can take buses along the winding mountain highway to the foot of the main peak and then cable cars along the 1,500-meter-long cableway for 20 minutes to the summit. On the cable cars, tourist can enjoy themselves in the beauty of scenery. It is an interesting way for tourists to relax themselves while roaming aimlessly on or galloping over the wide and soft grassland while smelling fragrant grasses and flowers on horseback.

It is a pleasure for you to rest or have a picnic in the birch forest in Lingshan Mountain. If you do not bring along enough food, you can buy a cup of tasteful Tibetan buttered tea, Qingke (highland barley) wine and a piece of roast meat from a whole sheep.

Lingshan's Tibetan Folklore Festival lasts through the whole summer. It takes three hours to drive westward along Shijingshan Road and Mentougou Highway to the destination. Individual tourists can take the subway to the terminal at Pingguoyuan and then change a special tourist bus leading directly to the mountain. The bus one-way fare is 15 yuan and the admission fee is 30 yuan, not including the one-way cable fare of 30 yuan.

Advice: The temperature at Lingshan is low after dark, so you should bring more clothes, and sneakers will be helpful for you to go sightseeing.

In order to protect the grassland, you must not pick flowers or litter after picnicking.

Questions:
1. What is the Tibetan Folklore Festival?
2. List some foods or drinks there.
3. How is the weather after dark at Lingshan?
4. Is it allowed to pick flowers on the grassland?
5. How long does the Tibetan Folklore Festival last?

Part Ⅲ

Task 1 Warm-Up

1. Most of the Pavilions are sharp at the top while the highest point of Snow Fragrance Cloud Blue Pavilion in the Humble Administrator's is flat, why?
2. When your guests are visiting Suzhou, it is raining. What would you introduce in the Humble Administrator's Garden?

Task 2 Words and Expressions

banquet	[ˈbæŋkwɪt]	n.	宴会
delicate	[ˈdelɪkət]	adj.	精美的,微妙的
entitle	[ɪnˈtaɪtl]	v.	取名为
block	[blɒk]	v.	阻塞
eave	[iːv]	n.	屋檐
vermilion	[vəˈmɪliən]	adj.	朱红的
resemble	[rɪˈzembl]	v.	像
facade	[fəˈsɑːd]	n.	建筑物的正面
bay	[beɪ]	n.	湾,分隔间
spacious	[ˈspeɪʃəs]	adj.	宽敞的
banister	[ˈbænɪstə]	n.	栏杆,扶手
cabin	[ˈkæbɪn]	n.	小木屋
gangplank	[ˈgæŋplæŋk]	n.	跳板
faithful	[ˈfeɪθfl]	adj.	忠诚的
endow	[ɪnˈdaʊ]	v.	赋予
conference	[ˈkɒnfərəns]	n.	会议
neat	[niːt]	adj.	整洁的
anchor	[ˈæŋkə]	v.	停泊
nobility	[nəʊˈbɪləti]	n.	崇高
indicate	[ˈɪndɪkeɪt]	v.	指示
prominence	[ˈprɒmɪnəns]	n.	突出
prose	[prəʊz]	n.	散文
cloister	[ˈklɔɪstə]	v.	回廊
obstruction	[əbˈstrʌkʃn]	n.	障碍
promenade	[prɒmɪˈnɑːd]	n.	散步场所
balustrade	[bæləˈstreɪd]	n.	栏杆
studio	[ˈstjuːdiəʊ]	n.	工作室
meticulous	[mɪˈtɪkjələs]	adj.	缜密的
stream	[striːm]	n.	小河,水流
uprising	[ˌʌpˈraɪzɪŋ]	n.	起义
shore	[ʃɔː]	n.	岸
deck	[dek]	n.	甲板
rebellion	[rɪˈbeljən]	n.	叛乱
residence	[ˈrezɪdəns]	n.	住宅
military	[ˈmɪlɪtəri]	adj.	军事的
exquisite	[ˈekskwɪzɪt]	adj.	精致的

succinct	[səkˈsɪŋkt]	adj.	简洁的
sanctity	[ˈsæŋktəti]	n.	神圣
shelter	[ˈʃeltə]	n.	庇护
Distant Fragrance Hall			远香阁
Little Gentle Waves Water			小沧浪
Mountain-in-View Building			见山楼
Little Flying Rainbow			小飞虹
Fragrant Islet			香洲
derive from			来自,起源于

Task 3 Dialogues

Scene: Now the group is standing in front of the Distant Fragrance Hall. (V = Visitor, G = Guide)

Travel Route: Distant Fragrance Hall—Little Flying Rainbow—Little Gentle Waves Water—Fragrant Islet—Mountain-in-View Building

Distant Fragrance Hall

G: Here is the main building of the central section, the Distant Fragrance Hall.

V: I think here is a guest house.

G: Yes, the owner used to give banquets and meet visitors here. The other buildings in the central section are all built facing to it and give prominence to it.

V: Why is it called the Distant Fragrance Hall, a very interesting name?

G: The name derives from one of the line "distant fragrance is all the more delicate and fresh", taken from a prose piece entitled "On Loving Lotus" by Zhou Dunyi, a writer of the Song Dynasty, about 1,000 years ago.

V: I see. So there is a big pond in front of the hall, where it is full of lotus.

G: That is the reason. In summer, we can enjoy delicate and sweet fragrance here, hence the name.

V: I find that it has long-windows but no walls on all four sides.

G: Yes, therefore it permits more natural day lighting inside. The pillars here are shifted to outside, making a cloister, so they won't stand in way and block the views outside.

V: You are right. Guests can command a nice view of the surrounding scenery without any obstruction.

G: Even in raining days, they can stand under the eaves and appreciate the nice scenery. The

design is very delicate.
V: That really is.

Little Flying Rainbow

G: This small bridge with a roofed promenade is the only one of this kind in Suzhou gardens.
V: What do you call it?
G: The Little Flying Rainbow.
V: Why?
G: Because the reflection of the vermilion balustrade in the water resembles a rainbow.
V: Yes, it is very beautiful, just like a traditional Chinese painting. I would like to take a photo here.
G: Yes, just enjoy yourself!

Little Gentle Waves Water

G: This is the Little Gentle Waves. It is a three-bay studio on water. With windows on its southern facade and banisters on the north, the studio faces water on two sides. Corridors on both eastern and western sides approach from a sort of courtyard on the water.

V: I feel the design is well organized.
G: You are so meticulous! From this angle, we can see the wisdom of the designer. Here is the end of the stream, but with these two buildings, one above the water the other beside the water, concealing the end of water; we feel that there is another part of scenery behind. This is a good example of the garden-building technique of contrasting the real with the unreal.
V: Yes, one side here is very spacious, but the other side is so close, very sharp contrast.
G: OK, let us move on.

Mountain-in-View Building

G: Here is the Mountain-in-View Building. This two-storied building had some historical significance.
V: Oh! Tell me more.
G: You must have heard about the great peasant uprising known as the "Taiping Rebellion" which took place in the mid-19th century.

V: I heard a little about that.
G: During that period, a popular government was set up in Suzhou under the command of Li Xiucheng, the Faithful Prince, as he was generally known among the Taiping. The official residence of the prince was located in east door, and this garden was endowed as his

backyard. It is in this very building that the prince often held military conferences. The upper room used to be his private study.

V: So it is a very important place.

G: Yes. The building has water on three sides. Interestingly, there is a stair inside. A rockery is piled up next to it and the stair was hidden inside for safety.

V: Such a hidden design.

G: The furniture in the hall is typically of the Ming Dynasty style, much different from the Distant Fragrant Hall we have visited just now, which is of the Qing Dynasty style. Qing Style is exquisite and rich in detail while Ming Style is neat and succinct.

V: I see. That really is.

Fragrant Islet

G: The boat-like structure in front of us is named the Fragrant Islet, which looks like a boat anchoring in shore.

V: The name is very special.

G: The name "Fragrant Islet" is borrowed from a famous poem. Chinese love lotus very much from ancient time, we regarded it as a flower of sanctity. And the owner loved it and named many architectures of the garden after lotus. He borrowed this flower to express his nobility of character.

V: The architectural style is very special!

G: Such a classical building is known as a dry boat. It combines four basic forms of Chinese architecture: pavilion, terrace, hall and tower. The terrace serves as the deck of a boat. Something linking the boat is a stone bridge without rails, which is regarded as the gangplank. The pavilion serves as the shelter in front of the cabin. The cabin is actually a water-side chamber. The tower with two stories indicates the boat is a double deck boat.

V: So nice! I would like to take a photo here.

G: OK!

Task 4 Useful Sentences

1. The terrace serves as the deck of a boat.
2. The name "Fragrant Islet" is borrowed from a famous poem.
3. You must have heard about the great peasant uprising known as the "Taiping Rebellion" which took place in the mid-19th century.
4. The upper room used to be his private study.
5. The reflection of the vermilion balustrade in the water resembles a rainbow.

Task 5　Listening

You will hear five sentences. Listen carefully and put down the whole sentences.

1. _____ .
2. _____ .
3. _____ .
4. _____ .
5. _____ .

Task 6　Role-Play

Situation 1: Arrange for the James a travel route: Distant Fragrance Hall—Little Flying Rainbow—Little Gentle Waves Water—Fragrant Islet—Mountain-in-View Building.

Situation 2: You are the local guide of a tourist group. After a day's sightseeing, some people in the group feel exhausted. They want to go back to the hotel immediately to have a rest before dinner. There will be a concert in the evening that they would like to attend. But some others say they haven't had enough time to go shopping since they arrived. Still a small portion of people suggest visiting another scenic spot since there is some time before dinner. Try to settle the problems.

Task 7　Translation

1. 它的建筑风格很特别。
2. 游客站在这里看周围的景色，一览无余。
3. It combines four basic forms of Chinese architecture: pavilion, terrace, hall and tower.
4. The name derives from one of the line "distant fragrance is all the more delicate and fresh", taken from a prose piece entitled "On Loving Lotus" by Zhou Dunyi, a writer of the Song Dynasty, about 1,000 years ago.
5. Even in raining days, they can stand under the eaves and appreciate the nice scenery.

Task 8 Supplementary Reading

Earthen Dwellings in Kunming

In Kunming, there are various kinds of restaurants, such as the "Cross-Bridge Garden Restaurant" and the "Cross-Bridge Capital Restaurant" which serve Yunnan cuisine, and the "Happy Restaurant" and the "Seeking Dream Garden" on the roadside which serves coffee and desserts, and there are also seafood restaurants run by people from coastal areas.

Eight kilometers from Kunming on the highway between Kunming and the Stone Forest, a group of earthen dwellings have appeared, offering local food and aboriginal performances which attract many tourists.

All the buildings are earthen. Climbing up the steps, there are huge group sculptures in the form of primitive totems, reminding people of ancient times. Stone-slab paths divide the earthen dwelling an aboriginal museum, aboriginal pottery workshops, a clay sculpture workshop, and an aboriginal wine tavern. Each earthen house looks mysterious but intimate.

Most of the exhibits in the aboriginal museum are sculptures, including clay sculptures and baked works of art. A group sculpture, called "Dongshi Meeting", shows the meeting of the chiefs of a tribe, and the expressions of the figures are ferocious. The "Woman and Horse" sculpture shows a horse made up of pottery fragments and parts of a human body. The sculpture is incomplete, but it can be recognized as a horse and a person. The two legs of the woman show the horse is galloping or maybe just relaxing. The sculpture is incomplete, but the artistic expression is exquisite.

The aboriginal wine tavern can seat 800 customers at a time, mainly serving the local foods of Honghe Prefecture in Yunnan Province. Pork, beef and mutton are roasted in pottery jars, with mushrooms, wild celery, and ferns collected from the mountains. Potatoes, pumpkins and other vegetables are green, golden yellow, brown, etc., and are all natural produce. The pottery jars, earthen bowls, just like they would have been in primitive society. The aboriginal performances given at the wine tavern ignite the audience's imagination. Tourists can also dance together with the "aboriginal dancers".

> Questions:
> 1. Introduce the varieties of restaurants in Kunming.
> 2. How does earthen house look?
> 3. What parts could the earthen dwelling be divided into by stone-slab path?
> 4. Say something about the exhibits in the aboriginal museum.
> 5. Are there any restaurants run by foreigners in Kunming?

Part Ⅳ

Task 1   Warm-Up

1. Introduce the features of the Fragrance Islet.
2. The Humble Administrator's Garden is constructed in full accordance with the traditional idea of garden building; please explain the embodiment of this concept in the central part.

Task 2   Words and Expressions

wave	[weɪv]	n.	波浪
reputation	[ˌrepjuˈteɪʃn]	n.	声誉
straightness	[ˈstreɪtnɪs]	n.	正直
folding	[ˈfəʊldɪŋ]	adj.	折叠的
suit	[sjuːt]	v.	适合
convey	[kənˈveɪ]	v.	传达
purity	[ˈpjʊərəti]	n.	纯净
ridge	[rɪdʒ]	n.	脊
partition	[pɑːˈtɪʃn]	n.	隔离物
gnarled	[nɑːld]	adj.	树木多瘤节的
cluster	[ˈklʌstə]	n.	群,簇
blossom	[ˈblɒsəm]	n.	开花
tile	[taɪl]	n.	瓦片
acoustics	[əˈkuːstɪks]	n.	音响效果
auspicious	[ɔːˈspɪʃəs]	adj.	吉利的
rafter	[ˈrɑːftə]	n.	椽,屋梁
camellia	[kəˈmiːliə]	n.	山茶
leisurely	[ˈleʒəli]	adv.	悠闲地
bamboo	[bæmˈbuː]	n.	竹子
ceiling	[ˈsiːlɪŋ]	n.	天花板
fan	[fæn]	n.	扇子
terrain	[ˈtereɪn]	n.	地势,地域
lofty	[ˈlɒfti]	adj.	崇高的
overlap	[ˈəʊvəˈlæp]	v.	重叠
arched	[ɑːtʃt]	adj.	拱形的

ginkgo	[ˈɡɪŋkəʊ]	n.	银杏树
pine	[paɪn]	n.	松树
plum	[plʌm]	n.	李子
oddly-shaped		adj.	奇形怪状的
magpie	[ˈmæɡpaɪ]	n.	喜鹊
fidelity	[fɪˈdeləti]	n.	忠诚
companion	[kəmˈpænɪən]	n.	同伴
curve	[kɜːv]	n.	曲线,弧线
Above-Water Corridor			亲水走廊
Whom-to-Sit-with Pavilion			与谁同坐轩
Mandarin Ducks Hall			鸳鸯馆
Inverted Reflection Building			倒影楼
Stay-and-Listen Parlor			留听阁
in memory of			纪念

Task 3 Dialogues

Scene: Now the group is standing at the Moon Gate between the central part and the western part. (V = Visitor, G = Guide)

Travel Route: Above-Water Corridor—Inverted Reflection Building—Whom-to-Sit-with Pavilion—Stay and Listen Parlor—Mandarin Ducks Hall

Above-Water Corridor

G: Now we are in the western part of the garden. Different from former parts, here, the architectural style is the Qing Dynasty, very elegant.

V: The corridor we are standing in now is so beautiful. It rises and falls so that we feel as if we were walking on waves.

G: Yes, it is one of the most exquisite corridors in Suzhou. The corridor is a very common architectural pattern in classical Suzhou gardens.

V: Oh, tell me more about that.

G: Firstly, it links different scenic spots in gardens. For example, this one links the moon gate and the Inverted Reflection Building. Secondly, it separates space, now this one divides the central part and the western part of the garden. Thirdly, the corridor provides visitors with shelter; even in raining days, we still can walk leisurely and enjoy the scenery. Fourthly, corridors lead our travel route; for any experienced travelers, to find the corridor and walk along it is a good way to visit the whole garden and enjoy the nice view.

Inverted Reflection Building

G: Here is the Inverted Reflection Building. There is a piece of broad water land in front of it. Standing beside it, we can enjoy the water view and the reflection of the building. Hence the name.

V: What is the function of this building?

G: It was built in memory of the garden's designer Wen Zhengming and his teacher Shen Zhou. Both are painters with national reputation in the Ming Dynasty.

V: I found two stone tablets carved with figures. Are these their pictures?

G: Right, on the east side of the wall, there is a stone tablet; it is Wen's portrait. On the west side, it is Shen's. On the central lacquer, a bamboo picture is carved. It is painted by Zhen Banqiao, a famous national painter in the Qing Dynasty about 200 years ago, who was famous for painting bamboo.

V: I've heard you Chinese love bamboo very much since ancient time.

G: Right, we regarded it as a plant of honesty and straightness.

V: That is very interesting!

Whom-to-Sit-with Pavilion

G: Hello! Everyone, this is the Whom-to-Sit-with Pavilion. Its popular name is the Fan Pavilion.

V: Yes, its ground, ceiling and windows are all in the shape of a folding fan.

G: Exactly. We can see that it was laid out in the shape of a folding fan to suit the terrain. Even the stone table inside it looks like the surface of a folding fan, too.

V: The name is very interesting.

G: It was inspired by a poem written by Su Dongpo, a famous poet. By this name, the owner conveyed the idea that he was a lofty person with spirit of purity, but there were few such kind of people in the realistic world. So he felt very lonely.

V: What is the special thing about this pavilion?

G: What is worth mentioning is the fact that when visitors stand on the corridor-over-water near the moon gate and look across the water, they will find that the roof of the fan pavilion overlaps the rounded top and ridge tiles on the roof of the bamboo Hat Pavilion so as to form an inverted fan. Of course, it's a folding fan, not a round one.

Staying-and-Listening Parlor

G: Here is the Staying-and-Listening Parlor. The name was borrowed from a poem written by Li Shangyin in the Tang Dynasty.

V: What is the meaning of the name?

G: Outside is a lotus pond. In rainy days, the owner stayed here and listened to the raindrop beating the lotus leaves and making pleasant sound. How nice and peaceful it was. Hence the name.

V: The carving here is very nice!

G: Yes. What is worth mentioning is that the arched frame partition is from the Ming Dynasty. With exquisite carving on it, it was made from a kind of rare material ginkgo. Gnarled pine trees, nice bamboo, clusters of plum blossoms oddly-shaped rocks and lifelike birds. You see, in the center, a pied magpie is standing on the plum tree. It is a traditional Chinese auspicious picture, which means good luck and omen.

V: Good! I would like to take a photo of that.

G: Enjoy yourself.

Mandarin Ducks Hall

G: Here is the Mandarin Ducks Hall, which is the main building of the western part of the garden. In the Qing Dynasty, the owner here was Hong Jun, a famous literary man.

V: There are real mandarin-ducks in the pond outside.

G: To show the love to his wife, he named here the Mandarin Ducks Hall. You know that in China, mandarin-ducks always appear in pairs, symbolizing love, fidelity and faithful companions.

V: What is the use of the hall?

G: This hall was originally used for entertainment. The owner used to invite Suzhou Opera singers to perform for his guests here, so the rafters in the ceiling were made in curves and the front part of the hall was raised above the water to achieve better acoustic results.

V: I found the hall is divided into two parts.

G: Yes. Its northern part is known as the 36 Mandarin Ducks Hall and the southern part is called the 18 Camellias Hall. In ancient China, men and women were strictly separated from each other, so, in the southern hall the owner received his friends while in the northern part his wife met her friends. In the corners of the building are 4-side rooms, also known as ear rooms. They were originally used by servants or as make-up rooms for actors and actresses when the garden's owner held performances.

V: So special! So nice!

Task 4 Useful Sentences

1. It rises and falls so that we feel as if we were walking on waves.
2. This one links the moon gate and the Inverted Reflection Building.
3. It was built in memory of the garden's designer Wen Zhengming and his teacher Shen Zhou. Both are painters with national reputation in the Ming Dynasty.
4. In China, mandarin-ducks always appear in pairs, symbolizing love, fidelity and faithful companions.
5. Its ground, ceiling and windows are all in the shape of a folding fan.

Task 5 Listening

You will hear five sentences. Listen carefully and put down the whole sentences.

1. _____.
2. _____.
3. _____.
4. _____.
5. _____.

Task 6 Role-Play

Situation 1: Arrange for the James the following route: Above-Water Corridor—Inverted Reflection Building—Whom-to-Sit-with Pavilion—Staying and Listening Parlor—Mandarin Ducks Hall.

Situation 2: You are the local guide for Peter Smith. He wants to buy some gifts for his wife and children to take home. But he does not know where to buy something that is typically Chinese, so he comes to you for help. You take him to a downtown shopping center and give him some advice about what he should buy.

Task 7 Translation

1. 这是苏州最精致的长廊之一。

2. 廊是苏州古典园林中最常见的建筑形式。
3. We regarded it as a plant of honesty and straightness.
4. The rafters in the ceiling were made in curves and the front part of the hall was raised above the water to achieve better acoustic results.
5. You know that in China, mandarin-ducks always appear in pairs, symbolizing love, fidelity and faithful companions.

Task 8   Supplementary Reading

Local Product of Lijiang

Lijiang, in south China's Yunnan Province, is the only Chinese city listed on UNESCO's World Cultural Heritage list. It is home to the ancient Dongba culture and is a major scenic area in China. Whiling sightseeing, tourists are recommended to shop for some local products.

Cellared Liquor

Lijiang's cellared liquor is made by adding distiller's yeast and local spring water to highland barley, wheat and barley, the mix of which is then cellared for years. It is transparent, amber-colored and fragrant. It is honored as a provincial banquet drink and was served to British Queen Elizabeth during her trip to Yunnan.

Duolijibu (Dried Crabapple)

Crabapples are called duoli in Lijiang. The local breed is round in shape and somewhat larger than a grape. The skin is red and meaty. It blooms in March, and ripens in August. The dried ones taste sweet and sour, and have some medicinal effects, such as a diuretic, reducing thirst and strengthening the stomach. In the folk medicine of the local Naxi ethnic group, the dried crabapples are the main ingredient in prescriptions for urinary diseases. In the harvest season, almost every household in Lijiang dries crabapples in the sun. The dried fruit can be bought in Lijiang all year round.

Ciba (Cake)

The main ingredients are wheat flour, ham and edible oil. The cakes are either sweet or salty and taste sharp and crisp. They can be kept for several days. Local people often carry them while traveling, or send them to friends as a local specialty. It is, indeed, a local specialty because only local water and wheat can produce a wonderful taste, they say.

Rice-Filled Sausage

This is a traditional food of the Naxi people. When butchering a pig for the New Year, almost every Naxi household will make it. Rice is mixed with pig's blood and various spices, and is then stuffed into the pig's intestine. It is cut into slices and then deep-fried or steamed. It nourishes the blood and vital energy in the body.

Bean Jelly

In Lijiang, bean jelly, made from beans of a local breed, can be eaten either hot or cold. In summer it is very refreshing to have a bowl of cold bean jelly seasoned with red pepper, pepper, scallion and vinegar. In winter people like to have it hot, and visitors can often see on the street stoves made out of oil drums on which bean jelly is being grilled. A bowl of hot bean jelly is just what your stomach needs on a chilly day.

Snow Tea

This type of tea grows on snowy mountains, hence the name. The tea leaves are white, and look like they have been processed. The tea has a refreshing fragrance and a sweet aftertaste. It helps reduce inner heat, enrich the saliva and stabilizes the blood pressure. Tourists can try a cup of hot Snow Tea (using 2-4 grams of tea leaves) or mix other tea leaves with it to alleviate fatigue.

Ginseng

Lijiang ginseng grows on the sunny and temperate banks of the Jinsha River. Studies show that it contains various medicinal elements. It has great tonic value, and is good for those who suffer from cardiovascular, stomach, and liver diseases, or diabetes. It also helps fight cancer.

Sulima Liquor

When you visit a local family in the area of beautiful Lugu Lake, the host will present you with a bowl of sulima made by the local Mosuo and Pumi people. This fragrant alcoholic drink is orange-colored and of low proof. It is also nutritious.

Pig's Fat

If you have a chance to visit a Mosuo family, you will surely be treated to pig's fat preserved and made in a special local way. It is nutritious and tastes neither fatty nor greasy. It can keep for a long time. Besides treating guests with it, the Mosuo and Pumi people also send it as a gift.

Salted Sour Fish

This is a traditional food of the Mosuo and Naxi people to treat guests and send as gifts. Though the taste varies from home to home, one thing is common: fish from Lugu Lake weighing 250 grams are used. Whenever a fisherman catches such a fish, he will place it in a special wooden basin and bring it home. The housewife will clean the fish quickly and put the still struggling fish in an earthen jar, and season it with salt, pepper and cooking wine. When the jar is filled, it will be sealed and kept in a cool place. After about 10 days, the jar will be unsealed. The salted fish can then be eaten cooked or raw.

Questions:
1. What is salted sour fish?
2. Where is Lijiang located?
3. What is the significance of Lijiang City?
4. What will you be served if you visit a local family in the area of beautiful Lugu Lake?
5. Why does Snow Tea have such a name?

Project 3 Suzhou Gardens

Part Ⅰ Lingering Garden

Task 1 Warm-Up

1. What are the characteristics of the winding corridor in the Lingering Garden?
2. Which are the three treasures in the Lingering Garden? Please say something about the cultural significance of the Taihu Lake stone.

Task 2 Words and Expressions

tax	[tæks]	n.	税
brief	[briːf]	adj.	简短的,扼要的
UNESCO	[juːˈneskəʊ]	n.	联合国教科文组织
literary	[ˈlɪtərəri]	adj.	文学的
minister	[ˈmɪnɪstə]	n.	部长
linger	[ˈlɪŋɡə]	v.	逗留
major	[ˈmeɪdʒə]	adj.	主要的
particularly	[pəˈtɪkjələli]	adv.	尤其
worth	[wɜːθ]	adj.	值得的
pronunciation	[prəˌnʌnsiˈeɪʃn]	n.	发音
characteristic	[ˌkærəktəˈrɪstɪk]	n.	特征
infinite	[ˈɪnfɪnɪt]	a.	无限的
acre	[ˈeɪkə]	n.	英亩
variety	[vəˈraɪəti]	n.	多样,种类
highlight	[ˈhaɪlaɪt]	n.	精彩部分
quintessence	[kwɪnˈtesns]	n.	精髓
wind	[waɪnd]	v.	蜿蜒
corridor	[ˈkɒrɪdɔː]	n.	走廊
finance	[faɪˈnæns]	n.	金融
rockery	[ˈrɒkəri]	n.	假山
brook	[brʊk]	n.	小溪
rustic	[ˈrʌstɪk]	adj.	乡村的
inscribe	[ɪnˈskraɪb]	v.	题写,铭刻

various	[ˈvɛərɪəs]	adj.	各种各样的
official	[əˈfɪʃl]	n.	官员
private	[ˈpraɪvət]	adj.	私人的
ingeniously	[ɪnˈdʒenjuəsli]	adv.	巧妙地
composition	[ˌkɒmpəˈzɪʃn]	n.	成分,组织
ever-changing	[ˌevəˈtʃeɪndʒɪŋ]	adj.	不断变化的
natural scenery			自然风光
in charge of			负责
be noted for			以……闻名
World Cultural Heritage			世界文化遗产
Cold Azure Mountain Villa			寒碧庄
take over			接管
be composed of			由……组成

Task 3　Dialogues

Scene: Now the group is on the way to Hotel by coach. (V = Visitor, G = Guide)

G: Hi, my friends. Now we are going back to our hotel, I will make a brief introduction of the Lingering Garden for you!

V: What is the Lingering Garden?

G: The Lingering Garden is one of four major gardens in China and one of Suzhou gardens inscribed under the World Cultural Heritage of UNESCO. Together with the Humble Administrator's Garden we have visited today, these two gardens hold a particularly important place among the various gardens in Suzhou.

V: OK! I guess, just as its name suggests, the garden is well worth lingering in.

G: Exactly! It was first named East garden, as opposed to the west garden that was laid west of it at the same time by the same person, Xu Taishi, a high official of the government. In 1798 the garden was owned by Liu Rongfeng, an official in charge of the province's finances, taxes and personnel matters. It was repaired and renamed Cold Azure Mountain Villa. Local people thought it was too literary to remember, and called it Liu Family's Garden, or simply Liu Garden. In 1876 Sheng Xuren, Minister of Communication, took over the garden. The new owner, the Sheng Family, changed the garden's family name Liu into another Chinese character Liu with the same pronunciation. This character Liu means "linger or stray". Since then the garden has been known as Liu Garden or the Lingering Garden.

V: I see. That is very interesting. How big is this garden?

G: The garden covers an area of about five acres. It's composed of the central section, eastern, western, and northern sections. The western section is noted for natural scenery with rockeries, woods and brooks; and the northern part is famous for its rustic scenery, with the central and eastern sections being its quintessence.

V: It is quite a large private garden. Is there anything special about this garden?

G: Most buildings in the garden are naturally constructed by a 670-meter-long winding corridor. So the garden's main characteristics are well-knit composition and infinite variety. And groups of buildings are designed ingeniously to divide and compose the space into ever-changing garden scenes. What I am trying to say is that the highlight of the garden is the use of its space.

V: That sounds good. I would like to have a look of this beautiful garden.

Task 4 Useful Sentences

1. The Lingering Garden is one of the four major gardens in China and one of Suzhou gardens inscribed under the World Cultural Heritage of UNESCO.
2. The winding corridor is regarded as one of the three famous corridors in Suzhou.
3. It's composed of the central section, eastern, western, and northern sections.
4. The western section is noted for natural scenery with rockeries, woods and brooks; and the northern part is famous for its rustic scenery, with the central and eastern sections being its quintessence.
5. The three treasures in the Lingering Garden are the following: "Cloud-Crowned Peak", "Marble Block Screen" and "Fish Fossil".

Task 5 Listening

You will hear five sentences. Listen carefully and put down the whole sentences.

1. _____.
2. _____.
3. _____.
4. _____.
5. _____.

Task 6 Role-Play

Situation 1: Arrange a half-day tour of the Lingering Garden for the James.

Situation 2: You take three individual travelers to Shangri-la Hotel without having booked in advance.
- Ask for two rooms and tell the receptionist the duration of their stay.
- You are told there is one room available at present. Book it.
- You are told there will be another one later in the day, but the room faces the street. Ask the travelers whether or not they want this room, and let the receptionist know.
- Check the rate for the room.
- Check whether meals are included in the rate for the room.

Task 7 Translation

1. 这个园林很值得流连其中。
2. 这个园林的特点在于布局有致,层出不穷。
3. What I am trying to say is the highlight of the garden is the use of its space.
4. The new owner, the Sheng Family, changed the garden's family name Liu into another Chinese character Liu with the same pronunciation.
5. Together with the Humble Administrator's Garden we have visited today, these two gardens hold a particularly important place among various gardens in Suzhou.

Task 8 Supplementary Reading

Gulangyu Island

Gulangyu, separated from the main island by the 500-metre-wide Egret River, with an area of 177 square kilometres, enjoys a laudatory title "Garden on the Sea". The original name of the islet was Yuan Zhou Zi. In the Ming Dynasty it was renamed Gulang, meaning "drum waves", because the holes in the southwestern reefs hit by the waves will make sounds like the drum.

The Dragon Head Hill, Hoisting Flag Hill and Hen Hill stand in a line in the islet. Overlapping peaks foil the blue water, white clouds, green trees and bright flowers. The air in the islet is fresh. The entire place is free from any sorts of vehicles and is particularly quiet. All these render an atmosphere of a fairyland.

The architecture in the islet varies greatly in style, Chinese and foreign. Thus the islet has a laudatory title "the World Architecture Museum". The residents here love music very much, and the number of the pianos possessed is in the leading place in the nation, though there is only a population of 20,000 people. Thus the islet is praised as the "Piano Islet".

Today, Gulangyu is listed as one of the nation's major scenic spots. The main sites of interest here include the Sunlit Rock, Shuzhuang Park, Gangzihou Bathing Beach and Memorial Hall to Zheng Chenggong, which are visited annually by millions of people from all parts of the country and the world.

Riguang Rock is also called Yellow Rock. It is the summit of Gulang Islet. On the mountain, huge and precipitous rocks form many caves and gullies. Pavilions are hidden among green trees. If you go up the steps, you will come to the Lotus Flower Convent first, where a huge rock named "A Piece of Tile", sitting on the top, forms a hall below. On the large rocks beside the convent are inscribed "Wonderland of Gulang", and "Number One along the Egret River".

Behind the convent are "the Dragon's Cave of the Egret River", "the Cave of Summer Resort", and the scenic spots. Close to the convent is the historical site of Zheng Chenggong's Dragon Head Mountain Fastness and the platform for directing the raining of his seamen. Coming to the top of the mountain, you can see the beautiful views of the sea and the mountains, and the Xiamen Island and Gulangyu, Dadan and Erdan are all presented before your eyes.

Shuzhuang Park is situated on the seashore to the south of Riguang Rock. In the 21st year of the Guangxu period in the Qing Dynasty (1895), a rich merchant from Tainan came to Gulangyu with his family and made his home there. He began building the park in 1913 in memory of his native home in Banqiao, Taiwan, and used Shuzhuang, the homonym of his mother's name to name the park. Now a bronze statue of the former owner of the park stands in the park. Architecturally the park is very cleverly designed by taking advantage of the mountain and the sea. There you can feel a stillness in things moving, and a movement in things still. It presents such a unique scene that you might find it difficult to tear yourself away from it.

Inside the park there are several beautiful views such as Renqiu Pavilion, the Forty-four Bridge, the Piled-up Rocks, the artificial hills, Danying Veranda and the Insensate Rock Room. No wonder the park ranks first among the famous parks in Xiamen. To its left is Gangzihou bathing beach, which is marked by clear water and sand, and has the capacity of bathing thousands of people at a time. Nearby there is Yanping Park, which was set up in memory of Zheng Chenggong.

The Nine-bending Forty-four Bridge is the major view of Shuzhuang Park. This over-one-hundred-metre-long bridge looks like a dragon moving through the water. On the bridge there are Watching Fishing Stand, Ferrying-to-the Moon Pavilion, One-thousand-wave Pavilion and so on. If you are strolling about or taking a rest on the bridge when it is at full tide, you might have a feeling of walking on the sea, coming up and down with the waves.

On the Piled-up Rocks by the winding crossing-the-sea bridge are inscribed these words: "Vast Sea and Boundless Sky", and "Resting the Head on the Currents", which are so beautifully written and so vividly blended with the surroundings that you would find them pleasing both to the eye and to the mind.

> Questions:
> 1. When did Gulangyu Island get the present name? What's the meaning?
> 2. What are the main sites of interest?
> 3. List the laudatory title of this islet.
> 4. What is the summit of Gulang Islet?
> 5. Which park ranks the first among the famous parks in Xiamen?

Part Ⅱ The Lion Grove Garden

Task 1 Warm-Up

1. When was the Lion Grove Garden built? Why is the Lion Grove Garden known as "Master forest"?
2. What is the name of the main hall in Lion Grove? What's its meaning? What are its architectural features?

Task 2 Words and Expressions

representative	[ˌreprɪˈzentətɪv]	n.	代表
sightseeing	[ˈsaɪtsiːɪŋ]	n.	观光
inspection	[ɪnˈspekʃn]	n.	视察
ideal	[aɪˈdɪəl]	adj.	理想的
ornamental	[ˌɔːnəˈmentl]	adj.	装饰的
inscription	[ɪnˈskrɪpʃn]	n.	题字,碑铭
tablet	[ˈtæblɪt]	n.	匾
tourist destination			景点
Surging Wave Pavilion			沧浪亭
Yangtze River Delta			长江三角洲

Task 3 Dialogues

Scene: Now the group is on the way to Hotel by coach. Mr. White is interested in the gardens in Suzhou. They are discussing. (V = Visitor, G = Guide)

V: Susan, we have been talking about the Lingering Garden. Is there any garden which is quite different from the previous ones?

G: The Lion Grove Garden is one of the four most famous gardens in Suzhou and it is a representative of the Yuan Dynasty style of the 13th century. The other three are the Surging Wave Pavilion, the Lingering Garden and the Humble Administrator's Garden. Also, it's one of the World's Cultural Heritage of UNSCEO and 4A level national tourist destination.

V: Is there really a lion inside?

G: Its original name was Teacher's Garden. The Buddhist monk Tianru built this garden for his teacher Zhongfeng who lived at the Lion Cliff in West Tianmu Mountains in Zhejiang Province, hence the name. Because the garden has a large number of rocks shaped like lions and in Chinese, the pronunciation is the same as "Lion Forest Garden". Hence the name.

V: I see. That is very interesting.

G: The garden covers an area of about 2.5 acres. It is an ideal sightseeing site as it has richly ornamental pavilions and towers in different styles. Each has its own history and story.

V: Why is this garden so famous in Suzhou, even in the area of South Yangtze River Delta?

G: Because of Qianlong Emperor, in the 18th century. The emperor visited it five times during his six inspection tours in our area south of the Yangtze River. He even had the garden copied both in Beijing and Chengde. He liked the garden and its rockeries so much that he left three inscriptions, drew three paintings with the garden's scenery as the theme, and wrote ten poems, one of which was inscribed on a stele displayed in the garden. Furthermore, many rare tablets and steles, paintings and calligraphies are kept in the Lion Grove Garden.

V: I see. I can't miss this garden during my stay in Suzhou.

Task 4 Useful Sentences

1. The Lion Grove Garden is one of the four most famous gardens in Suzhou and it is a representative of the Yuan Dynasty style of the 13th century.
2. Also, it's one of the World's Cultural Heritage of UNSCEO and 4A level national tourist destination.
3. The garden has a large number of rocks shaped like lions; and in Chinese, the pronunciation is the same as "Lion Forest Garden".
4. It is an ideal sightseeing site as it has richly ornamental pavilions and towers in different styles; each has its own history and story.
5. He liked the garden and its rockeries so much that he left three inscriptions, drew three paintings with the garden's scenery as the theme, and wrote ten poems, one of which was inscribed on a stele displayed in the garden.

Task 5 Listening

You will hear five sentences. Listen carefully and put down the whole sentences.

1. _____.
2. _____.
3. _____.
4. _____.
5. _____.

Task 6 Role-Play

Situation 1: Arrange a half-day tour of the Lion Grove Garden for Mr and Mrs James and their kids, Tom and Kate.

Situation 2: A group of Australian students headed by Prof. James arrived in Suzhou during this summer vacation. They will stay here for a week. You are the guide. You invite Prof. James to discuss the travel arrangements of the group with him.

- Make some suggestions about tourist attractions that the visitors might be interested in seeing and say something about the special features of each place.
- The Australian students want to visit Suzhou University to experience the campus life of Chinese students. What might you say?
- Plan an itinerary for the group and discuss it with Prof. James.

Task 7 Translation

1. 园林占地2.5公顷。
2. 这个园林是世界文化遗产。
3. 这是个4A级国家旅游胜地。
4. He even had the garden copied both in Beijing and Chengde.
5. The emperor visited it five times during his six inspection tours in our area south of Yangtze River.

Task 8 Supplementary Reading

Mogao Grottoes

The Mogao Grottoes, also known as "the Thousand Buddha Caves", and praised as "a glittering pearl that adorns the Silk Road", are the most famous Buddhist grottoes in China. Located 15 km southeast of Dunhuang (25 km by road), these caves are carved out of the sandstone cliffs of the Singing Sand (Mingsha) Mountains.

The 1,600 m of grottoes in the south to north cliff were constructed in 10 dynasties from the 4th to the 14th century. The Mogao grottoes' 45,000 square meters (480,000 sq ft) of mural paintings and more than 2,000 color statues are regarded as the greatest treasure-house of Buddhist art existing in the world.

The first grotto was chiseled out in 366 AD. According to legend, a monk called Yue Zun dreamed of 1,000 golden Buddhas when he was traveling home across this region, and he decided to turn his dream into reality by painting them on the wall of a cave.

Over the next 1,000 years, 10 dynasties rose and fell, and artists of each dynasty contributed grottoes. Work on the grottoes ceased during the Yuan Dynasty (1206-1368), and ever since the grottos have remained through for hundreds of years, protected from natural erosion by their cave location. Today, 492 caves are still standing. Altogether there are 2,000 statues and over 45,000 separate murals.

> Questions:
> 1. What is the nickname of Mogao Grottoes?
> 2. When was the first grotto chiseled out?
> 3. How many caves are there now?
> 4. What is the significance of Mogao Grottoes?
> 5. Who has contributed to the grottoes?

Part Ⅲ The Garden of Cultivation

Task 1 Warm-Up

1. What's the origin of the name "Yi Pu" — the Garden of Cultivation?
2. State briefly the function of the pavilions in the architecture of the garden.

Task 2　Words and Expressions

distinctive	[dɪˈstɪŋktɪv]	*adj.*	独特的
occupy	[ˈɒkjupaɪ]	*v.*	占用
residential	[ˌrezɪˈdenʃl]	*adj.*	住宅的
offer	[ˈɔːfə]	*v.*	提供
distance	[ˈdɪstəns]	*n.*	距离,远方
luxuriantly	[lʌgˈʒuərɪəntli]	*adv.*	繁茂地
cottage	[ˈkɒtɪdʒ]	*n.*	村舍
terrace	[ˈterəs]	*n.*	平台
secondary	[ˈsekənderi]	*adj.*	从属的
artistic	[ɑːˈtɪstɪk]	*adj.*	艺术的
hectare	[ˈhekteə]	*n.*	公顷
comprise	[kəmˈpraɪz]	*v.*	构成
calm	[kɑːm]	*adj.*	平静的
mist	[mɪst]	*n.*	雾
courtyard	[ˈkɔːtjɑːd]	*n.*	庭院
pool	[puːl]	*n.*	水塘
in scale			在规模上

Task 3　Dialogues

Scene: Now the group is discussing the classical gardens on the coach. (V = Visitor, G = Guide)

G: Hi, my friends, now we are going back to our hotel. I'd like to make a brief introduction of the Garden of Cultivation for you!
V: What is the Garden of Cultivation?
G: The Garden of Cultivation is small in scale but of distinctive artistic characteristics of the Ming Dynasty (1368-1644).
V: Why it gets such a name?
G: This garden was firstly built in the Ming Dynasty; it was called Yaopu at first. During early Qing period, its name was changed to the present one, but was also called Jingting Mountain Cottage.

V: It is a small one. How about the area?
G: The garden occupies an area of 0.33 hectare, more than half of which are residential houses.

V: How about the layout of the garden?
G: The garden's arrangement is open and simple; buildings, ponds and mountain trees are laid out from north to south successively. This is the most basic method of arrangement of a Suzhou garden. In the southwestern corner there are some small courtyards comprising secondary views, which offer the visitors very calm and joyful feelings. All structures in the garden are used to create one artistic garden view with hills covered in mist, waves reaching far into the distance, and trees growing luxuriantly. There are also springs and deep pools, lofty pavilions and terraces.
V: I have heard of the Summer Palace in Beijing. What's the difference between them?
G: The Summer Palace is categorized to imperial gardens, which are large in area. It covers about 290 hectares and has three sections: the administrative section, residential section and recreational section. On the other hand, the gardens here were mostly built at one side or at the back of residential houses. In almost every case, there is a large space in the garden set in a landscape of artistically arranged rockeries, ponds, pavilions, bridges, trees and flowers. Surrounding the beautiful scene are small open areas partitioned by corridors through which visitors can enjoy the scenery. Buildings in the garden are open on all sides and are often situated near the water so that the whole scene can be enjoyed.

Task 4 Useful Sentences

1. I'd like to make a brief introduction of the Garden of Cultivation for you!
2. The Garden of Cultivation is small in scale but of distinctive artistic characteristics of the Ming Dynasty (1368-1644).
3. During early Qing period, its name was changed to the present one, but was also called Jingting Mountain Cottage.
4. In the southwestern corner there are some small courtyards comprising secondary views, which offer the visitors very calm and joyful feelings.
5. All structures in the garden are used to create one artistic garden view with hills covered in mist, waves reaching far into the distance, and trees growing luxuriantly.

Task 5 Listening

You will hear five sentences. Listen carefully and put down the whole sentences.

1. _____.
2. _____.
3. _____.

4. _____.
5. _____.

Task 6　Role-Play

Situation 1: Arrange a two-hour tour of the Garden of Cultivation for the James.

Situation 2: You are the local guide of a tour group. Your group is going to Nanjing today. You have already checked out from the hotel.

- As soon as you arrive at the railway station, you find out that the train is delayed to a very late time. On hearing the news, the group protests angrily for they have travel plans in Nanjing today. You try to explain the whole situation and comfort them.
- Negotiate with the person concerned to see whether it is possible for the group to take another train to Nanjing in time for the travel plan.
- Inform your travel service about the change and make sure that the travel service in Nanjing knows about the change.

Task 7　Translation

1. 这个园林的布局是如何的?
2. 这个园林规模很小,具有鲜明的明清艺术风格。
3. The garden occupies an area of 0.33 hectare, more than half of which are residential houses.
4. In the southwestern corner there are some small courtyards comprising secondary views, which offer the visitors very calm and joyful feelings.
5. This is the most basic method of arrangement of a Suzhou garden.

Task 8　Supplementary Reading

Hangzhou

　　Hangzhou is the capital of Zhejiang Province and its political, economic and cultural center. With enchanting natural beauty and abundant cultural heritages, Hangzhou is known as "Heaven on Earth" and one of China's most important tourist venues. The City, the southern terminus of the Grand Canal, is located on the lower reaches of the Qiantang River in southeast China, a superior position in the Yangtze Delta and only 180 kilometers from Shanghai. Hangzhou has a subtropical monsoon type climate with four quite distinct seasons. However, it is neither too hot in summer nor too cold in winter, making it a year round destination.

The West Lake is undoubtedly the most renowned feature of Hangzhou, noted for the scenic beauty that blends naturally with many famous historical and cultural sites. In this scenic area, Solitary Hill, the Mausoleum of General Yue Fei, the Six Harmonies Pagoda and the Ling Yin Temple are probably the most frequently visited attractions. The "Ten West Lake Prospects" have been specially selected to give the visitors outstanding views of the lake, mountains and monuments.

A number of national museums can be found in Hangzhou and are representative of Chinese culture. Fine examples are the National Silk Museum and the National Tea Museum. Along with the other museums in Hangzhou, they provide a fascinating insight into the history of Chinese traditional products.

One of the most important parts of traveling is tasting the local delicacies. Hangzhou dishes are noted for their elaborate preparation, sophisticated cooking and refreshing taste. Many local specialties will be sure to make your trip a cultural experience. We recommend that you try Beggar's Chicken (a chicken baked in clay), West Lake Fish in Sweet Sour Source (vinegar coated fish fresh caught from the lake), Dongpo Pork (braised pork) and Fried Shrimps with Longjing Tea, etc.

The shopping environment in Hangzhou is exciting and convenient. Travelers and tourists like to go to Qing He Fang Street. It is one of the most famous and historic streets in the city and reflects many of the features of the Southern Song Dynasty (1127-1279). Shoppers will admire the antique buildings while purchasing items from a wide range of local goods such as silks, tea or maybe a silk parasol, brocade or a beautiful Hangzhou fan. These are just some of the items to be found but there are many more.

At night Hangzhou has much to offer and teahouses and various kinds of pubs are both plentiful and popular. Choosing one overlooking the West Lake for a pleasant chat over a cup of tea is sure to make you feel totally relaxed and refreshed.

While much of the ancient city that had been the capital of the Southern Song Dynasty was destroyed during the Taiping Rebellion in the mid-nineteenth century, today's Hangzhou is a modern and vibrant economical center. As such it provides a base for many talented and skilled people. Nevertheless, thanks to its unique setting by the West Lake it continues to enjoy the many benefits of the natural surroundings that have delighted visitors for centuries. Not only was it much vaunted in his writings by the 13th century explorer Marco Polo, but the lake and its environs have inspired poets of great renown such as Bai Juyi and Su Dongpo down the ages. There can be no doubt that visit here is certain to be a memorable one.

Questions:
1. Tell the status of Hangzhou in tourist attractions nationwide.
2. Which site is the most renowned feature of Hangzhou?
3. What are the Hangzhou dishes famous for?
4. How is the shopping environment in Hangzhou?
5. List some places of interest in the West Lake area.

Project 4　Old City Center Canal Cruise

Part Ⅰ

Task 1　Warm-Up

1. What's the difference between the ancient city of Central River and Shantang River?
2. How does the name "Midu Bridge" come from?

Task 2　Words and Expressions

yacht	[jɒt]	n.	游艇,快艇
intersection	[ˌɪntəˈsekʃn]	n.	十字路口,交叉点
distinctive	[dɪˈstɪŋktɪv]	adj.	独特的
total	[ˈtəʊtl]	adj.	总的
prosperous	[ˈprɒspərəs]	adj.	繁荣的,兴旺的
local	[ˈləʊkl]	n.	当地人
diligent	[ˈdɪlɪdʒənt]	adj.	勤奋的
canal	[kəˈnæl]	n.	运河
greedy	[ˈgriːdi]	adj.	贪婪的
eliminate	[ɪˈlɪmɪneɪt]	v.	除去
ceremony	[ˈserəməni]	n.	仪式,典礼
pulse	[pʌls]	n.	脉搏
essence	[ˈesns]	n.	精髓
ferry	[ˈferi]	n.	渡船
salutatory	[səˈluːtətəri]	n.	开幕词
moat	[məʊt]	n.	护城河
renowned	[rɪˈnaʊnd]	adj.	有名的
region	[ˈriːdʒən]	n.	地区
vehicle	[ˈviːɪkl]	n.	车辆,交通工具
gentle	[ˈdʒentl]	adj.	温和的
tough	[tʌf]	adj.	强硬的
cruise	[kruːz]	n.	巡航,漫游
blackmail	[ˈblækmeɪl]	v.	勒索,讹诈
reproduce	[ˌriːprəˈdjuːs]	v.	再生,复制

soul	[səʊl]	n.	灵魂
delicate	[ˈdelɪkət]	adj.	精美的
Grand Canal			大运河
be similar to			与……相似
make an acquaintance of			认识
Seeking-Ferry Bridge			觅渡桥
Osmanthus Park			桂花公园
ahead of			在……前面
Oriental Venice			东方威尼斯
be connected with			与……有关
make up one's mind			决定
in terms of			就……而言
in brief			简单地说

Task 3   Dialogues

Scene: Now the group is on the yacht. (V = Visitor, G = Guide)
Travel Route: Seeking-Ferry Bridge—Chi Men—Osmanthus Park—Southern-Park Bridge—Ren-Min Bridge—Su-Lun Factory

Salutatory

G: Hello, everyone! Welcome on board. Now we are at the intersection of the moat and the Grand Canal. From here we are going to enjoy the distinctive water-view of Suzhou.
V: Yes, I have already heard that Suzhou is a famous water city.
G: Yes. About 700 years ago, Marco Polo, the renowned traveler came to Suzhou and praised it as the Oriental Venice. The total area of Suzhou is 8,488 square kilometers and the water covers 3,609 square kilometers, almost the half. There are about 300 lakes and 20,000 rivers in the region, big or small. So, Suzhou is actually a water city.
V: Can you say something about the relationship between Suzhou and the water?
G: Yes. In Chinese handwriting, Su means fish and rice. So you can understand that Suzhou is a land of fish and rice, it is a very rich and flourishing place from ancient times. Suzhou has very close relationship with the water. We live near water, depend on water, and boat is our main transportation vehicle in ancient times. Many customs are connected with water. Because of the water, Suzhou can be a prosperous place for long time. Chinese think the character of Suzhou locals is similar to water, being gentle, diligent and tough. So, since you

have been in Suzhou, if you want to make a full acquaintance of Suzhou culture and customs, you cannot miss the canal cruise. Only in this way, to be close with Suzhou water, can you enjoy the real beauty of Suzhou.

V: I can't wait for that!

Seeking-Ferry Bridge

G: Now, everyone, we are in the southeast of Suzhou. We can see two bridges.

V: Yes.

G: The larger one is named New Seeking-Ferry Bridge, and the smaller one Old Seeking-Ferry Bridge, which was built in the Yuan Dynasty, about 700 years ago.

V: Why did this bridge have such a name?

G: At that time, Suzhou was a prosperous place. Many people need to cross the river very often. But there was no bridge here; ferry was the only way to cross the canal. So the owner of ferry was greedy, often blackmailed travelers. A monk named Jinxiu was blackmailed several times. So he made up his mind to build a bridge here, which was good for people to cross the river. After that, people had no need to ferry any longer. Therefore, the bridge was firstly named Eliminating-Ferry Bridge. In Suzhou dialect, "eliminating" is similar to "seeking". Gradually, the name was changed to Seeking-Ferry Bridge.

V: I see now. How big is this bridge?

G: The bridge is 81.3 meters long with arch span of 19.8 meters and has 53 steps on both sides. What is worth mentioning, among the existing ancient bridges in Suzhou, this bridge is the thinnest one in terms of the thickness, only 30 cm of the arch top. Now, this bridge was listed as the historical site under the protection of Jiangsu Provincial Government.

V: I found there is a set of statues over there.

G: Yes. Along the canal bank, there is a set of statues reproducing the historical scenery: one is the ferry transporter, one is the female traveler waving to the ferry and the other is Jingxiu, the monk, sitting collecting money. Here's a nice place to appreciate the full moon. At night, the reflections of the bridge arches and the full moon on the water surface form entertaining scenery.

Chi Men—Osmanthus Park—Southern-Park Bridge

G: Now, we can find a red-brick building over there.

V: Yes, what is it?

G: In the Tang Dynasty, about 1,300 years ago, this was an old city gate, called Chi Men. This one is rebuilt in 2004 in the shape of the original one. It's altogether 225 meters long, about 8 meters high. In 1895, here was the oldest customs house in Suzhou.

V: It is very elegant. I think there is a park over there.

G: Yes, you are right. We called it the Osmanthus Park. In 1983, Suzhou local government chose osmanthus as our city flower. Inside the park, there are more than 200 kinds of osmanthus trees. Suzhou locals love osmanthus flower very much. Many of our habits and customs have close relationship with osmanthus. What's more, the spirit of osmanthus is similar to Suzhou locals. So we regard it as our city flower, and this park is named the Osmanthus Park.

V: Very interesting. A nice big bridge is ahead of us.

G: That is the Southern-Park Bridge.

V: Is there something special about it?

G: The opening ceremony of China International Tourism Festival was held here in April 16, 2004. Hopefully this canal cruise can also let you feel the heavenly unique charm, which is based on water and takes the water as her soul and pulse.

Ren-Min Bridge—Su-Lun Factory

G: Now, it is Ren-Min Bridge, which is 62 m long, the span is 23.4 m and height is 4 m. Attention please, we can see 16 delicate stone-carvings at two sides. Each has a name. Each reflects a period of history of Suzhou in brief, an important essence.

V: Look, a huge old factory building. What is it?

G: It's the Su-Lun Factory. This factory takes a very important role in Suzhou history. It's the first national industry factory in Suzhou. Through it, Suzhou locals see the brightness of electronic firstly. At last, it was constructed by Lu Runxiang, Zhuang Yuan (the No. 1 scholar in national entrance exam) of the Qing Dynasty in 1894.

 Task 4　Useful Sentences

1. Now we are at the intersection of the moat and the Grand Canal.
2. From here we are going to enjoy the distinctive water-view of Suzhou.
3. About 700 years ago, Marco Polo, the renowned traveler came to Suzhou and praised it as the Oriental Venice.
4. Since you have been in Suzhou, if you want to make a full acquaintance of Suzhou culture and customs, you cannot miss the canal cruise.
5. Now, this bridge was listed as the historical site under the protection of Jiangsu Provincial Government.

Task 5 Listening

You will hear five sentences. Listen carefully and put down the whole sentences.
1. _____.
2. _____.
3. _____.
4. _____.
5. _____.

 Task 6 Role-Play

Situation 1: Arrange a cruise tour containing Seeking-Ferry Bridge—Chi Men—Osmanthus Park—Southern-Park Bridge—Ren-Min Bridge—Su-Lun Factory.

Situation 2: Mr. Smith bought a sandal wood fan. When he comes back to the hotel, he finds that the fan is broken on the side. He is very upset and comes to you for help. You go with him to the shop and talk to the shop assistant to see whether he can change the fan for Mr. Smith.

 Task 7 Translation

Put the following sentences into Chinese.
1. Chinese think the character of Suzhou locals is similar to water, being gentle, diligent and tough.
2. Only in this way, to be close with Suzhou water, can you enjoy the real beauty of Suzhou.
3. In Suzhou dialect, "eliminating" is similar to "seeking". Gradually, the name was changed to the Seeking-Ferry Bridge.
4. At night, the reflections of the bridge arches and the full moon on the water surface form entertaining scenery.
5. Hopefully this canal cruise can also let you feel the heavenly unique charm, which is based on water and takes the water as her soul and pulse.

Task 8 Supplementary Reading

Crescent Moon Tour

Ninxia Hui Autonomous Prefecture in Gansu Province has long been eulogized as a "Little Mecca in China". The 800,000 Muslims belong to ethnic groups of the Hui, Dongxiang and Salar, accounting for over 50 percent of the total population in this prefecture. The prefecture has 1,700 mosques. Of these, 100 are located in Ninxia City, scattered over its 80 square kilometers of land. Because of this, Ninxia has become the prefecture with the most mosques in China. Every year numerous Muslims stream into Ninxia to pay homage. Meanwhile, more than over hundred local people go to Saudi Arabia on pilgrimages.

When our car entered the Ninxia area, we found that every mosque caught our eye. Unlike other places, the people we passed in the streets were dressed differently. The men were wearing white hats and the women were wearing white veils. The roof of each mosque was decorated with treasure vases, one piled on top of another no matter what architectural features the mosques represented. On top of the highest vase was a crescent moon. Hence, the name of the tour.

In the Dagongbei Mosque stands a glazed pagoda. Its base is made of large bricks with carved designs that constitute its unique style. We found that the Chinese wisteria on either side of the hall where religious services are held, were blooming. It is said that the Chinese wisteria has been there for centuries, and is regarded as the guardian of the ancient building.

The famous Nanguan Mosque was constructed in the Yuan Dynasty (1206 – 1368), and was rebuilt in 1997. On top of the palace hall where religious services are held, there are three green dome towers in the distinctive Arabian style. The one in the center is 32 meters high, and is called the Huanxing (Waking-Up) Pavilion, or Looking-Moon Pavilion. There are more Muslims here than in other mosques.

Ancient Cultural Arts

The decorative pottery on the mosques in Ninxia City reminds me of pottery wares from Ninxia displayed in Beijing's Palace Museum. When I was there, I could see the pottery in various shapes in stores and on various buildings. Paying a visit to the Ninxia Museum, I was allowed to view the Ma Family Kiln first discovered in the Hehuang region. As early as 5,000 years ago, ancestors of the Chinese people in Gansu Province began constructing their houses with loess earth to make walls and purple grass to make the roofs. They lived and worked in round and rectangular houses.

The Pottery Hall in Ninxia Prefecture Museum is the place with the most exhibits. It has various kinds of pottery, covering different periods from the Panshan Culture to Qijia Culture. Whenever visitors enter the hall, they feel as if they are stepping back in time. They are fascinated with the scenes depicting people fishing, cooking, hunting, doing farm work, wearing bone decorations and clothing made from animal skin, pottery making and stone tool polishing.

The museum curator is an experienced pottery maker himself. He showed me to his workshop in his courtyard, where he often receives visitors from far away. I was deeply impressed by the methods our Chinese ancestors used in making pottery while he explained to us the various procedures. When I was about to leave, he gave me a small piece of pottery as a token of my trip to his workshop.

It seems to me that Ninxia is the best place to cultivate cultural arts. Hezhou bricks with carved designs, as both building materials and decorations, are used to lay paths in parks, and to construct public facilities such as mosques. Even in ordinary people's families, bricks with special carved designs are inlaid on top of gates and roofs.

Many brick workshops stood on both sides of the highway we traveled on. We could not help but stop and visit one. The worker who was busy with his graver in the gloomy light stopped working. He told us that Hezhou bricks with carved designs serve as a folk cultural art with a history of several hundred years. The art originated in the Northern Song Dynasty (960-1127) and became mature in the late Ming and early Qing Dynasties. One piece of brick consists of three or four layers of patterns which create a unique three dimensional effect.

Bottle Gourd with designs from the hands of the Hui people are widely known. The manufacture of bottle gourds has history of more than one hundred years. The bottle gourds can be as small as a pearl or as large as one's fist. Their designs are about traditional Chinese operas, classic literature, fairy tales and local legends. In the Ninxia Handicraft Factory, everyone of us witnessed how the women workers exquisitely made their articles, and we were deeply impressed by their excellent workmanship.

Grottoes and Pagodas

Ninxia is not only famous for its numerous mosques, but also for its Buddhist and Taoist temples, and churches which have been well preserved. Due to the influence of different religions, the culture there is very unique.

The Bingling Grottoes located in Ninxia Prefecture's Qingyuan County, are a good combination of Western and Oriental culture. Visitors can take a speed ship at the Lotus Flower Terrace in Less Jishi Mountain which is 25 kilometers from Ninxia. It takes about an hour by ship to get to the grotto site which has been eulogized by the noted historian Fan Wenlan as, as famous as the Mogao Grottoes, and Maijishan Grottoes.

With successive construction in the Northern Wei (386-534), Northern Zhou (557-581) in the Northern and Southern Dynasties, Sui Dynasty (581-618), Tang Dynasty (618-907), and Yuan (1206-1368), Ming (1368-1644) and Qing (1616-1911) Dynasties, the grottoes have become their present size, consisting of the three sites of the Upper Temple, a cave valley, and Lower Temple. According to statistics, the grottoes have 183 caves containing about 800 statues, and the murals cover more than 900 square meters. Tourists are very surprised by the Giant Buddha, similar to the Leshan Grand Buddha.

The Grottoes have many Buddhist pagodas with stone carvings and relief sculptures. Each stone pagoda has a unique feature, and the most distinctive one was built with stones from cliffs in the Tang Dynasty. The upper part looks like a typical Indian pagoda while the lower part is more like a pottery storehouse popular in the Han Dynasty (206 B. C. - 220. A. D). It is so well integrated that it is very impressive.

The Wanshou (Ten-Thousand Longevity) Taoist Temple is the largest in Ninxia City. Since its establishment in the Ming Dynasty, it has been attracting a large number of pilgrims. It has left some trances of reconstruction; however, there is no information about this.

(Source: http://chinavista.com/travel/linxia/content.html)

Questions:
1. Could you explain where the phrase "Crescent Moon Tour" comes from?
2. When could the manufacture of bottle gourds be dated back?
3. What is Ninxia famous for?
4. Among the grottoes, which one is the most distinctive?
5. Which temple is the largest one in Ninxia?

Part Ⅱ

Task 1   Warm-Up

1. What are three scenic spots at the Pan Gate Three Scenic Zone?
2. How does the name of Shantang Canal and Shantang Street come from?

Task 2   Words and Expressions

auspicious	[ɔːˈspɪʃəs]	adj.	吉利的,幸运的
strategic	[strəˈtiːdʒɪk]	adj.	战略的,重要的
appreciation	[əˌpriːʃiˈeɪʃn]	n.	欣赏,鉴识
story	[ˈstɔːri]	n.	楼层(= storey)
era	[ˈɪərə]	n.	纪元,时代
remove	[rɪˈmuːv]	v.	搬迁
relic	[ˈrelɪk]	adj.	神圣的遗物,遗迹

precious	[ˈpreʃəs]	adj.	宝贵的
pearl	[pɜːl]	n.	珍珠
unearth	[ˌʌnˈɜːθ]	v.	发掘
urn	[ɜːn]	n.	瓮
strobe	[strəʊb]	n.	闸门
steep	[stiːp]	adj.	险峻的，陡峭的
guard	[gɑːd]	v.	守卫，保卫
defeat	[dɪˈfiːt]	v.	战胜
stripe	[straɪp]	n.	条纹
liberation	[ˌlɪbəˈreɪʃn]	n.	解放
motto	[ˈmɒtəʊ]	n.	座右铭
progress	[prəˈgres]	n.	进步
spacious	[ˈspeɪʃəs]	adj.	宽敞的
exquisite	[ˈekskwɪzɪt]	adj.	精致的
luxurious	[lʌgˈʒʊəriəs]	adj.	奢侈的
accommodations	[əˌkɒməˈdeɪʃn]	n.	膳宿，住处
tale	[teɪl]	n.	故事
seal	[siːl]	v.	密封
engrave	[ɪnˈgreɪv]	v.	雕刻，刻上
well-preserved		adj.	保存得很好的
survive	[səˈvaɪv]	v.	幸免于难，存活
resort	[rɪˈzɔːt]	n.	胜地
stagnant	[ˈstægnənt]	adj.	不景气的
emit	[iˈmɪt]	v.	发出
demolish	[dɪˈmɒlɪʃ]	v.	拆毁，破坏
sutra	[ˈsuːtrə]	n.	佛经
nickname	[ˈnɪkneɪm]	n.	绰号，昵称
trap	[træp]	v.	设圈套，陷入
isolate	[ˈaɪsəleɪt]	v.	隔离
cliff	[klɪf]	n.	悬崖，峭壁
defender	[dɪˈfendə]	n.	防卫者
intruder	[ɪnˈtruːdə]	n.	入侵者
fortress	[ˈfɔːtrɪs]	n.	堡垒，要塞
invade	[ɪnˈveɪd]	v.	侵略
motivate	[ˈməʊtɪveɪt]	v.	激发（兴趣）
decade	[ˈdekeɪd]	n.	十年
pray	[preɪ]	v.	祈祷
means	[miːnz]	n.	方法，手段

wharf	[wɔːf]	n.	码头
renovation	[ˌrenəˈveɪʃn]	n.	整修
overwhelm	[ˌəʊvəˈwelm]	v.	淹没
merit	[ˈmerɪt]	n.	功绩
legendary	[ˈledʒəndəri]	adj.	传说的
refer to			涉及,指的是
dumplings wrapped in bamboo leaves			粽子
Dragon Boat Festival			端午节
Warring States Period			战国时期

Task 3 Dialogues

Scene: Now the group is on the yacht. (V = Visitor, G = Guide)
Travel Route: Three Attractions of Panmen City Gate—Hong-Sheng Match Factory—Cang-Lang Children's Palace—Bai Hua Zhou Park—Imperial Pavilion—Wan Nian Bridge—Xu Portal

Three Attractions of Panmen City Gate

G: Dear friends, on the right is the world famous Three Attractions of Pan Portal.

V: What are they referring to?

G: It includes the Auspicious Light Pagoda, Wu-men Bridge and Pan-men Gate, covering an area of about 24 hectares. The resort is situated at southeast corner of Suzhou.

V: I guess it is a very famous scenic spot.

G: Yes. 2,500 years ago, here is an important strategic position of Suzhou. The Grand Canal passes the portal from the west to the east, so it is also a busy trade centre of Suzhou. Before the war, the local marketplace was stagnant; less people came here. The local residents therefore started to call it "Cold-Water Pan Portal". Nowadays, however, this resort has become one of the most popular tourist attractions in Suzhou. Here, you can enjoy the small bridges, flowing water, and traditional household of Suzhou. In 2001 the Eighth APEC Finance Ministers Informal Convention was held in a five-star hotel near here. With this opportunity, Pan Portal resort has gained attention and appreciation from all over the world.

V: The pagoda is the Auspicious Light Pagoda.

G: Yes. It is an ancient seven-story and eight-side pagoda. It is built by bricks and woods, 53.57-meter tall. In the era of Three Kingdoms around 1,800 years ago, the king of Wu

State Sun Quan built a pagoda and a temple for his beloved mother. Legend has it that, when it was completed, the pagoda did emit beautiful light at night. Therefore it got such a name. It was removed during the Northern Song Dynasty, about 1,000 years ago. The temple was later demolished during the war time in 1860, but the pagoda survived very luckily. In April 1978, a number of precious cultural relics were discovered in this pagoda. One of them, a pearl pagoda of 1.22 m high is an extremely rare object. And a Buddhist sutra, which was written on a blue paper, was also unearthed. Many other relics were found, too. All these relics are exhibited in Suzhou Museum. It was very rare to discover these well-preserved Buddhist relics with this large amount and of such high class.

V: I see the bridge. Is this Wu-Men Bridge?

G: Yes, it is the highest existing ancient single-arch stone bridge in Suzhou. It is 66.3 m long and the span of its arch is 16 m while the height of its arch is about 9 m. It is said that Marco Polo, the world famous traveler, once came here and praised the beautiful scenery; the nickname of the bridge is Marco Polo Bridge.

V: A portal over there, I think that is Pan-men Gate.

G: Yes, it contains the land gate and water gate.

V: Tell me more.

G: The land portal has two layers of wall. In the centre, there is a mouth-shaped square, which is called Urn City. The purpose is to trap the enemy. As soon as the enemy entered the first gate, the defenders can lay down strobe to isolate them. The walls are as steep as cliffs, and the Urn City was heavily guarded at that time. In such case, to defeat the intruders would be, if we use a Chinese saying here, as easy as "to catch a turtle in an urn".

V: So interesting! How about the water gate?

G: Beside the land portal is the water. The double-layered arch was built with stripe stones, big enough to let two boats pass through side by side. Like the Land Portal, the Water Portal also has two gates (east and west) and an Urn City, which is much smaller though. In connection with the Land Urn City in the north, the Water Portal forms a fortress on the moat.

Hong-Sheng Match Factory—Cang-Lang Children's Palace

V: On our left hand, we can see a set of red-brick old buildings in the style of pre-peaceful liberation period.

G: That's the relic of the Hong-Sheng Match Factory, which was built by Chinese famous entrepreneur, Liu Hongsheng in 1920. This western-style house was originally the warehouse. It reminds us of the important history of national industry fight against the western invading economy.

V: OK, I like the idea.

G: OK, ladies and gentlemen. Here, the newly-built building is the Cang-Lang Children's Palace. The famous motto of "study well and make progress everyday", which has been motivating numerous Chinese youth for decades, was given by Chairman Mao to a local Suzhou boy, named Chen Yongkang in the 1950s. This is built for those children to develop their wisdom and skills after school.

V: The sentence is also famous in our country.

Bai Hua Zhou Park

V: There is a spacious park.

G: It's Bai Hua Zhou Park. Lunar Feb 12th is the birthday of the hundred-flower fairy. So many young girls and women would come here to pray. They hope they would become more beautiful. Hence the name. In Southern Song Dynasty, about 800 years ago, the capital of China is Hangzhou. Suzhou is the only way which must be passed for different ranks of officials and foreign envoys to Hangzhou by boats. To make it even more convenient, Suzhou Post House and exquisite accommodations were built nearby. Suzhou Post House was the largest and most luxurious one in China at that time. Also, here is a main wharf in Suzhou at that time. You know the means of transportation in Suzhou was mainly boat in the canals. So it is a busy and prosperous market place.

Imperial Pavilion—Wan Nian Bridge

G: My friends, we can find a pavilion over there. We call it "Imperial Pavilion". In the Qing Dynasty, Emperor Kangxi came here on his trip to the south. He required that officials love people; this tale was recorded and carved on the steles. Later a pavilion was built. Local residents started to call the street "Imperial Pavilion Street" since then.

V: I think this is an important place.

G: Yes.

V: A very big and nice bridge.

G: Ahead of our boat is the bridge called Wan Nian Bridge, which was first built in the Ming Dynasty, about 400 years ago. It had not been rebuilt until the reign of Emperor Qianlong in the Qing Dynasty. A number of renovations took place in 2004. This bridge is very important in Suzhou.

Xu Portal

V: There is another ancient portal.

G: This is Xu Portal.

V: Is there any relationship between it and the Pan Portal we have passed just now?

G: Like other portals, it was originally constructed with land portal and water portal. About 2,500 years ago, in the Spring and Autumn Period, the founder of Suzhou, Wu Zixu constructed 8 such kind of portals to defend Suzhou City. Xu Portal is among them.

V: I wonder why only the land portal left. Where is the water portal?

G: Good question! During the Warring States Period, the ruler of Suzhou, Chun Shenjun, found that the city was well below the water surface of Taihu Lake. To protect the city from being overwhelmed, the water portal was sealed ever since. You can see a statue over there, that's the statue of Wu Zixu. Behind it, a piece of city wall with the height of 4.5 m, covering over hundred square meters, was engraved with the legendary stories of Wu Zixu. Eight Chinese characters, embodying his great efforts and historical merits during the city construction, were carved on the back side of the wall. Suzhou locals admire and miss him very much even now. A traditional festival Duan-Wu (Dragon Boat Festival) in Suzhou has been connected with him. On that day, people threw Zongzi (dumplings wrapped in bamboo leaves) into Xu River in ancient times. Meanwhile a competition of dragon boat was held here too. This custom continues today.

Task 4 Useful Sentences

1. About 2,500 years ago, in the Spring and Autumn Period, the founder of Suzhou, Wu Zixu constructed 8 such kind of portals to defend Suzhou City.
2. Legend has it that, when it was completed, the pagoda did emit beautiful light at night.
3. On our left hand, we can see a set of red-brick old buildings in the style of pre-peaceful liberation period.
4. The double-layered arch was built with stripe stones, big enough to let two boats pass through side by side.
5. The walls are as steep as cliffs, and the Urn City was heavily guarded at that time.

Task 5 Listening

You will hear five sentences. Listen carefully and put down the whole sentences.

1. _____.
2. _____.

3. _____.
4. _____.
5. _____.

Task 6 Role-Play

Situaiton 1: Make an introduction of Three Attractions of Panmen City Gate—Hong-Sheng Match Factory—Cang-Lang Children's Palace—Bai Hua Zhou Park—Imperial Pavilion—Wan Nian Bridge—Xu Portal.

Situation 2: You are going to arrange a concert for your group in the evening, but the tour members want to see something typically Chinese. And you agree to change the plan, and select to have a cup of tea in Chun Lei (Spring Blossom) Tea House and enjoy Suzhou Pingtan, the local art form of story telling and ballad singing. Explain the content of the story.

Task 7 Translation

Put the following sentences into Chinese.
1. In such case, to defeat the intruders would be, if we use a Chinese saying here, as easy as "to catch a turtle in an urn".
2. The famous motto of "study well and make progress everyday", which has been motivating numerous Chinese youth for decades, was given by Chairman Mao to a local Suzhou boy, named Chen Yongkang in the 1950s.
3. To protect the city from being overwhelmed, the water portal was sealed ever since.
4. As soon as the enemy entered the first gate, the defenders can lay down strobe to isolate them.
5. It was very rare to discover these well-preserved Buddhist relics with this large amount and of such high class.

Task 8 Supplementary Reading

Caishi Island and Swan Lake Tours

On the Shandong Peninsula, the landscapes of Caishi (colored stone) Island on the southeast of Yandunjiao Village near Rongcheng City's Madao Town and Chengshanwei Swan Lake are relatively unknown. Other attractions include Penglai Pavilion, Changshan Islands and Yantai's beaches in the province.

Caishi Island has Shidao Harbor in the south and faces the Yellow Sea to the east. Across the bay is Chengshantou National Tourist Zone. Located at a middle latitude, it belongs to the temperate monsoon humid climate with four clear seasons and mean temperature of 12℃. Pleasant weather and beautiful landscapes are ideal for sightseeing, summer holiday-making and recuperation.

It will cost you 18 yuan to take the mini-bus from Yantai's Long-Distance Bus Station to Madao Town.

On the first day you can walk for ten minutes or take a special bus directly from the town's Jintai Hostel to the island. Every winter from November to March due to the rising tide, a large number of swans can be seen here, adding charm and vigor to the island.

Early morning on the second day, you can go to the seashore and enjoy the beach when the tide is out. History has honored the island as one of the eight scenes of Rongcheng and it is known at home and abroad for is beauty, steep gradients and interesting shape. The island's red, orange, yellow, white and black stones complement each other and form various lines in natural patterns. They can look like characters, animals, rivers and mountains or whatever you perceive them to represent.

Later, you can take the Madao Town-Longxu Island mini-bus for three yuan to the Chengshanwei Swan Vacationing Village, which has various levels of accommodation and has a variety of recreational facilities. Especially in summer, tourists are in large numbers. This place is the best scenic spot to watch swans.

A "T" shaped sea gulf, the Swan Lake, originally named Rongcheng Cove, is located one kilometer east of Chengshanwei and covers a dozen square kilometers. It is not too cold in winter with the lowest temperature at 1 ℃ below zero. To the east of the lake is flat sandy beach with sea weed, a good place for swans to winter. From November to March, swans come from northern areas to winter here for dozens of years. The number has increased year by year, reaching 10,000 at the most.

At 4 pm the sun set and the day was fine. We went to the eastern side of the lake. A landscape of lakes and mountains and the beautiful sunset glow form a delightful contrast. Swans, wild ducks and other birds cry and play with each other and the others fly high in the sky. What a beautiful and harmonious picture!

After visiting Swan Lake, you should go to Chengshantou because of its special geographical position and natural landscape. It is more than ten kilometers from Swan Lake. Weihai-Rongcheng mini-bus goes all the time.

Chengshantou is on the eastern tip of the Jiaodong Peninsula and also is the easternmost point of China's coastline. It is surrounded on three sides by sea and reefs and the current rushes and circles around. Even if there is no wind the sea waves can be dangerous. A local proverb says that nine out of ten sailors worry about passing Chengshantou.

According to historical records, in 219 B. C. and 210 B. C. Qinshihuang visited Chengshan twice. To its south there are four huge strangely shaped rocks that are splashed by the ebb and flow of the tide. People called it Qinrenqiao. It was built to honor Qinshihuang's search for the God of the Sea. After the 14th century, Chengshantou became a strategic area and the Yellow-Sea Battle during the Sino-Japanese War of 1894-1895 took place in nearby waters.

Chengshantou, now a famous national scenic area, is also called the "end of the world". It is known as China's Cape of Good Hope, with its green hills, blue sea, precipitous cliffs and momentous waves.

(Source: http://www.chinavista.com/travel/swan/content.html)

Questions:
1. Where is Caishi Island?
2. What is the climate like on the island?
3. Which place is the best one for people to watch swans?
4. When do the swans come from the northern area to spend winter here?
5. Which place is the easternmost point of China's coastline?

Part Ⅲ

Task 1 Warm-Up

1. Please introduce Ancient Xumen Gate and Ancient Xumen Gate Square.
2. What is the unique landscape and urban layout of the old city in Suzhou? How should the tourists be guided to enjoy it?

Task 2 Words and Expressions

portal	[ˈpɔːtl]	n.	入口,大门
depict	[dɪˈpɪkt]	v.	描述,描绘
renew	[rɪˈnjuː]	v.	更新
immortal	[ɪˈmɔːtl]	adj.	不朽的
		n.	神
omen	[ˈəʊmən]	n.	征兆,预兆

auspicious	[ɔːˈspɪʃəs]	adj.	吉利的,幸运的
sandalwood	[ˈsændlwʊd]	n.	檀香木
lunar	[ˈluːnə]	adj.	月亮的,阴历的
commercial	[kəˈmɜːʃl]	adj.	商业的
jammed	[dʒæmd]	adj.	被卡住的,塞满的
repair	[rɪˈpeə]	v.	修理,修补
geomancy	[ˈdʒiːəmænsi]	n.	土占,地卜,风水
hang	[hæŋ]	v.	悬挂
noble	[ˈnəʊbl]	adj.	高贵的,宏伟的
turret	[ˈtʌrət]	n.	小塔,角楼
fan	[fæn]	n.	扇子
calendar	[ˈkæləndə]	n.	日历,历法
lunar calendar			农历
by chance			偶然,碰巧

Task 3　Dialogues

Scene: Now the group is on the yacht. (V = Visitor, G = Guide)
Travel Route: Chang Portal—Immortal Temple—Nan-Hao Street—Diao Bridge—Portal Building

Chang Portal

G: We have just mentioned, a reputation of Suzhou is "Silver Xu Portal, gold Chang Portal".

V: Yes.

G: We have already visited Xu Portal, now we are in the area of Chang Portal, which was the richest and busiest and the most prosperous commercial area not only in Suzhou, but also in China. You must know the world famous Chinese traditional novel *The Story of the Stone*.

V: Yes, of course.

G: It depicts the true society of the Ming and Qing Dynasties. The first sentence in the novel is: "Chang portal must be the most flourishing place in the world."

V: So amazing!

G: According to the historical record, a 5-kilometer long street is jammed with more than ten thousand different shops. All kinds of trades can be found, for example, silk, rice, medicine, tea and so on. Besides, the locals believe that the *fenshui* (geomancy) here is wonderful, so we all like coming here nowadays. The local government tried its best to renew the original style of Chang Portal. Many old buildings have been repaired and are open to the public, attracting many tourists and travelers.

Immortal Temple—Nan-Hao Street

V: The architecture with yellow walls must be a temple.

G: It is the Immortal Temple. It was firstly built in the Southern Song Dynasty, about 800 years ago, in memory of Lv Dongbing, one of the eight traditional immorals in China. Suzhou locals like him very much.

V: What is the name of the street in front of the temple?

G: The street along the Immortal Temple is Nan-Hao Street. In Suzhou, we have a very famous traditional festival called Immortals' Festival, which is held every year. This festival has a very long history. On the fourteenth day of fourth month of lunar  calendar, Lv Dongbing would change into a common person, walking in street of Suzhou. It's said that if you could meet him and touch him, you will have good luck. But we don't know what he would be like. So people rush out and crowd into the street, hoping to touch Lv Dongbing by chance and bring good omen home. Until now we keep this custom. When the festival is held, the street becomes a busy commercial street. You can find many handcrafts, silks, sandalwood fans, and so on.

V: I hope I could enjoy this busy meeting.

Diao Bridge—Portal Building

G: The bridge hung over ahead of us is called Diao Bridge.

V: Suzhou is really a water city, with so many bridges.

G: Here is boundary line of Suzhou City in ancient times. Cross the bridge, you leave Suzhou City. In the Ming and Qing Dynasties, Suzhou is a major place of jade carving in China. This bridge is the main trade market of jade handcrafts in Suzhou. Now the bridge was rebuilt in 2000. It's a corridor bridge with a classical style.

V: It is very beautiful.

G: Hello, my friends, in the Spring and Autumn Period, about 2,500 years ago, the founder of Suzhou, Wu Zixu constructed 8 portals to protect the city of Suzhou, Chang Portal is among them. The name means being noble and auspicious, the one we see now was rebuilt in 2006. It's 10 meters high, 156 meters wide, 84 meters deep. There is a tea house in the turret on upstairs. Climb up, and you can enjoy the whole beautiful scenery of this area.

V: I need to take some photos here.

G: OK.

Task 4 Useful Sentences

1. We have already visited Xu Portal, now we are in the area of Chang Portal, which was the richest and busiest and the most prosperous commercial area not only in Suzhou, but also in China.
2. It depicts the true society of the Ming and Qing Dynasties.
3. It's a corridor bridge with a classical style.
4. It was firstly built in the Southern Song Dynasty, about 800 years ago, in memory of Lv Dongbing, one of the eight traditional immortals in China.
5. Many old buildings have been repaired and are open to the public, attracting many tourists and travelers.

Task 5 Listening

You will hear five sentences. Listen carefully and put down the whole sentences.

1. _____.
2. _____.
3. _____.
4. _____.
5. _____.

Task 6 Role-Play

Situation 1: Arrange an introduction of Chang Portal—Immortal Temple—Nan-Hao Street—Diao Bridge—Portal Building.

Situation 2: Mr. Smith wants to buy some presents for his friend Mr. White's family. Please help Mr. Smith select presents with Chinese flavor or Suzhou flavor.
- Mr. White is his classmate in college.
- Mr. White is an engineer, and his wife is a college teacher of Arts.
- The Whites have two kids, Tom, 17 years old, and Alice, 10 years old.

Task 7　　Translation

Put the following sentences into Chinese.
1. Silver Xu Portal, gold Chang Portal.
2. You must know the world famous Chinese traditional novel *The Story of the Stone*.
3. The first sentence in the novel is: "Chang portal must be the most flourishing place in the world."
4. Besides, the locals believe that the *fenshui* (geomancy) here is wonderful, so we all like coming here nowadays.
5. So people rush out and crowd into the street, hoping to touch Lv Dongbing by chance and bring good omen home.

 Task 8　　Supplementary Reading

Quanzhou

A Famous Historical City Built of Stone

　　Those who had been to Quanzhou are all enchanted by the stone buildings with the influence of the Tang and Song Dynasties. The bridges, pagodas and awe-inspiring temple halls there are all imbued with ancient culture.

　　Bordering the sea, Quanzhou is a time-honored city of culture. As early as over 2,000 years ago, Quanzhou was inhabited by the Minyue tribe, a branch of the "Hundred Yue" people. After the unification of China by the First Emperor of the Qin Dynasty, a prefecture was set up here. The city was officially named Quanzhou in 711 A. D., the second year of the reign of Jingyun of the Tang Dynasty. As the shape of the city looked like a carp, it was also called the City of the Carp. Again, as coralbean trees were planted all around the city, it was also called the Coralbean City in history.

　　Quanzhou started trading with foreign countries in the Southern Dynasty, and during the Song and Yuan Dynasties its foreign trade flourished unprecedentedly. It had trade relations with over 100 countries and regions, becoming the biggest sea port in the East and one of the starting points of the "Silk Road on the Sea".

　　Quanzhou was reputed as a "Holy City". It boasts the existence of a great many historical sites and scenic spots relating to religion. And the flourish of religions in Quanzhou in those days was matchless.

　　The Kaiyuan Temple on West Street in the city, first built in the year 686 A. D. and covering an area of 78,000 square meters, are equally famous as the Quangji Temple in Beijing and the Lingyin Temple in Hangzhou. The Main hall of the temple, the "Purple Cloud Hall", is 20 meters in total height, 9-bay in width and 6-bay in depth, with an area of 1,287 square meters. It is large in scale and has three distinguished features rarely seen in other temples: 100 heavy stone columns supporting the roof of the hall—the Hall of One Hundred Pillars; five huge Buddha statues standing in the same hall; and most admirable being the flying musicians carved on some of the pillars. The 24 flying musicians supporting the beams have the upper part of their bodies that of a beautiful woman and the lower part that of a bird. Wearing thin skirts and holding musical instruments or sacrificial objects, they seem to be singing and dancing among the beams. The ancient artists thus skillfully used these 24 figures to support the beams and to symbolize 24 solar terms, and made them wait upon the buddha day and night. This masterpiece ingeniously embodies the harmonious unity of mechanics, aesthetics and Buddhism.

The city of Quanzhou was not the only host to Buddhism but was a friendly harbour to other religions, including Christianity, Islamism and Manicheism. Along with the development of economy, foreigners kept pouring in to do business, to preach or to settle down. Many splendid cultural and religious relics bear witness, among which the most famous are the Qingjing (lustration) Mosque of Islamism and the "holy tombs" on the Lingshan Hill.

The Qingjing Mosque in Quanzhou is one of the five most time-honored, best preserved and biggest Qingjing Mosques in the Islamic world. It was designed after the mosque in Damascus, Syria, and built with pure granite. Its pointed-arch portal, 20 meters high, has three layers, outer, middle and inner. The outer and middle layers are similar to the caisson ceiling in the Chinese ancient architecture. The vaulted inner layer took on the architectural style of the ancient Arab. Standing under the vault, you can realize the time-honored cultural exchange between China and foreign countries.

In the "holy tombs" on the Lingshan Hill are buried the disciples of Mohammed, founder of Islam, who travelled with difficulties to China across vast ocean to preach. This is one of the few existing relics in the Islamic world. In the shape of a crescent, the winding stone corridor at the "holy tombs" signifies the purity and holiness of the disciples. The "Zheng He Burning Incense Tablet" records the prayer of a pious Chinese Moslem. The huge stone that shakes slightly when strong winds blow is said to be the relic of the holy sage... Over many years, countless Moslems came here to worship.

At the foot of Mt. Qingyuan in the northern suburbs of Quanzhou there is a huge "Yuhua Rock", which was carved into a seated statue of the founder of Taoism, Lao Zi who has left hand on his knee, his right hand against a small table, his eyes looking straight forward and his beard flowing, in a leisurely and carefree manner. Five meters high, the statue is the biggest stone statue of Lao Zi in China.

The stone of Quanzhou has contributed much to the brilliance of the culture of religion in the city.

The East and West pagodas are also known as the Zhenguo Pagoda and the Renshou Pagoda. First built with wood during the Five Dynasties at the end of the Tang Dynasty, the pagodas were later rebuilt with bricks and finally rebuilt with stone in the Southern Song Dynasty. The two pagodas have been standing erect there for nearly 800 years despite earthquake, typhoon and storm. Both pagodas were built in the style of tower, the West Pagoda being 44.6 meters in height and the East Pagoda 48.4 meters. They are octagonal in shape, five tiers high with five layers of eaves. The 39 granite carvings in relief at halfway up the East Pagoda depict the stories in the Buddhist scriptures and Indian folklores, done in the traditional way of painting and carving China mixed with the art of a foreign country. According to records, when the East Pagoda was built up the fourth tier, abbot Faquan passed away. It happened that an eminent monk Tianxi of India arrived in Quanzhou at that time to preach scriptures. The last part of the construction project was then accomplished under his guidance. This unusual episode has made the East Pagoda a historical evidence of the friendly cooperation between China and foreign countries.

It is said, "The bridges in central Fujian are second to none under heaven." The most representative one is Luoyang Bridge. In 1053, the 5th year in the reign of Huangyou of the Northern Song Dynasty, the people of Quanzhou, who are good at manipulating stones, built a dike by throwing stones into the sea where the Luoyang River empties itself into the sea, on the initiative of Quanzhou Prefect Cai Xiang. The foundation of the piers was ingeniously designed: shaped like a raft to ward off the pressure of the currents. Oysters were cultivated at the base of the piers to help glue them to the bedrock. This is the first sea port bridges in China, Luoyang Bridge. A grand project when built, the bridge, 834 meters in length, 7 meters in width, had 31 piers, seven pavilions, nine stone pagodas and carved balustrades on either side with 28 stone lions. Verdant pines were planted in the north and south of the bridge. Luoyang Bridge spanning the Luoyang River has been described as a magnificent view like a rainbow spanning the sky.

The history of human being began with stone. It is again stone, Quanzhou, that enables you to feel the greatness of the ancient culture of China.

(Source: http://www.chinavista.com/travel/quanzhou/quanzhou.html)

Questions:
1. What does the city look like?
2. Does the city have any nicknames? What are they?
3. When did Quanzhou begin to trade with foreign countries? When did the trade come to a flourishing point?
4. Which temple in Quanzhou is equally famous as Quangji Temple in Beijing and Linyin Temple in Hangzhou?
5. How do you understand "The stone of Quanzhou has contributed much to the brilliance of the culture of religion in the city"? Illustrate your idea with examples.

Part Ⅳ

Task 1   Warm-Up

1. Suzhou is regarded as the Oriental Venice. Please use specific figures to explain the origins of the name.
2. What names does Suzhou have in the history? Try to give two examples to show the relationship between these names and water.

Task 2   Words and Expressions

inconvenient	[ˌɪnkən'viːnɪənt]	adj.	不方便的
facilitate	[fə'sɪlɪteɪt]	v.	促进,帮助
surpass	[sə'pɑːs]	v.	超越,胜过
epitome	[ɪ'pɪtəmi]	n.	缩影,化身
makeup	['meɪkʌp]	n.	化妆品
deal	[diːl]	n.	协定,交易
representative	[reprɪ'zentətɪv]	adj.	代表的,典型的
jasmine	['dʒæsmɪn]	n.	茉莉
pagoda	[pə'gəʊdə]	n.	宝塔
construct	[kən'strʌkt]	v.	建造
lane	[leɪn]	n.	航道
showpiece	['ʃəʊpiːs]	n.	展览品
bargain	['bɑːgɪn]	v.	讨价还价
rope	[rəʊp]	n.	绳索
export	['ekspɔːt]	adj.	出口的
fragrance	['freɪgrəns]	n.	香味
afar	[ə'fɑː]	adv.	在远处,从远处
remind ... of ...			使……想起……
in terms of			在……方面

Task 3   Dialogues

Scene: Now the group is on the yacht. (V = Visitor, G = Guide)

Travel Route: Shantang River—Residential House—Tonggui Bridge—Yangjiabang—Star Bridge—Bantang Pond—Yefang Bang—Puji Bridge—Green Hill Bridge and Blue Water Bridge

Shantang River—Residential House

V: The scenery here is very charming.

G: Yes, we are moving into a traditional water lane, the Shantang River, a very narrow lane. It is 3.5 kilometers long.

V: Is it a natural river?

G: No, man-made. This river reminds us of a famous poem by Bai Juyi in the Tang Dynasty, 1,300 years ago. At that time, he was the governor of Suzhou. He found that it was inconvenient for locals to go to the Tiger Hill, the No. 1 scenic spot in Suzhou, so he ordered a canal to be dug to facilitate people to go to the Tiger Hill. The bank he ordered to be constructed was called Shantang Street. The local people called it the bank of Master Bai to thank him. From the Tang Dynasty it was a shopping street as famous as Chang Men Portal we said just now.

V: OK, can you tell me more?

G: The very short street is jammed with many different kinds of shops, for example, silk, dying, rice, tea, fans and so on. It surpassed any other streets in terms of flourish in the Ming and Qing Dynasties. Following the pattern and style of this street, a street called Suzhou Street was constructed in the Summer Palace, so you can understand the importance of Suzhou. Now this street was listed as historical street under the protection of Suzhou Government, known as the "epitome of ancient Suzhou, showpiece of Suzhou culture, traditional street of Modern City".

V: OK, nice.

G: Ladies and gentlemen, now I will make a brief introduction of the traditional residential houses of Suzhou.

V: OK.

G: In Suzhou, there are all together 3 kinds of residential houses. They are houses facing to the river, along the river or across the river. If there is a street in front of the house and a river behind it, that's a house along the river. If rivers and streets are all in front of the house, that's a house facing to the river. If there is a corridor across the river connecting two parts, that's the house across the river. All these 3 traditional kinds of houses can be found here.

V: Yes.

G: Even if we insert some pillars into the water, above which terrace, pavilion or small houses were built we live inside. That's the traditional daily life of local people in Suzhou. So you can see our life has closely connected with water. So boats are our main transportation vehicles. What's more, boats are a moving market, carrying different goods, for example, vegetables, fruits, makeup and so on. The seller cried out when moving in the river. If she needs anything, the housewife would push out the window to ask the seller and bargain. When the deal was done, the housewife would put down the basket by rope, with money inside. Then the seller took the basket and money, put the goods inside, finally the woman pull up the rope and took the basket. That's a real picture of local life.

V: So interesting.

Tonggui Bridge—Yangjiabang and Star Bridge

G: There is a small bridge ahead of us.

V: Yes.

G: The bridge in front of us is Tonggui Bridge. It was built in the Ming Dynasty, about 400 years ago. The one we see now was rebuilt in 1880. Its length is more than 20 m. It is one representative single arch stone bridge in Suzhou.

V: Another bridge. Here, the scene is so nice.

G: Here is Yangjiabang. The hall is Yuhan Hall in 1990's. Here is a warehouse of Suzhou tea factory. Suzhou is a famous export city of flower tea, especially jasmine tea. From here one third of tea is carried to countries all over the world. If you like, you can buy some to have a try. The fragrance of the tea is nice. (*A few minutes later*) Ahead of us is Star Bridge, similar to Tonggui Bridge. It was firstly built in the Tang Dynasty when Bai Juyi had the river dug. This one was rebuilt in 1866.

Bantang Pond—Yefang Bang—Puji Bridge

G: Hello, everyone, it is the Bantang Pond. We can see the river get narrow; here, the scene changes to another kind of flavor, from busy city to rural sight. Clean water, small bridge, woods, temples, green houses, everything is so beautiful, everything is so nice, and everything is so peaceful. In the center of the Pond is Caiyun Bridge, another is Tongqiao Bridge. In the Ming and Qing Dynasties, Tongqiao is the

highest one in Shantang area. This is also a good place for enjoying moon on the night of Mid-Autumn Day. It's one of the most important traditional festivals of Chinese.

V: We have already known that.

G: We Chinese believe the moon is the biggest on that night around the whole year, so we need to celebrate it with moon cakes, enjoying the moon, wishing every member of the family happiness. But now, we don't do that on the bridge, because it has been long neglected. The local government is planning to rebuild it after the original pattern.

V: That is so good!

G: After Caiyun Bridge, the river becomes narrower. This is Yefang Bang. At first it used to gather many smelting workshops; later because of the beautiful scenery, locals like to come here to enjoy the peach flowers and willows. In early spring of every year, locals like to come here to have a picnic.

V: Ha-ha, so charming.

G: The three-arch stone bridge is Puji Bridge. It is the biggest one also the highest one in Shantang area. This bridge was firstly built in 1710 and rebuilt in 1841. From here we can see the Tiger Hill Pagoda from afar.

V: Yes.

G: On our right hand there are two bridges. One is Green Hill Bridge, the other is Blue Water Bridge. Go along the river we can go to the Tiger Hill, which is regarded as No. 1 scenic spot in Suzhou. Later, I will make a brief introduction of the Tiger Hill.

Task 4 Useful Sentences

1. From the Tang Dynasty it was a shopping street as famous as Chang Men Portal we said just now.
2. Go along the river we can go to the Tiger Hill, which is regarded as No. 1 scenic spot in Suzhou.
3. It is one representative single arch stone bridge in Suzhou.
4. Suzhou is a famous export city of flower tea, especially jasmine tea.
5. It surpassed any other streets in terms of flourish in the Ming and Qing Dynasties.

Task 5 Listening

You will hear five sentences. Listen carefully and put down the whole sentences.

1. _____.
2. _____.
3. _____.
4. _____.
5. _____.

Task 6　Role-Play

Situation 1: Make an introduction of the residential houses in Suzhou.

Situation 2: It happens to be the Dragon Boat Festival when the tour group arrives. Please take your group to have a peculiar festival, including activities and food arrangement, and tell them the customs and stories of the festival.

Task 7　Translation

Put the following sentences into Chinese.
1. We can see the river get narrow; here, the scene changes to another kind of flavor, from busy city to rural sight.
2. Now this street was listed as historical street under the protection of Suzhou government, known as the "epitome of ancient Suzhou, showpiece of Suzhou culture, traditional street of Modern City".
3. If she needs anything, the housewife would push out the window to ask the seller and bargain.
4. In Suzhou, there are all together 3 kinds of residential houses, they are houses facing to the river, along the river or across the river.
5. What's more, boats are a moving market, carrying different goods, for example, vegetables, fruits, makeup and so on.

Task 8　Supplementary Reading

Si Guniang (Four Girls) Mountains

　　Si Guniang (Four Girls) Mountains Scenic Area is situated in Xiaojin County of the Aba Tibetan and Qiang Autonomous Prefecture, Sichuan Province, China. It was listed as the National Scenic Resort in 1994 and as the National Nature Reserve in 1996. The area consists of Mt. Si Guniang, Mt. Balang and Changping, Haizi, Shuangqiao gulleys, covering an area of 2,000 sq km. Featuring primitive ecological condition and exquisite scenery, the area is reputed to be the Queen of Sichuan's Mountains and the Oriental Alps Mountain. It is also a center of attention for scientists.

　　Mt. Si Guniang encompassing 4 peaks perennially covered with snow soars high with maximum 62,500 m above sea level in the northwest of Western Sichuan Plain. There exist the remains of glaciers formed in the remote antiquity and vertical distribution of vegetation and rare wildlife. Additionally, there are Mt. Wuse (Five colors), Lieren (Hunter) Peak, Laoying (Eagle)

Cliff, Mt. Niuxin(Ox's Heart), which are shrouded in clouds and mists the year round, presenting an atmosphere of a fairyland.

Mt. Balang stands 5,040 m above sea level between the Wolong Nature Reserve and Rilong Town of Xiaojin County. Here is the only way which must be passed leading up to Mt. Si Guniang. The high mountain and deep gulley is veiled in the boundless sea of clouds. A road runs zigzag up. Seeing all this, one feels as if he were in a fairyland.

Guozhuang (a Tibetan folk dance) Terrace sits between Changping and Haizi gulleys, covering an area of 1 sq km. Locals gather here after making a pilgrimage to the mountain every year to hold rituals and celebrations and perform Guozhuang dance, offering a scene of bustle and excitement.

Haizi (Lake) Gulley is 19.2 km long with an area of 126.48 sq km. The gulley contains a dozen plateau lakes, such as Multi-colored Lake, White Lake, Blue Lake, Yellow Lake. In these lakes, the water is so clear that one can see the bottom and briskly swimming fish. People feel completely relaxed and happy at the scene.

Changping (Long Terrace) Gulley is 29 km long with an area of 100 sq km. In the gulley, there are ancient cypress tree-lined roads, lamaseries, grotesque crags, waterfalls dashing from on high and other wonderful views.

Shuangqiao (Double Bridges) Gulley is 34.8 km long with an area of 216.6 sq km. The gulley is flat with brooks flowing crisscross murmuring. The slopes are densely covered by primitive forest. Dozens of mountains including Mt. Wuse, Lieren Peak thrust themselves towards the sky, some like rhinoceros looking at the moon, some like lion roaring, all with different postures and colors, presenting a likeness both in shape and spirit.

In the scenic area, Shidiaolou (stone constructed building) is where Jiarong Tibetan people live generation after generation. Jiarong people's splendid ethnic costumes and ornaments, solemn rituals, melodious folk songs and cheerful dances form the touching picture scrolls of local conditions customs.

(Source: http://www.chinavista.com/travel/sigu/sight.html)

Questions:
1. Where are Si Guniang Mountains located? What are Si Guniang Mountains?
2. What is the status of this scenic area?
3. What does the name of Guozhuang Terrace come from?
4. List some local customs of the scenic area.
5. Could you guess the meaning of "Haizi"?

Project 5　Zhou Zhuang

Part Ⅰ

Task 1　Warm-Up

1. Why is Zhou Zhuang considered as the No. 1 water town in China?
2. What's the other name of Chinese Twin Bridge? Talk about other ancient bridges in Zhou Zhuang.

Task 2　Words and Expressions

junction	[ˈdʒʌŋkʃn]	n.	连接,会合处,交叉点
squire	[ˈskwaɪə]	n.	乡绅,大地主
migrate	[ˈmaɪgreɪt]	v.	迁移,迁徙
waterway	[ˈwɔːtəweɪ]	n.	水路,航道
grain	[greɪn]	n.	谷物,谷类
handicraft	[ˈhændɪkrɑːft]	n.	手工艺品,手艺
prosperous	[ˈprɒspərəs]	adj.	繁荣的,兴旺的
peculiar	[pɪˈkjuːliə]	adj.	特殊的,独特的
cottage	[ˈkɒtɪdʒ]	n.	小屋,村舍
humanity	[hjuːˈmænəti]	n.	人类,人性
phenomena	[fɪˈnɒmɪnə]	n.	现象（phenomenon 的复数）
forge	[fɔːdʒ]	v.	锻造,建立
sedan	[sɪˈdæn]	n.	轿子
paddle	[ˈpædl]	v.	划桨
private	[ˈpraɪvɪt]	adj.	私人的,个人的
residence	[ˈrezɪdəns]	n.	住宅,住处
excavate	[ˈekskəveɪt]	v.	挖掘
impress	[ɪmˈpres]	v.	使……有印象
reputation	[ˌrepjuˈteɪʃn]	n.	声誉
premier	[ˈpremiə]	n.	总理,首相
convention	[kənˈvenʃn]	n.	大会
wonderland	[ˈwʌndəlænd]	n.	仙境,奇境
award	[əˈwɔːd]	v.	授予

committee	[kəˈmɪti]	n.	委员会
valuables	[ˈvæljuəblz]	n.	(pl.)贵重物品
coach	[kəʊtʃ]	n.	大巴
replica	[ˈreplɪkə]	n.	复制品
boundary	[ˈbaʊndəri]	n.	边界,分界线
interior	[ɪnˈtɪəriə]	n.	内部
exterior	[ɪkˈstɪəriə]	n.	外部
feature	[ˈfiːtʃə]	n.	特征,特色
archway	[ˈɑːtʃweɪ]	n.	拱门,拱道
antithetical	[ˌæntɪˈθetɪkl]	adj.	对偶的,对立的
couplet	[ˈkʌplɪt]	n.	对句,对联
shoot	[ʃuːt]	v.	拍照
jade	[dʒeɪd]	n.	玉石,翡翠
outline	[ˈaʊtlaɪn]	v.	画出轮廓
tile	[taɪl]	n.	瓦片
Venice	[ˈvenɪs]	n.	威尼斯(意大利港市)
fossil	[ˈfɒsl]	n.	化石
deem	[diːm]	v.	认为,视作
elegant	[ˈelɪgənt]	adj.	优雅的,雅致的
stretch	[stretʃ]	v.	伸展,延伸
creek	[kriːk]	n.	小湾,小溪
embody	[ɪmˈbɒdi]	v.	代表
sensation	[senˈseɪʃn]	n.	轰动
occidental	[ˌɒksɪˈdentl]	adj.	西方的
petroleum	[pəˈtrəʊliəm]	n.	石油
process	[ˈprəʊses]	v.	加工,处理
symbol	[ˈsɪmbəl]	n.	象征,标志
have access to			接近(的机会),进入
the Spring and Autumn Period			春秋时期
keep away from			远离,回避
the reform and opening-up policy			改革开放政策
foreign minister			外交部部长
World Cultural Heritage			世界文化遗产
as to			至于,说到
mass media			大众传媒,新闻界
trace back to			追溯
APEC(= Asia-Pacific Economic Cooperation)			亚洲太平洋经济合作组织

Task 3　Dialogues

Scene: Now the group is on the way to Zhou Zhuang by coach. (V = Visitor, G = Guide)
Travel Route: Coach—Archway—Screen Wall—Taiping Bridge—Double Bridge

On the Coach

G: Hello, everyone. Now we are on the way to Zhou Zhuang. I will make a brief introduction about this famous water town to you.

V: OK, very good!

G: Zhou Zhuang is located at the junction of Kunshan, Wujiang of Suzhou and Qingpu District of Shanghai. With water on three sides, Zhou Zhuang has access to Cheng Lake, Bai Lake, Dianshan Lake and Nan Lake. The town covers an area of 36 square kilometers, with a population of about 20,000.

V: Why do you call it Zhou Zhuang?

G: Zhou Zhuang has a long history and bright culture. The history can be traced back to the Spring and Autumn Period. At first, it was called Zheng Fengli. In the first year of Yuanyou of the Song Dynasty, the officer named Zhou changed the house into a temple, and named it Zhou Zhuang for the first time. Till now, it has more than 900-year history.

V: I see. Is it an important town in Suzhou?

G: Yes. In the Ming Dynasty, Shen Wansan and his son who were rich squires in Southern Yangtze River Delta migrated to Zhou Zhuang, trading with foreigners through good waterway of Yangtze River. Zhou Zhuang became the trade center of grains, silk and handicrafts. During the Ming and Qing Dynasties, Zhou Zhuang had prosperous industries and 8 long street shops, and became a big town beyond Fengmen of Suzhou city.

V: But why is Zhou Zhuang so special in China?

G: Nice question. Zhou Zhuang kept away from wars with peculiar natural environment: being surrounded by water, natives communicated with each other by boat. The typical style and feature of water town in south Yangtze River is small bridge, flowing water and cottages. The long history brought up many celebrities: Zhang Han, litterateur in Western Jin Dynasty; Liu Yuxi and Lu Guimeng, poets in the Tang Dynasty. Zhang Hall is the architecture in the Ming Dynasty, and its feature is "the sedan can enter from doorway; the boat can paddle across the house". The No. 1 private residence in south Yangtze River is Shen Hall. Under the reform and opening-up policy, Zhou Zhuang makes use of beautiful natural scenery and rich historical human landscape, excavates cultural expert, forms Zheng Feng street, gathers the traditional cultures and passes on classical Kun Opera. The more than 1,000-year historical culture of Zhou Zhuang has formed the romantic charm of rivers and lakes, which impresses foreign visitors with the growing reputation. Many famous persons and experts come here. Wu Guanzhong praises it as "Zhou Zhuang gathers together all the beauty of water towns in China". The famous architect Luo Zhewen highly praises Zhou Zhuang as a treasure not only in Jiangsu, but across the whole country. During recent years, leaders, whether at home or from abroad, have all come to Zhou Zhuang, such as former Premier Zhu Rongji, Singapore President Nadan, the Foreign Minister of Russia. In 2000, the former president of China Jiang Zhemin visited it. The convention of APEC was also held in Zhou Zhuang. At that time, first-ladies from different countries came to this wonderland where they have daydreamt for long.

V: That is so wonderful! I can't wait for that!

G: What is more, Zhou Zhuang wins many special honors, which was awarded one of 100-famous towns of Jiangsu in 1991. Zhou Zhuang was listed on the preparation list by World Cultural Heritage committee of UNECSO in 1999, and was awarded the Best Practice in human settlement improvement by human settlement of UN. And in 2006, Zhou Zhuang was among the first batch of national five A-class scenic areas. Because of these, Zhou Zhuang is accepted by the whole world.

OK. Here we are. The park is over there. Please take away your valuables and get off the coach.

Archway

G: The front decorated ancient archway is the gate of the old town. Actually, this is a replica of the ancient one, and this was built in 1991. The archway is the boundary between the old town district and the new one.

V: I guess the interior is the old town district.

G: Right. It is only 0.47 square kilometers, whose feature is small bridge, flowing water and some cottages. There are some ancient architecture of the Yuan, Ming and Qing Dynasties. The exterior is new district. The four letters "Zhen Feng Ze Guo" on the decorated archway was written by Shen Peng, former chairman of Chinese Calligraphy Association.

V: What is the meaning?

G: "Zhen Feng" is the original name of Zhou Zhuang. After Mr. Zhou changed the house into a temple, "Zhen Feng Li" was changed into "Zhou Zhuang". Therefore, the name "Zhou Zhuang" has been called by us for more than 900 years. As to "Ze Guo", Zhou Zhuang is like an island, being surrounded by water. People went out all by boat 89 years ago. The old town is well-protected; more than 60% of the architecture is in the original styles of the Yuan, Ming and Qing Dynasties.

Passing the archway, we enter the old town district. Please turn back and see the four letters "Tang Feng Jie Yi".

V: What's the meaning?

G: It means that you can also see some ancient traditional folk culture and ancient style and grace. This is written by Fei Xinwo when he was aged, and there is his signature at the left-hand corner, Xin Wo Zuo Bi. The antithetical couplet is written by well-known reporters, describing the beautiful scenery of Zhou Zhuang. If you want to take photos, this angle is best. You can also shoot that replica of running water tower.

V: That is a good idea.

Screen Wall

G: In the front, there is a screen wall facing the gate of a house, which is made of white jade of the Han Dynasty. It was built 900 years ago.

V: What is this pattern?

G: It outlines the miniature of the special feature of Zhou Zhuang: small bridges, flowing water and the cottages. Please look up, you can feel the historical sense from walls and tile.

Zhou Zhuang is the typical water town alongside Yangtze River, being regarded as "Venice" by someone. The four rivers cross each other and form the Chinese character "井 jing", which cut apart Zhou Zhaung into 8 parts and 14 kinds of bridges. Most of folk houses are built between streets and rivers. For many special styles and features, Zhou Zhuang is deemed as the living fossil of water towns and ancient towns in China. A certain professor says that Mount Huang gathers the beauty of mountains and rivers in China, and Zhou Zhuang gathers the beauty of water towns in China.

Taiping Bridge

V: I've found an old bridge. It's so elegant!

G: It is named Taiping Bridge, which was built in the Qing Dynasty. And now you are facing the moving picture of south Yangtze River. This old bridge was once drew in the picture "someday of Zhou Zhuang" by Japanese female painter Qiaoben Xinquan, which is showed in the second floor of Zhou Zhuang Museum.

Attention please, this old street is called One-step Street because you can pass it through walking for only one step. It is also called Friendship Street.

V: Why?

G: Because it is so narrow that the shop owners on both sides can shake hands from their own side.

V: Ha-ha.

Double Bridge

V: I have seen these two bridges on many magazines and photo-cards.

G: Yes. That is Double-Bridge. If you travel to Zhou Zhuang, this is a must. You can see the difference between them. One is from left to right, the other is from top to bottom. One is square, and the other is circle. They look like the shape of ancient keys, so local people also call them "Key Bridge". These two bridges were built 400 years ago, Wanli period of the Ming Dynasty (1573-1619 AD). This bridge is named "Shi De Bridge". It stretches across the river from north to south: 16 meters long, 3  meters wide and 5.9 meters high. The other is crossing the Yinzi Creek: 13.3 meters long, 2.4 meters wide and 3.5 meters high. Double Bridge fully embodies the romantic charm; you can take photos here.

V: Yes, I will. But can you tell me why Double-Bridge is so famous?

G: OK! There is a story. In 1984, the famous painter residing in America Chen Yifei came to Zhou Zhuang. Because of the limited time, he could not paint Zhou Zhuang right away but only took some photos. After going back to America, he focused on these two bridges and created the oil painting "the memory of hometown". Afterward, this oil painting was exhibited in America and caused a sensation. This oil painting "the memory of hometown" is collected by Armand Hammer, the chairman of the board of American Occidental Petroleum Corporation. In November 1984, he gave it to Chinese former president Deng Xiaoping as a present when he visited China. In 1985, this painting was processed again by Chen Yifei, and it was used as the picture of UN first-day cover. Zhou Zhuang became well-known in the world under the mass media's influence. Key Bridge is a key which opens the door between Zhou Zhaung and the world.

V: Now I can understand. This Double Bridge is the symbol of Zhou Zhuang. I should take some photos here.

 ### Task 4 Useful Sentences

1. Now we are on the way to Zhou Zhuang, I will make a brief introduction about this famous water town to you.
2. With water on three sides, Zhou Zhuang has access to Cheng lake, Bai lake, Dianshan Lake and Nan Lake.
3. The town covers an area of 36 square kilometers, with a population of about 20,000.
4. The history can be traced back to the Spring and Autumn Period.
5. Zhou Zhuang kept away from wars with peculiar natural environment: being surrounded by water, natives communicated with each other by boat.

Task 5   Listening

You will hear five sentences. Listen carefully and put down the whole sentences.
1. _____.
2. _____.
3. _____.
4. _____.
5. _____.

Task 6   Role-Play

Situation 1: Introduce Zhou Zhuang briefly.

Situaiton 2: You take a foreign visitor for one-day Suzhou tour. He has never been to Suzhou before and is curious about almost everything. Tell him briefly the history of Suzhou, select one or two key scenic spots, and try your best to answer his questions.

Task 7   Translation

Put the following sentences into Chinese.
1. In the Ming Dansty, Shen Wansan and his son who were rich squires in Southern Yangtze River Delta migrated to Zhou Zhuang, trading with foreigners through good waterway of Yangtze River.
2. The typical style and feature of water town in south Yangtze River is small bridges, flowing water and cottages.
3. Zhang Hall is the architecture in the Ming Dynasty, and its feature is "the sedan can enter from doorway; the boat can paddle across the house".
4. They look like the shape of ancient keys, so local people also call them "Key Bridge".
5. Afterward, this oil painting was exhibited in America and caused a sensation.

Task 8   Supplementary Reading

Earth Buildings

The Yongding landscape fascinates tourists with its enchanting mountains and waters. What adds charm to the scenery is the groups of earth buildings strewed over the valley and on the riverside. The unique style of these high, heavy, unsophisticated and imposing human habitations has always been a wonder to tourists.

Most of the earth buildings are either circular or quadrangular. Many of them are a few hundred years old. The circular ones have a very special flavour. Those built in ancient times all consist of inside buildings enclosed by huge peripheral ones. Such a combined building holds hundreds of rooms and dwellers. With all the halls, storehouses, wells and bedrooms inside, the huge tower-like building is almost a small fortified city. It is well lighted, well ventilated, windproof, quakeproof, warm in winter and cool in summer. Structurally, it incorporates the merits of different dwelling houses. In these buildings one can also find cultural treasures, such as sculpture, mural paintings, antithetical couplets and work of calligraphy.

The peculiar earth buildings and the beautiful scenery have attracted scholars and tourists from home and abroad. A worldwide interest in the "earth building tour" has emerged.

Zhencheng is an important building under provincial protection. It consists of two rings, both designed according to the Eight Diagrams (eight combinations of three lines formerly used in divination). The outer ring has four storeys—kitchens on the first floor, granaries on the second, and bedrooms on the third and the fourth. Between each "diagram" is a fire wall. The meeting hall and reception rooms are in the two-storeyed inner ring, in which one hall, two wells, three gates and four stairs are reasonably designed and symmetrically located. On its sides there is a school and a garden. Admiring such structure art, a foreign expert referred to Zhencheng as "mythological architecture". In 1985, a model of Zhencheng was exhibited on an international architecture model show in Los Angeles.

Huanji was built in the Qing Dynasty during Kangxi's reign (1662-1723). As is recorded, an earthquake in 1940 cracked the wall, making a crevice a foot wide and a dozen yards long. After the quake, however, the crevice closed up on its own, leaving a clear scar on the wall.

Earth buildings are made of earth, stone, bamboo and wood, all easily available in the construction. The walls are built with rammed.

(Source: http://travel.chinavista.com/destination-sight-18.html?pagenum)

Questions:
1. Where are the earth buildings mentioned in the article located?
2. What is the shape of the earth building?
3. What kind of cultural treasures could one find in such earth buildings?
4. Which building is under the provincial protection?
5. What happened to Huanji in 1940 and what is the most amazing part of it?

Part II

Task 1　Warm-Up

1. What honor has Zhou Zhuang won so far?
2. Talk about the architectural features of Zhang Hall.

Task 2　Words and Expressions

notable	[ˈnəʊtəbl]	adj.	著名的
offspring	[ˈɔːfsprɪŋ]	n.	后代,子孙
workmanship	[ˈwɜːkmənʃɪp]	n.	手艺,技巧,工艺品
decline	[dɪˈklaɪn]	v.	下降,衰退
surname	[ˈsɜːneɪm]	n.	姓
residential	[ˌrezɪˈdenʃl]	adj.	居住的
feature	[ˈfiːtʃə]	n.	特征,特色
decoration	[ˌdekəˈreɪʃn]	n.	装饰,装饰品
decorate	[ˈdekəreɪt]	v.	装饰,布置
marble	[ˈmɑːbl]	n.	大理石
swallow	[ˈswɒləʊ]	n.	燕子
conception	[kənˈsepʃn]	n.	概念,观念
descendant	[dɪˈsendənt]	n.	后裔,子孙
jade	[dʒeɪd]	n.	玉石
funeral	[ˈfjuːnərəl]	adj.	葬礼的
ritual	[ˈrɪtʃuəl]	n.	仪式,典礼
distinguished	[dɪˈstɪŋgwɪʃt]	adj.	卓越的
prominent	[ˈprɒmɪnənt]	n.	显著的
ellipsoid	[ɪˈlɪpsɔɪd]	n.	椭圆
gauze	[gɔːz]	n.	薄纱,纱布
threshold	[ˈθreʃhəʊld]	n.	门槛,开端
indicate	[ˈɪndɪkeɪt]	v.	指示,象征
symmetrical	[sɪˈmetrɪkl]	adj.	对称的
lath	[læθ]	n.	木板条
rotten	[ˈrɒtn]	adj.	腐烂的
preserve	[prɪˈzɜːv]	v.	保护,保存

couplet	[ˈkʌplɪt]	n.	对句,对联
paddle	[ˈpædl]	v.	划桨
peculiar	[pɪˈkjuːlɪə]	adj.	奇怪的,特殊的
flee	[fliː]	v.	逃走,逃离
squire	[ˈskwaɪə]	n.	乡绅,大地主
dock	[dɒk]	n.	码头,船坞
considerate	[kənˈsɪdərət]	adj.	考虑周到的
enshrine	[ɪnˈʃraɪn]	v.	奉为神圣
sage	[seɪdʒ]	n.	圣人
exile	[ˈeksaɪl]	v.	放逐,流放
feudalistic	[ˌfjuːdəˈlɪstɪk]	adj.	封建制度的
reserved	[rɪˈzɜːvd]	adj.	保留的
convey	[kənˈveɪ]	v.	表达,传达
slippery	[ˈslɪpəri]	adj.	滑的
distant	[ˈdɪstənt]	adj.	遥远的
soundness	[ˈsaʊndnɪs]	n.	健康,完好,完整
in case of			防备,假如

Task 3   Dialogues

Scene: Now the group is in front of Zhang Hall. (V = Visitor, G = Guide)
Travel Route: Zhang Hall—Fu'an Bridge

Zhang Hall

G: Hello, everyone, this is the notable Zhang Hall.

V: Is Zhang the family name of the owner?

G: Yes. Zhang Hall was built by Xu Mengqing's offspring who is the younger brother of Xu Da, King Zhongshan of the Ming Dynasty. But why was it called Zhang Hall? In early Qing Dynasty, Xu family declined, and sold the houses to a person with the surname Zhang. So it changed the name into Zhang Hall.

V: Is this residential house very typical?

G: The ancient Chinese architecture appears as a group of buildings, including palaces, temples and folk houses, which are not standing tall and erect of main building, but is the level surface of symmetry. These buildings stand alone, but connect with each other. Zhang Hall also has this feature which is the typical house of "Tianjing Yuan".

V: How big is this residential house?

G: The whole hall covers an area of 1,800 square kilometers, having more than 60 rooms and a private garden, which is divided into 6 parts. Let us visit this big family.

V: OK!

G: When you pass the gate, you can see the first part which is the entrance hall. It functions as a decoration. Zhang family, for example, will decorate the front of the gate when they have happy events.

V: Very interesting!

G: The second part is sedan hall; it is also called tea hall. On the left, there is an 8-bearer sedan. The sedan hall is the place where the guests and visitors get off the sedan. And on the right, there is the place where the sedan-chair bearers, boatmen and ordinary visitors have a rest or drink. In folk houses in ancient China, the master want to get a realm different from the outside world, so they set up a screen wall facing the gate of a house. And where is Zhang's? There is a natural and marble one, which functions as "going straight to the point".

V: I remember, many rich families have such style.

G: Here is the third part, which is the main hall, Yulan and Swallow Hall, which is originally called "Happy Hall". In the early time there were two Yulan trees. The flowers attracted many swallows when spring came. The master saw this and changed the name. Yulan and Swallow Halls have the conception of having the hall and descendants filled with gold and jade.

V: What is the function of this?

G: The main hall is the place for the master to hold happy events and funeral rituals and to receive the distinguished guests. There is Ming-style furniture in the main hall. Please look at them carefully.

V: Is there something special?

G: There are two prominent ellipsoid carving boards. You can image, this is like the wing of an officers' hat in ancient time, so this hall is called "black gauze cap hall". This can explain that the earliest master is an officer.

V: Yes.

G: Let's turn back to look at the threshold, the height of which can indicate the rank of official title of the owner. According to the historical records, this master is "Sipin", which is something like the vice provincial governor now.

V: So funny!

G: Now we have come to the 4th part, "Da Tang Lou".

V: I think this is the living-room.

G: Right. It has two floors. The female members of the family live on the upper (second) floor and the hostess entertained the female visitors on the first floor.

V: The layout here is classical.

G: All the furniture is symmetrical. The long lath is the most important furniture, which is particular in workmanship and carving. There is a vase on one side and a mirror on the other side, meaning safety and soundness of the family. And now please look at this.

V: What?

G: Something under pillars, which firmly supports the pillars. Can you guess what it is made of?

V: I have no idea.

G: Generally, it's made of stone, but this one is made of rare Nanmu, which won't rot. So these can be preserved for 500 years. Meanwhile, this can also explain the long history of Zhang Hall. Next, Let us look at the couplet that was made by Prof. Wu Guanzhong of Central Art and Design Technology Institute, which is "the sedan enters from the gate, and the boat is paddled across the house". Now let's look at the most distinct feature.

V: OK, very good.

G: Here is the 5th part. The daughters of rich families couldn't go out in ancient times. Therefore here is the recreation center for girls such as playing musical instrument and chess.

V: Yes. Very interesting.

G: Let's go further. The sixth part is the study, which is built near the river. It has bright light, and the environment is quite quiet and elegant. Therefore, the master can read or work, and open the windows to see the scenery of the back yard of the garden.

V: A small river and a boat at the back of the room.

G: Yes, now we reach the "the boat can be paddled across the house" place. The river in front of you is called "Zhujing River". Although it's very narrow, it connects with the big lake, so it's a flowing river. It gathers the features of water towns, including small bridge, flowing water and household. This architecture is quite peculiar in south Yangtze River.

V: Why did they dig this river?

G: There are two reasons: one is to transport the everyday applicants by boat; the other is for fleeing in case of wars. The boat can change the directions in this square pool, which is Zhang's private dock. The raised part of stone at the opposite side, which ties the rope, is called "cow nose" during ancient times.

V: Considerate!

G: Now we've reached the back yard of the garden. There is a Buddha hall inside, for the hostess worships the Buddhist, and prays for safety and health. She enshrines and worships "three western sages" in Buddha hall. The middle one is the founder of this Budda and his two servants, Avalokitesvare Buddhisattva and Bodhisattva of Great Power. This side is the private school.

Fu'an Bridge

G: Now we are on Fu'an Bridge, which was built in 1355 (in the Yuan Dynasty). It's the oldest bridge in the town.

V: What is the meaning of its name?

G: Its original name is Manager Bridge which was built by Shen Wansi, who didn't want to follow his brother (he was sent to a distant exile, so he offered the money to build bridges and pave the roads for the town). And he changed the name into "Fu'an Bridge", which means to live safely and freely. Later he became a rich man.

V: I like the idea, being rich and safe.

G: Its feature is that it has a tall building on each side, but there is no stair between the first floor and second floor. You must go round the stairs of bridge.

V: Yes, I see.

G: These structural bridges are called "bridge-building architecture" by experts. Professor Chen Congzhou of Tongji University said, these structural bridges were very common in feudalistic time, but the four "bridge-building architectures" being reserved so completely is very rare. There are rare Wukang stone on it; this can convey the bridge's long history. Wukang stones, with many tiny holes, are from Deqing, Zhejiang. During the rainy or snowy days, these stones can't be slippery. Zhou Zhuang is the region of rivers and lakes, with no big mountains near it. So the stones that they used to build the houses and bridges were carried here by water. It's very difficult. I wish Fu'an Bridge can bring each visitor safety and richness.

V: Thank you very much.

 Task 4　Useful Sentences

1. Zhang Hall was built by Xu Mengqing's offspring who is the younger brother of Xu Da, King Zhongshan of the Ming Dynasty.
2. Wukang stones, with many tiny holes, are from Deqing, Zhejiang.
3. The whole hall covers an area of 1,800 square kilometers, having more than 60 rooms and a private garden which is divided into 6 parts.
4. The sedan hall is the place where the guests and visitors get off the sedan.
5. The main hall is the place for the master to hold happy events and funeral rituals and to recieve the distinguished guests.

Task 5 Listening

You will hear five sentences. Listen carefully and put down the whole sentences.
1. _____ .
2. _____ .
3. _____ .
4. _____ .
5. _____ .

Task 6 Role-Play

Situation 1: Arrange an introduction of Zhang Hall and Fu'an Bridge.

Situation 2: There are three vegetarians and two Moslems in your group and another member who has high blood pressure and must have no salt in his diet. It is already five o'clock and the group is scheduled to have dinner at Suzhou Tourism Restarurant. Find a way to handle this situation.

Task 7 Translation

Put the following sentences into Chinese.
1. He changed the name into "Fu'an Bridge", which means to live safely and freely.
2. During the rainy or snowy days, these stones can't be slippery.
3. In the early Qing Dynasty, Xu family declined, and sold the houses to a person with the surname Zhang.
4. There is a vase on one side and a mirror on the other side, meaning safety and soundness of the family.
5. The sedan enters from the gate, and the boat is paddled across the house.

Task 8 Supplementary Reading

Looking for the Secret of Longevity

In Guangxi, southwest China, there is a world-famous longevity hometown—Bama Yao

Autonomous County.

According to a survey in 1994, among the county's 230,000 inhabitants, the people aged over 100 numbered 81, with the oldest aged 130. Old people from the age of 90 to 99 numbered 226. Such a record is very rare not only in China, but also in the world. On November 1, 1991, at the Japanese Tokyo World Natural Science Convention, Bama was elected as the fifth hometown of longevity in the world.

The county is located 300 kilometers northwest of Nanning, the capital of Guangxi. Every morning, there are long-distance buses running from Nanning Bus Station and Nanning Passenger Transportation Center to Bama.

Deluxe bus starts from Nanning at 8:00 am and arrives at Bama at 3:00 pm. To visit centenarians, tourists need to contact the county government beforehand.

The Panyang River is the main river of the county. It starts from the foot of the mountains in the western areas, runs through the central area of the county (a total length of 143 kilometers), and flows finally into the Hongshui River. About 62 percent of the centenarians live along the Panyang River. The river starts from the high mountains and deep valleys, so the water is very clear.

The Panyang River is not a large river, but it is surrounded by green mountains, and looks full of vigor and vitality. The small public buses can stop on demand, so passengers can get on at anytime. After more than one hour, we got to our destination—Poyue. It took more than 20 minutes to get to the Baimo Cave from there on foot. The Panyang River passes in front of the cave, and meets with the spring water from the cave. Usually few tourists come to visit so they must pay the administrative staff 10 yuan to turn on the light if they want to go into the cave. We visited the cave from nine o'clock in the morning to three o'clock in the afternoon. There are large stalagmites and stalactites in the cave, and all kinds of other formations. There is very large hall in the cave capable of holding 10,000 people at one time, with small stone peaks and stream in it. The Baimo Cave has small caves inside (the small cave has smaller caves inside), and some plants also grow there. The Baimo Cave was called "No. 1 cave in the world" by British explorers.

The Panyang River meets with the spring from the Baimo Cave, flowing through the White Bear Cave, then forming a 2,000-meter-long underground river. The exit of the underground river is the famous scenic spot, Bainiao Cave.

We got on a mini-bus from Bama County to Jiazhuan, then walked over a small bridge on the Panyang River to reach the exit of the Bainiao Cave after a two-kilometer tour. The entrance of the cave is a 50-meter-wide and 15-meter-high triangle. The ticket fee is 5 yuan. Tourists go along a 50-meter-long and 0.5-meter-wide drifting bridge to the exit of the cave. The cave has a sandy beach. Going ahead, tourists will see various formations. The cave there can hold several hundred people, and

visitors can hear the sound of birds. If visitors pay another 5 yuan, they can take a bamboo raft and drift along the underground river. The 40-meter-wide and 2,500-meter-long river has a depth of 21 meters at the deepest spot. In the cave, tourists also can see swallows, bats, kingfishers and hawks. When the rosy dawn emerges or the sun sets, thousands of birds fly out from the cave, playing and looking for food.

Bama is also called Wangang, meaning hundreds of mountains. Because Bama is surrounded by green mountains, the Panyang River is pollution-free. The main food of the Bama people is yellow corn, beans, potatoes, vegetables and the oil produced from tea-oil trees. These plants and food have many trace elements and more vitamins, carotene, and minteral elements than the plants produced in other places. Probably that's one of the reasons for people's long lives.

Bama is located in the mountainous area and most of people live among the mountains and valleys. They have to climb mountains or walk for a long time to go shopping, or to get to their fields, and some people's fields are several kilometers away from their houses. They must work hard on their field. A life time of hard work has given the people strong muscles and bones, which is another reason for their long life span. The Bama people's living standards are not high, but they like to help others and are satisfied with their current situation. Centenarians thought that the secret of longevity is to do good deeds, help others, be kind, have confidence, and never give up. These centenarians all have good families, they get along well with their family members, and their children treat them well. Their lives are very happy.

(Source: http://chinavista.com/travel/bama/bama.html)

Questions:
1. What is the oldest age in this longevity hometown according to the 1994 survey?
2. What is the name of this longevity hometown? What is the location?
3. Could you guess the meaning of the word "centenarian" from the context?
4. What kind of animals could people see in Bainiao Cave?
5. Could you elaborate on the secret of longevity in this place?

Part III

Task 1 Warm-Up

1. What is "Grandma's Tea" like in Zhou Zhuang?
2. Who praised Zhou Zhuang as a natural studio? What movies have been filmed in Zhou Zhuang?

Task 2 Words and Expressions

layer	[ˈleɪə]	n.	层
residence	[ˈrezɪdəns]	n.	住宅,住处
distribute	[dɪˈstrɪbjuːt]	v.	分配,分布
axis	[ˈæksɪs]	n.	轴
magnificent	[mægˈnɪfɪsnt]	adj.	壮丽的,宏伟的
exuberant	[ɪgˈzjuːbərənt]	adj.	兴高采烈的,繁茂的
pine	[paɪn]	n.	松树
reign	[reɪn]	n.	君主统治,在位期
annals	[ˈænəlz]	n.	纪年表,年鉴
depraved	[dɪˈpreɪvd]	adj.	堕落的,颓废的
bandit	[ˈbændɪt]	n.	盗匪,歹徒
recklessly	[ˈrekləsli]	adv.	不顾后果地
anchor	[ˈæŋkə]	v.	抛锚,停泊
lantern	[ˈlæntən]	n.	灯笼
crude	[kruːd]	adj.	天然的,未加工的,粗糙的,简陋的
status	[ˈsteɪtəs]	n.	地位
mahogany	[məˈhɒgəni]	n.	红木
Phoenix	[ˈfiːnɪks]	n.	凤凰,不死鸟
kirin	[ˈkiːrɪn]	n.	<日>麒麟
rear	[rɪə]	adj.	后面的
		n.	后部
integral	[ˈɪntɪgrəl]	adj.	构成整体所必需的
peep	[piːp]	v.	窥视
betroth	[bɪˈtrəʊθ]	v.	同……订婚
maid	[meɪd]	n.	女仆
sought	[sɔːt]	v.	搜索(seek 的过去式和过去分词)
kinship	[ˈkɪnʃɪp]	n.	血缘关系
tie	[taɪ]	n.	束缚,使人结合在一起的事物
enlightened	[ɪnˈlaɪtnd]	adj.	开明的
miserable	[ˈmɪzərəbl]	adj.	痛苦的,悲惨的
upturned	[ˌʌpˈtɜːnd]	adj.	仰着的,向上翘的
eave	[iːv]	n.	屋檐
bracket	[ˈbrækɪt]	n.	档次,括号,支架
drooping	[ˈdruːpɪŋ]	adj.	下垂的,无力的
lotus	[ˈləʊtəs]	n.	荷花

virtuous	[ˈvɜːrtʃuəs]	adj.	有道德的
plum	[plʌm]	n.	李子
porcelain	[ˈpɔːslɪn]	n.	瓷器
ingot	[ˈɪŋɡət]	n.	锭，铸块
forehead	[ˈfɔːrɪd]	n.	前额，前部
opium	[ˈəʊpiəm]	n.	鸦片，麻醉剂
bench	[bentʃ]	n.	长凳
tutor	[ˈtjuːtə]	n.	家庭教师
squat	[skwɒt]	v.	蹲下，蹲坐
scroll	[skrəʊl]	n.	卷轴，画卷，名册
snail	[sneɪl]	n.	蜗牛
commemorate	[kəˈmeməreɪt]	v.	纪念
extend	[ɪksˈtend]	v.	延伸，扩展
warehouse	[ˈwɛəhaʊs]	n.	仓库
manual	[ˈmænjuəl]	adj.	手工的
stringed	[strɪŋd]	adj.	有弦的
tofu	[ˈtəʊfuː]	n.	豆腐
iron	[ˈaɪən]	n.	铁
prosperous	[ˈprɒspərəs]	adj.	繁荣的，兴旺的
glorious	[ˈɡlɔːriəs]	adj.	光荣的，辉煌的
brilliant	[ˈbrɪliənt]	adj.	卓越的，杰出的
frequently	[ˈfriːkwəntli]	adv.	频繁地
lotus root		n.	莲藕
match-maker		n.	媒人
gateway	[ˈɡeɪtweɪ]	n.	门，通路
bankrupt	[ˈbæŋkrʌpt]	adj.	破产的
wharf	[wɔːf]	n.	码头
reception	[rɪˈsepʃn]	n.	接待
hanging	[ˈhæŋɪŋ]	n.	悬挂物
boa	[ˈbəʊə]	n.	蟒蛇
spy	[spaɪ]	v.	监视，看到
plaque	[plɑːk]	n.	匾
prosperity	[prɒˈsperəti]	n.	繁荣，兴旺
statue	[ˈstætʃuː]	n.	雕像，塑像
bald	[bɔːld]	adj.	秃头的
clan	[klæn]	n.	氏族，宗族
plinth	[plɪnθ]	n.	柱脚，底座
buffalo	[ˈbʌfələʊ]	n.	水牛，野牛

specialty	[ˈspeʃəlti]	n.	特产
layout	[ˈleɪaʊt]	n.	安排，布局
litterateur	[ˌlɪtərəˈtɜːr]	n.	文学家，文人
successive	[səkˈsesɪv]	adj.	连续的
commercial	[kəˈmɜːʃl]	adj.	商业的
dulcimer	[ˈdʌlsɪmə]	n.	扬琴
bowed	[bəʊd]	adj.	弯如弓的
workshop	[ˈwɜːkʃɒp]	n.	工场，车间
unexpected	[ˌʌnɪkˈspektɪd]	adj.	想不到的
annals of local history			地方志
be bent on			专心致志于，决心要
be composed of			由……组成
be up to			由某人决定
do one's bidding			按……的吩咐去做
be impressed by			对……印象深刻
fried bean curd			油炸豆腐
pass away			去世，逝世
consist of			由……组成

Task 3 Dialogues

Scene: Now the group is in front of Shen Hall. (V = Visitor, G = Guide)
Travel Route: Shen Hall—Quanfu Temple—the Culture Street—Sanmao Teahouse

Shen Hall

G: Now we are visiting Shen Hall, the biggest one of southern Yangtze River.
V: That is great. How big is it?
G: Facing to the south, with 7 layers and 5 gateway arches in between, Shen's Residence has over one hundred rooms distributed on both sides of a central axis, altogether one hundred meters in length, covering an area of more than 2,000 square meters.
V: Wow, so magnificent. Like Zhang Hall, Shen is the family name of the owner, I think.
G: Yes, Shen's residence, first known as the Hall to Respect Work, was changed to the name of the Hall of Exuberant Pine Trees at the end of the Qing Dynasty. It was set up by Shen Benren, Shen Wansan's descendant during the reign of Qianlong in the Qing Dynasty. There is a story about it.

V: Tell me now, please.

G: According to the annals of local history, Shen Benren led a depraved life and was keen on making friends with bandits when he was young. After his father passed away, hearing that the family was certain to become bankrupt in less than 3 years, Shen Benren held a party to entertain his friends, gave every one of them some money as a present and told them that he would stop acting recklessly in order to maintain the family. From then on, shutting his door and declining to see any visitor, he was bent on engaging in farm work and had his residence built in such a large scale.

V: A moving story.

G: Shen's residence is composed of 3 sections. The front section is a covered wharf, it was for the family to anchor the boats and do some washing in the ancient time. The mid-section consists of the entrance hall, the tea room and the main reception hall. Let's have a visit one by one.

V: OK!

G: The entrance hall used to be decorated with lanterns and hangings. If the passers-by saw the red lanterns and colored hangings, they knew the family was holding wedding ceremony or birthday celebration. If they saw the white lanterns and hangings, they knew someone of the family had been dead.

V: The same with the Zhang Hall.

G: Right. The tea room was for parking sedan-chairs of the distinguished guests when they came to visit the owner. The sedan-chair carriers or the boatmen waited here for their masters, having a cup of tea. In general, the ordinary visitors used to be met in this room. That's why the furniture in the room is simple (shabby) and crude.

V: It is up to the social status.

G: Now we are in the main hall, the Hall of Exuberant Pine Trees. Those VIPs were entertained here.

V: I find that the mahogany furniture is exquisitely made in the Qing style.

G: Yes, the beams are carved with patterns of phoenix, cranes, Kirin, boa (not dragon, which was only used by the emperor). At the rear of the hall stand two huge round marbles, on which draws natural Chinese shan-shui paintings. The mahogany stands are carved delicately with meaningful patterns and one Chinese character "longevity". On the walls are wall-hangings inlaid with marbles, round one above, square one below.

V: Yes, but why?

G: In ancient times, Chinese people thought that the sky was round and the earth square, expressing the theory that man is an integral part of nature.

V: OK, I see.

G: Please look up, there are two moving windows.

V: Is there something special?

G: Yes. As we know, man and woman were unequal in feudal society, in which women's social status was low. It was improper for men and women to touch each other's hand when passing objects. When the distinguished guests came and were seated, the girls of the family were never allowed to meet them. Full of curiosity, the girls wanted to know who had come; they could only stay near the windows to peep on the second floor. If the girl had yet not been betrothed to anyone, when a match-maker found her a boyfriend and took him here to the future parents-in-law, the girl could not come downstairs but only stayed there spying and listening. If the boy looked nice and conversation was satisfactory, the girl would ask her maid to make a cup of tea to serve the boy, which meant the girl was satisfied with him and agreed with this marriage.

V: Ha-ha, clever idea!

G: At that time, marriage was decided by the parents and much up to the words of a match-maker. A boy or a girl, whether he or she was from the family of high position or not, had no freedom to choose his or her lover. Some parents sought a marriage among families of equal social rank; some parents claimed ties of kinship with someone of a higher social position, ignoring their daughters' real happiness, or even not caring whether they live or die. Some girls could do nothing but do their parents' bidding, but some girls refused to marry and committed suicide for love, or ran away with their lovers. Of course, there were parents who were well-educated and enlightened, they would listen to the daughter's opinions, but the final decision was still certain to be made by the parents.

V: So miserable!

G: Yes. Please look back. The gateway facing the reception room is the biggest and the most magnificent one among the fire gateways in this family.

V: It is very elegant and nice.

G: It's 6 meters in height, from top to bottom are exquisite stone carvings, such as the stone upturned eaves, stone bracket sets, drooping lotus on both sides, four Chinese characters carved on the horizontal plaque in the middle meaning a virtuous family enjoys long prosperity for generations, around which are patterns of plum blossoms. In addition, we can see the figures, animals and buildings.

V: I think this is the sitting room.

G: Yes. In the past, the female guests were received here. On the beam is the Chinese characters "longevity" in round. Three porcelain statues on the long table at the rear are gods of happiness (with a boy in his arm), wealth (with a gold ingot in his hand), and longevity (bald head, broad forehead, with a peach in the hand). The chairs are smaller and narrower, for ladies. And on the left is the opium bed.

V: I have seen it before.

G: This is the small room.

V: Who is the sitting statue?

G: Shen Wansan, the ancestor of the family.

V: On both sides are some desks and benches. I think this room used to be the classroom; the children of the family (or of the clan) were given lessons by the private tutor here.

G: Perfectly right. The columns in the front are based with wooden plinths, which were made in the Ming Dynasty. This wooden plinth is rare in this area. Outside in the yard is a stone squatting buffalo, which always reminds the descendants of the fact that the wealth of the family depends on farming.

V: Yes, they should.

G: Now the dining hall.

V: On the walls are four scrolls, what do they mean?

G: They are Chinese characters: Happiness, Wealth, Longevity and double happiness. Every one is written in one hundred different handwritings.

V: On the tables are the home-made dishes the family used to eat in their daily life, I think.

G: Yes, the fish, eel, snails, fried bean curd, lotus roots, especially the pig's elbow (or chunk) in the middle, which has been the specialty in Zhou Zhuang. It's the waiting place for the servants who could walk out quickly to serve any wants.

V: So interesting.

G: The one next to the dining hall is the kitchen. It's spacious and bright. The old-fashioned kitchen layout used in the farmers' families is rarely seen now.

Quanfu Temple

G: After Shen Hall, we'll visit Quanfu Temple, which is the typical garden temple.

V: OK.

G: This temple is divided into 3 parts. The east and west parts are to commemorate the famous poet Liu Yuxi and Lu Guimeng of the Tang Dynasty and the litterateur Zhang Jiying of the Western Jin Dynasty. The middle part is the key to visit.

V: Why is the temple so famous?

G: We have mentioned the story that Mr. Zhou changed the houses into the temple. This temple has more than 900-year history. After it had been built in the Song Dynasty, it was extended in the successive dynasties and became famous in southern Yangtze River. Unfortunately, it was destroyed and changed into food warehouse during the "Cultural Revolution". The present temple was built by Shanghai Huaxia Company in 1995 and moved from Baiyan Lake to South Lake.

Culture Street—Sanmao Teahouse

V: So busy here.

G: Now we are in Zhenfeng Street which was a commercial street. Later it was changed into the street with the manual arts, gathering the folk and commercial culture, so it's also called "the street of the cultures". Here's the instrumental shop which sells traditional Chinese instruments such as two-stringed bowed instrument and dulcimer. That's the cloth shop. Now please smell carefully, yeah, it's the bean curd. In front of you, there's the Zhang family Tofu workshop. On the opposite side is the wood shop. Look, this is the sight of A Po Tea. Listen, where is the voice from? Behind you, there is an iron work shop.

V: I love here. I need to take a photo here.

G: That is the Sanmao Teahouse. Taiwan female writer Sanmao visited Zhou Zhuang in 1989, and said she would come to Zhou Zhuang again. But she passed away. Mr. Zhang Jihan was to commemorate this friend, and opened the teahouse. The fans of Sanmao can sit here to read her books when they are drinking tea.

V: OK. Very good.

G: Every visitor, this is the visit to Zhou Zhuang, which was prosperous, is glorious, and will be brilliant. I hope you'll be impressed by this visit, and come to Zhou Zhuang frequently. Maybe you can also get an unexpected fortune.

Task 4 Useful Expressions

1. Facing to the south, with 7 layers and 5 gateway arches in between, Shen's Residence has over one hundred rooms distributed on both sides of a central axis, altogether one hundred meters in length, covering an area of more than 2,000 square meters.
2. It was set up by Shen Benren, Shen Wansan's descendant during the reign of Qianlong in the Qing Dynasty.
3. Shen's residence is composed of 3 sections.
4. The sedan-chair carriers or the boatmen waited here for their masters, having a cup of tea.
5. Full of curiosity, the girls wanted to know who had come; they could only stay near the windows to peep on the second floor.

Task 5 Listening

You will hear five sentences. Listen carefully and put down the whole sentences.

1. _____.
2. _____.

3. _____.
4. _____.
5. _____.

 Task 6　Role-Play

Situation 1: Arrange a two-hour tour of Shen Hall—Quanfu Temple—the Culture Street—Sanmao Teahouse.

Situation 2: Most of the foreign guests don't know how to use chopsticks. You come over to demonstrate and tell them something about the history of Chinese chopsticks.

 Task 7　Translation

Put the following sentences into Chinese.
1. According to the annals of local history, Shen Benren led a depraved life and was keen on making friends with bandits when he was young.
2. After his father passed away, hearing that the family was certain to become bankrupt in less than 3 years, Shen Benren held a party to entertain his friends, gave every one of them some money as a present and told them that he would stop acting recklessly in order to maintain the family.
3. On the walls are wall-hangings inlaid with marbles, round one above, square one below.
4. If the boy looked nice and conversation was satisfactory, the girl would ask her maid to make a cup of tea to serve the boy, which meant the girl was satisfied with him and agreed with this marriage.
5. Some girls could do nothing but do their parents' bidding, but some girls refused to marry and committed suicide for love, or ran away with their lovers.

Task 8 Supplementary Reading

A "Retreat Away from the World"

The Yesanpo Scenic Area on the banks of the Juma River in Laishui County, Hebei Province is titled a "retreat away from the world". It is enclosed by mountains on four sides with the river flowing around three of the sides. The scenic area boasts unique natural scenery, rich historic and cultural connections, a beautiful environment and cool and fresh air.

The Bofeng Holiday Resort is located at the center of the Yesanpo. It is constructed with the investment of Beijing Bofeng Industry and Trade Group. Now the holiday resort has become a large tourism reception base integrating food and lodging, transportation and entertainment. The holiday resort receives tourism groups and individual tourists, where people can spend holidays, recuperate, explore and hold meetings. The principle of the Bofeng Holiday Resort is: Win your trust and support; win your satisfaction and smile.

The Yesanpo Canyon in the scenic area is only one kilometer from the Yesanpo Holiday Resort. It is composed of some ten natural valleys including the Baifo (A Hundred Buddhas) Valley, the Lovers valley and the "Tianting Xianjing" (Fairyland of Heaven). There are exotic peaks, stones of various fancy shapes, groups of caves, and precipitous cliffs. There are also four Buddha's sculptures, including the Manjusti Buddha of the Wutai Mountain and the Ksitigarbha Buddha of the Jiuhua Mountain, and four gardens including Jingxin Garden and Wuyou Garden. From February to November every year various kinds of flowers in these gardens bloom alternatively. In addition to the precious primitive plants, all kinds of wild animals add great fun for visitors and provide an ideal natural place for scientific investigation on plants and animals.

Bofeng Lake, in the shape of a ring on the banks of the Juma River, covers several square kilometers. The clear water blends into the green mountains around it. The Water Amusement Garden in the holiday resort offers a number of entertainment programs such as boating, rafting, swimming and fishing. The colorful and exotic peddles on the riverside are great for stone collectors.

Jinghuayuan Palace is named after the novel written by Li Ruzhen, a novelist of the Qing Dynasty. The construction covers an area of 3,000 square meters and includes 28 scenic spots such as "Strange Fowl in fight" and "Fairyland of Penglai". Electronic technologies are used to create an exciting effect inside the palace by making use of sound, light and waves. And the exquisite and lifelike works of ancient art vividly represent historic scenes.

Food and Lodging in Bofeng Holiday Resort

Bofeng Holiday Inn: 3-star. Two building with 200 rooms including luxury suits and standard guestrooms can accommodate 650 guests at the same time. The restaurant can serve 300 guests simultaneously, with 6 independent dining rooms. Three meeting rooms can hold 50 – 150 people. Ballroom, karaoke, chess and poker room, and sauna are also available. Dinners can taste all kinds of game in the restaurant or try Sichuan and Guangdong style dishes.

Bofeng Hotel: 230 beds. The restaurant can serve 100 guests simultaneously.

Entertainment

The holiday resort has an Ethnic Minority Folklore Garden, Waterfall Waterwheel Garden, Fishing Garden, Barbecue, Fireworks and Bonfire Garden, a racecourse, a swimming pool, sand baths, a paragliding field, a sand surfing field and a water amusement park. Entertainment items include horse racing, sand surfing, parachuting, rock climbing, boating, fishing, rafting, swimming, bumper boating. The holiday resort also organizes bonfire, barbecue, and fireworks parties for tourists in groups. And there are all kinds of entertainment performances and a tour of the Miao folklore.

(Source: http://chinavista.com/travel/yesanpo/enhead.html)

Questions:
1. Which place is titled "a retreat away from the world"?
2. What is the principle of Bofeng Holiday Resort?
3. Say something about the Yesanpo Canyon.
4. What does Bofeng Lake look like?
5. Which special tour of a certain ethnic group could the visitors enjoy in the resort?

Project 6 Tongli

Part I

Task 1 Warm-Up

1. What are the features of the Retreat and Reflection Garden?
2. What's the ancient name of Tongli?

Task 2 Words and Expressions

thatch	[θætʃ]	v.	用茅草等盖(屋顶)
locate	[ləʊˈkeɪt]	vt.	使坐落于
bank	[bæŋk]	n.	岸
worth	[wɜːθ]	n.	价值,财富
adjacent	[əˈdʒeɪsnt]	adj.	邻近的
luxuriant	[lʌɡˈʒʊəriənt]	adj.	繁茂的,肥沃的
flaunt	[flɒnt]	v.	挥动,夸耀
pretty	[ˈprɪti]	adj.	漂亮的
unsophisticated	[ʌnsəˈfɪstɪkeɪtɪd]	adj.	不谙世故的,不复杂的
boast	[bəʊst]	v.	以……为荣
paddy field	[ˈpædi fiːld]	n.	稻田
crown	[kraʊn]	vt.	居……之顶
ancestral	[ænˈsestrəl]	adj.	祖先的
archway	[ˈɑːtʃweɪ]	n.	拱门
imitate	[ˈɪmɪteɪt]	vt.	仿制
interior	[ɪnˈtɪəriə(r)]	adj.	内部的
inscribe	[ɪnˈskraɪb]	v.	题写
integrated	[ˈɪntɪɡreɪtɪd]	adj.	综合的,融合的
witness	[ˈwɪtnəs]	vt.	目击,见证
significance	[sɪɡˈnɪfɪkəns]	n.	重要性,意义
roof	[ruːf]	n.	屋顶
current	[ˈkʌrənt]	adj.	现在的
fertile	[ˈfɜːtaɪl]	adj.	肥沃的
reserved	[rɪˈzɜːvd]	adj.	保留的

celebrity	[səˈlebrəti]	n.	名人
Small Oriental Venice			小威尼斯
belong to			属于
trace back to			追溯到
Standing Committee of the National People's Congress			全国人民代表大会常务委员会
key cultural relic protection unit at the provincial level			省级重点文物保护单位
after a storm comes a calm			否极泰来
make a brief introduction			做简要介绍

Task 3　Dialogues

Scene: Now the group is on the way to Tongli by coach. (V = Visitor, G = Guide)
Travel Route: Coach—Archway—Tailai Bridge

On the Coach

G: Hello, everyone. Today we will visit another famous water town of Suzhou, Tongli. Now I will make a brief introduction about this famous water town for you.

V: OK, very good!

G: Tongli, which belongs to Wujiang in Jiangsu Province, is located along the bank of Taihu Lake and to the east of the ancient canal, surrounded with eight lakes. So you see, it is worth the name, "Small Oriental Venice". Tongli has a very good location, it is 80 kilometers away from Shanghai Hongqiao Airport in the east and 18 kilometers away from Suzhou in the north, adjacent to 318 national highway in the south and Suzhou-Jiaxing Expressway in the west.

V: How big is this town?

G: Not very big. It covers an area of about 102 square kilometers with a population of 58,000.

V: Why do you call it Tongli? Is there some special meaning in it?

G: In the beginning, it is known as Futu, which means a very rich and prosperous land. In the early Tang Dynasty, some 1,300 years ago, local people changed its name to "Cuprum Town", because "Futu" is too luxuriant and flaunt. The current name "Tongli" can be traced back to the Song Dynasty about 1,000 years ago, when people recreated the two characters "Fu" and "Tu".

V: I see. Is it an important and very rich town in Suzhou?

G: Yes. Pretty and unsophisticated Tongli town boasts fertile paddy fields, rich resources and outstanding natives, thus crowned as "Small Oriental Venice".

V: What is Tongli famous for?

G: Tongli is characterized by a large number of architectures in the Ming and Qing Dynasties, small bridges and outstanding celebrities. Tongli boasts 38 residences in the Ming and Qing Dynasties, 47 temples and ancestral halls and around 100 residences of rich and powerful local people as well as former residences of celebrities.

Archway

G: The front ancient decorated archway is the gate of the old town. It is imitating the Ming style.

V: I guess the interior is the old town district, like Zhou Zhuang.

G: Right. The eight characters on its beam are inscribed by Fei Xiaotong, a celebrity of Wujiang, who is the former deputy head of the Standing Committee of the National People's Congress.

V: I have heard of him before.

G: Now we set foot in the town of more than 1,000 years history. Tongli Town with beautiful scenery is surrounded by eight lakes, namely Tongli, Jiuli, Yeze, Nanxing, Pangshan and so on. The town is divided into 7 small islands by 15 rivers arranged like the Chinese character "川" and connected by 49 ancient bridges of different dynasties and styles, making these islands an integrated area. Each bridge has its own formation and style. All these graceful stone bridges of different shapes witness the history and culture of greatest significance in Tongli.

V: That is so wonderful!

Tailai Bridge

V: The bridge on our left is very interesting! It has a roof!

G: That is Tailai Bidge, which is originally built in the Yuan Dynasty, about 700 years ago.

V: What is the meaning of Tailai?

G: "Tailai" means that after a storm comes a calm. The architectures built by riverside, famous for "small bridge, flowing stream and thatched households", make Tongli the best-reserved ancient town by riverside as well as the key cultural relic protection unit at the provincial level. It has also been listed as one of the 13 scenic spots of Taihu Lake.

V: I need to take a photo here!

G: Enjoy yourself!

Task 4 Useful Sentences

1. That is Tailai Bidge, which is originally built in the Yuan Dynasty, about 700 years ago.
2. The eight characters on its beam are inscribed by Fei Xiaotong, a celebrity of Wujiang, who is the former deputy head of the Standing Committee of the National People's Congress.
3. Each bridge has its own formation and style.
4. Tongli, which belongs to Wujiang in Jiangsu Province, is located along the bank of Taihu Lake and to the east of the ancient canal, surrounded with eight lakes.
5. Tongli is characterized by a large number of architectures in the Ming and Qing Dynasties, small bridges and outstanding celebrities.

Task 5 Listening

You will hear five sentences. Listen carefully and put down the whole sentences.

1. _____.
2. _____.
3. _____.
4. _____.
5. _____.

Task 6 Role-Play

Situation 1: Arrange a travel route of Coach—Archway—Tailai Bridge for the James.

Situation 2: You are the guide of a foreign group. There are 4 American college students who study Chinese culture in Suzhou University. They want to have a chance of a boat trip around Tongli after visiting all the places of interest. What is more, they'd prefer to have a local boat aunt accompanying to sing the local opera.

- You inquire the boat owner of the price and ask him to help you find an aunt who could sing the local opera.
- You discuss the charge, and tell the 4 tourists that the fee would be extra charged.
- When the local boat aunt sings the local opera, explain the story and discuss about some local language with the 4 tourists.

Task 7　Translation

1. "泰来"意为否极泰来。
2. 这些形状各异、精巧的石桥见证了同里的历史和文化。
3. The architectures built by riverside, famous for "small bridge, flowing stream and thatched households", make Tongli the best-reserved ancient town by riverside as well as the key cultural relic protection unit at the provincial level, it has also been listed as one of the 13 scenic spots of Taihu Lake.
4. Tongli Town with beautiful scenery is surrounded by eight lakes, namely Tongli, Jiuli, Yeze, Nanxing, Pangshan and so on.
5. Pretty and unsophisticated Tongli town boasts fertile paddy fields, rich resources and outstanding natives, thus crowned as "Small Oriental Venice".

Task 8　Supplementary Reading

"Duan Wu"—a Day in Memory of a Patriotic Poet

The 5th day of the 5th month of the lunar year is an important day for the Chinese people. The day called "Duan Wu" (meaning Day of Right Mid-Day) or the Dragon Boat Festival, is observed everywhere in China. This unique Chinese celebration dates back to earliest times and a number of legends explain its origins. The best known story centers on a patriotic court official named Qu Yuan, of the State of Chu during the Warring States Period more than 2,000 years ago. Qu tried to warn the emperor of an increasingly corrupt government, but failed. In a last desperate protest, he threw himself into the river and drowned. The State of Chu was soon annexed by the State of Qin. Later Qu Yuan's sympathizers jumped into boats, beat the water with their oars. They made rice dumplings wrapped in reed-leaves (Zongzi) and scattered them into the Miluo River in the hope that fish in the river would eat the rice dumplings instead of the body of the deceased poet.

The custom of making rice dumplings spread to the whole country. Today, people eat glutinous rice cakes to mark the occasion.

At the news of the poet's death, the local people raced out in boats in an effort to search his body. Later the activity became a boat race and the boats gradually developed into dragon-boats. In many places along rivers and on the coast today, the holiday also features dragon-boat races. In these high-spirited competitions, teams of rowers stroke their oars in unison to propel sleek, long vessels through the water.

(Source: http://travel.chinavista.com/show_culture-37.html)

Questions:
1. Which day does "Duan Wu" fall on?
2. Among many legends centering on "Duan Wu", which story is the best known?
3. How do people celebrate "Duan Wu"?
4. Who is Qu Yuan?
5. Do you know another name of "Duan Wu"?

Part Ⅱ

Task 1　　Warm-Up

1. What are the nine scenic spots open to tourists in Tongli?
2. What are the features of old bridges in Tongli?

Task 2　　Words and Expressions

elegant	[ˈelɪgənt]	adj.	优雅的
float	[fləʊt]	v.	漂浮
accountant	[əˈkaʊntənt]	n.	会计人员
fete	[feɪt]	n.	庆祝,节日
celadon	[ˈselədɒn]	n.	青瓷
placidity	[pləˈsɪdəti]	n.	平静
philosophical	[ˌfɪləˈsɒfɪkl]	adj.	哲学的
wooden	[ˈwʊdn]	adj.	木制的
theft	[θeft]	n.	偷窃
stern	[stɜːn]	n.	尾部,船尾
magnolia	[mægˈnəʊliə]	n.	木兰
vessel	[ˈvesl]	n.	船
couch	[kaʊtʃ]	n.	长椅,睡椅
pavement	[ˈpeɪvmənt]	n.	路面
cobblestone	[ˈkɒblstəʊn]	n.	圆石,鹅卵石
massage	[ˈmæsɑːʒ]	n.	按摩
porch	[pɔːtʃ]	n.	门廊
landscaper	[ˈlændskeɪpə]	n.	园林学家

womenfolk	[ˈwɪmɪnfəʊk]	n.	女人们
wing-room	[ˈwɪŋˈruːm]	n.	厢房
furnish	[ˈfɜːnɪʃ]	v.	布置
pebble	[ˈpebl]	n.	鹅卵石
veranda	[vəˈrændə]	n.	阳台,游廊
board	[bɔːd]	n.	木板
fireproof	[ˈfaɪəpruːf]	adj.	防火的
hospitality	[ˌhɒspɪˈtæləti]	n.	款待,殷勤
shipboard	[ˈʃɪpbɔːd]	n.	舷侧
chilliness	[ˈtʃɪlɪnəs]	n.	寒气
bat	[bæt]	n.	蝙蝠
subdrain	[sʌbˈdreɪn]	n.	暗沟
bare	[beə(r)]	adj.	赤裸的
central courtyard			中庭
sedan hall			轿厅
land boat			旱船
Sui Hanju			岁寒居
Visiting Scenic Spot			览胜阁
A Naohong Barge			闹红一舸
Osmanthus Hall			桂花厅
Ren Lansheng			任兰生
Chen Congzhou			陈从周
Outer house			外庭

Be loyal to the emperor when serving the court and reflect upon oneself when retreating from the post.
进思尽忠,退思补过。

Retreat and Reflection Garden	退思园
tea lounge	茶厅
Wanxiang Building	畹香楼
Zuo Chun Wang Yue Building	坐春望月楼
Shuixiang Pavilion	水香榭
Tuisi Thatched Cottage	退思草堂
Laoren Peak	老人峰
Gu Yu Sheng Liang Pavilion	菰雨生凉
Waterside Garden	贴水园
inner chamber	内庭

Task 3 Dialogues

Scene: Now the group is going to visit the Retreat and Reflection Garden. (V = Visitor, G = Guide)

Travel Route: Main Gate—Tea Lounge—Sedan Hall—Grand Reception Hall—Wanxiang Building—Land Boat—Zuo Chun Wang Yue Building—Sui Hanju—Shuixiang Pavillion—Visiting Scenic Spot—Tuisi Thatched Cottage—A Naohong Barge—Laoren Peak—Gu Yu Sheng Liang Pavillion—Osmanthus Hall

Main Gate—Tea Lounge—Sedan Hall

G: Hello, everyone. Now we come to the Retreat and Reflection Garden. It was built in the Qing Dynasty from 1885 to 1887. The First owner was Ren Lansheng.

V: The name is very interesting. What is its meaning?

G: The name comes from a saying "Be loyal to the emperor when serving the court and reflect upon oneself when retreating from the post" in *Zuo Zhuan*.

V: I see. I have already visited many classical gardens in Suzhou. Can you tell me something special about this one?

G: Its designer was Yuan Long, a famous garden designer. The garden covers an area of 9.8 mu, simple, quiet and elegant. It is a typical Qing Dynasty style garden. Tuisi Garden has a unique layout; pavilion, terrace, tower, porch, bridge, hall and house are centered by the pond as if these architectures are floating on it. Chinese landscaper Chen Congzhou regards Tuisi Garden as "Waterside Garden". In 2001, Tuisi Garden was listed as a site of World's Cultural Heritage.

V: OK! I understand. Where are we now?

G: The whole garden can be divided into four sections, which are the outer house, inner chamber for womenfolk, the central courtyard and the garden from west to east. The outer house has three halls; they are the Main Gate Hall, the Tea Lounge and the Sedan Hall. Now we are at the second part, the Tea Lounge.

V: What is its function?

G: It was used to receive ordinary guests. The part behind us is the Sedan Hall. The wing-rooms on the right and left are the places of accountant's office.

V: OK. Very nice.

G: Now please follow me to the third part, the Grand Reception Hall. The owner used to receive his honored guests and hold important ceremonies for wedding, funeral and fete.

V: The gate is closed.

G: Yes. The gate is not open in normal times except when there come distinguished guests.

V: I see that the hall is furnished and decorated interestingly.

G: There are a celadon vase on the right and a marble top mirror on the left on the long narrow table, implying the meaning of placidity. There are a large clock at the north left corner and a mirror at the right corner, meaning being utterly loyal. All these show that the owner had a heart to be fully loyal to the court.

V: Ha-ha. That is typical Chinese philosophical idea.

Wanxiang Building

G: Now we have reached at the second section of the garden—the inner chamber for womenfolk, also named "Wanxiang Building".

V: I've found the architecture style is much different from the former ones.

G: The building has the Anhui style. It is because Ren Lansheng was an official in Anhui at one time. He liked the architectural style of Anhui so much that he shifted it here.

V: I've noticed there are two verandas on both sides.

G: Yes. That is the typical Anhui architecture style. The double verandas on both sides have two advantages: It can keep the sun out in summer, keep off the rain on rainy days. Under the porch are two stairs, making it convenient for people to go upstairs and downstairs.

V: I see. Very clever designing. The door over there is very special, flashed bricks stuck on the thick wooden board.

G: Yes. Wanxiang Building is the inner chamber for womenfolk's daily life. Safety is very important. Flashed bricks stuck on the thick wooden board, which makes the door heavier. Locals commonly call it brick door. By doing this, there are two advantages. Firstly it can guard against theft because the door is very heavy; secondly it can avoid the fire. So they can be called a fireproof door.

V: The ancient wisdom of Chinese.

Land Boat—Zuo Chun Wang Yue Building—Sui Hanju

G: After visiting the second part, let's continue to go to the third part—the central courtyard. Here is a land boat without stern.

V: Why did the owner build such kind of building?

G: This land boat can express the hospitality of the owner, because boat is the main means of transportation at that time. The owner hoped his guests could come here often.

V: I found in many Suzhou gardens, there is such kind of trees.

G: They are called magnolia trees. In China it has the meaning of being auspicious.

V: I see. What are the halls over there?

G: The six-side-base and six-story building on both sides of us is Zuo Chun Wang Yue Building, which serves as the guest house. Opposite to it is the Suihanju, which was used to receive visitors in winter by the owner.

Shuixiang Pavillion—Visiting Scenic Spot—Tuisi Thatched Cottage—A Naohong Barge—Laoren Peak

G: Now we come to the fourth section of this garden—back garden, it is the first building—Shuixiang Pavilion.

V: I see there is a mirror.

G: Yes, it can reflect the whole back garden. On its northern corner stands a small and exquisite pavilion named "Visiting Scenic Spot", which is the highest point of the garden. Standing on it, you will have a whole view of the garden scenery. It is the best place for us to stay indoors to visit the garden.

V: OK.

G: Here is the main building—Tuisi Thatched Cottage.

V: The cottage is laid out as the pattern of a house with two rooms.

G: There is a precious stele behind it on which the "homeward bound" was inscribed by Zhao Mengfu, a calligrapher in the Yuan Dynasty, about 700 years ago.

V: The scenery outside is very beautiful.

G: Yes. Now please look upward from here. You will find a building in ship form. It was called Soundly Water Vessel.

V: Where does the sound come?

G: That is because there are Taihu rockeries beside its shipboards, as if waves were up during the boat sailing. The boat appears to be floating because the goldfish is swimming in water. The scenery is named "A Naohong Barge".

V: Over there is a peak, looking like an old man with a stick.

G: Yes. At first sight it also looks like the traditional character "寿", so it is called "Laoren Peak". Peering at it, you can find a tortoise standing on it, so the stone enjoys the fame of good health and a long life.

Gu Yu Sheng Liang Pavilion—Osmanthus Hall—Pavement

G: Now we are in the "Gu Yu Sheng Liang Pavilion", which is the place for the owner to enjoy coolness in summer.

V: A bright mirror was inlaid amidst it.

G: It seems that there is another garden beside this one. Looking far into the distance, you will find yourself in the midst of lotus pool. If you eat melon and enjoy coolness here in midsummer, you will experience naturally coolness and refreshing when you are calm. Besides, three subdrains were designed under the whole building. The master could hear the clear ripples lying in Xiangfei couch, which adds slighter chilliness in the air. It is said that the mirror was taken back by the son of the owner when he returned to China after studying abroad.

V: So comfortable.

G: Now we will visit Osmanthus Hall. There are all kinds of osmanthus, so the hall will be full of the strong fragrance of osmanthus in autumn.

V: I see. The pavement over there looks very nice.

G: A round "寿" meaning longevity is in its center and five bats are flying surrounding the character. The pattern means enjoying both richness and longevity. There are many copper coins in ancient time. In addition the ground is paved with cobblestones. You can benefit from walking on it with bare feet because the pebbles can give your foot massages. Since you get there today, you may as well have a try.

V: Ha-ha. So interesting!

Task 4 Useful Sentences

1. The garden covers an area of 9.8 mu, simple, quiet and elegant.
2. Tuisi Garden has a unique layout: pavilion, terrace, tower, porch, bridge, hall and house are centered by the pond as if these architectures are floating on it.
3. In 2001, Tuisi Garden was listed as a site of World's Cultural Heritage.
4. Standing on it, you will have a whole view of the garden scenery.
5. Looking far into the distance, you will find yourself in the midst of lotus pool.

Task 5 Listening

You will hear five sentences. Listen carefully and put down the whole sentences.

1. _____.
2. _____.
3. _____.
4. _____.
5. _____.

Task 6　Role-Play

Situation 1: Arrange a half day travel of the Retreat and Reflection Garden for the James.

Situation 2: A group of Australian tourists come to Suzhou, and you are the guide. Today, your group travel to Tongli. When the bus runs on the road, a kid named Tom find something interesting. You explain that it is gorgon fruit, something like a water lily plant. In order to well explain the food, you take the group to the market. You tell the foreign visitors that gorgon fruit could be made in different dish and dessert. When the group are having lunch in the restaurant, you order the dish and dessert made of gorgon fruit.

 Task 7　Translation

1. 进思尽忠，退思补过。
2. 地面铺满了鹅卵石。
3. You can benefit from walking on it with bare feet because the pebbles can give your foot massages.
4. Peering at it, you can find a tortoise standing on it, so the stone enjoys the fame of good health and a long life.
5. On its northern corner stands a small and exquisite pavilion named "Visiting Scenic Spot", which is the highest point of the garden.

 Task 8　Supplementary Reading

Suzhou Embroidery

　　Suzhou embroidery, Hunan embroidery, Sichuan embroidery and Guangdong embroidery are the four most famous in China. Suzhou embroidery has a long history. It has been excavated in Auspicious Tower and Mount Tiger Tower made in Northern Song in the Five Dynasties. The embroidery was made in rather professional ways, which is believed to be the earliest by now. It is recorded that Suzhou embroidery was very prosperous and the art reached perfection after the Song Dynasty. Each family bred silkworms and made embroidery. There appeared embroidery thread lanes, brocade mills, embroidery flower streets, etc., in the city. That proved the prosperity of Suzhou embroidery. Some lived by embroidering. Daughters in rich families were engaged in it as a way of killing time and molding their experiment. That's how "popular embroidery", "boudoir embroidery" and "palace embroidery" came into being. Suzhou embroidery in the Qing Dynasty reached its culmination. Suzhou was called the "market of embroidery", famous both at home and abroad. There were various ways of knitting and they were applied widely. Mountains, rivers, lakes, pavilions, flowers and birds, characters were all embroidered. Suzhou embroidery was largely needed in the palace. Therefore wonderful and magnificent embroidery sprang up.

At the end of Qing Dynasty and the beginning of the Republic of China, Shen Shou, an expert at embroidery, renovated the traditional way of knitting. Flowers and birds, characters embroidered in new ways, or endowed with new meaning were very characteristic. The image of Elina, the queen of Italy absorbed the theory of chiaroscuro. Close attention was paid to the vividness of the images. Such embroidery was called "art embroidery" or "emulation embroidery". Shen Shou combined the previous art and her own experience, classified the way of knitting into 18 varieties, as recorded by Zhang Sui in a book. Thus the way of knitting was systematized. Her own embroidery won several awards for the country in International Fairs.

The pieces of embroidery on characters, animals and flowers, mountains and water are for appreciation. They can also be made into pictures, book marks, a set of hanging scrolls, etc. There are also the varieties of embroidery: single-side embroidery, double-side embroidery of different colors. Double-side embroidery, the specific style of Suzhou embroidery can be appreciated from both sides. Pictures look exactly the same and wonderful on both sides. Special ways are used in knitting instead of knotting. There the end of silk threads is invisible. It is knitted in the right angle without piercing the other side. Both sides will present the same excellent effect. The Nangjing Bridge, Xiangjun, the peony, the cat and the goldfish are the masterpieces in double-side embroidery.

(Source: http://travel.chinavista.com/show_culture - 171.html)

Questions:
1. What are the four most famous embroideries in China?
2. How do people find proofs of prosperity of Suzhou embroidery in China?
3. When did Suzhou embroidery reach its culmination?
4. Who is the person making great contribution to Suzhou embroidery?
5. Tell the varieties of embroidery.

Part Ⅲ

Task 1　Warm-Up

1. Talk about the tradition of "walking on Ternate Bridges".
2. What does the "one garden, two halls and three bridges" in Tongli refer to?

Task 2　Words and Expressions

renowned	[rɪˈnaʊnd]	adj.	有名的
triangle	[ˈtraɪæŋgl]	n.	三角形
booming	[ˈbuːmɪŋ]	adj.	兴旺的
auspiciousness	[ɔːsˈpɪʃəsnəs]	n.	吉兆
resident	[ˈrezɪdənt]	n.	居民
residential	[rezɪˈdenʃl]	adj.	居住的
symbolize	[ˈsɪmbəlaɪz]	v.	象征
connotation	[kɒnəˈteɪʃn]	n.	含义
promising	[ˈprɒmɪsɪŋ]	adj.	有前途的
luxurious	[lʌgˈʒʊəriəs]	adj.	奢侈的
revolve	[rɪˈvɒlv]	v.	旋转,围绕
reputation	[repju(ː)ˈteɪʃn]	n.	名誉
convergence	[kənˈvɜːdʒəns]	n.	汇合点
hilarious	[hɪˈleərɪəs]	adj.	欢闹的
everlasting	[ˌevəˈlɑːstɪŋ]	adj.	永恒的
extend	[ɪkˈstend]	v.	表示,提供
endow	[ɪnˈdaʊ]	v.	赋予
proverb	[ˈprɒvɜːb]	n.	谚语
meteoric	[ˌmiːtɪˈɒrɪk]	adj.	流星的
newlywed	[ˈnjuːliwed]	adj.	新婚的
axle	[ˈæksl]	n.	轮轴
Three Bridges			三桥
Chongben Hall			崇本堂
Jili Bridge			吉利桥
Liu Bingnan			柳柄南
Jiayin Hall			嘉荫堂
Taiping Bridge			太平桥
Changqing Bridge			长庆桥
live as long as the Southern Mountain			寿比南山
be blessed with			幸运地享有

Task 3 Dialogues

Scene: Now the group is in Tongli Town. (V = Visitor, G = Guide)
Travel Route: Three Bridges—Jiayin Hall—Chongben Hall

Three Bridges

G: Now what you have seen is the renowned Three Bridges, which has a good reputation among bridges.

V: What are their names?

G: Three Bridges indicate Taiping Bridge, Jili Bridge and Changqing Bridge which are arranged in a triangle at the convergences of three rivers, forming ring roads in the town.

V: What is the special meaning of these three bridges?

G: Tongli people like walking across Three Bridges. If someone celebrates marriage, the celebration group will walk across Three Bridges full of joy, accompanied by hilarious drum music and fireworks, praying aloud, "Peace, auspiciousness and everlasting happiness!" Residents along the street will come out to view the occasion, extending their congratulations. If old people celebrate their 66-year-old birthday, they will certainly walk across Three Bridges after lunch for auspiciousness. It is unknown to all when the custom of "walking across Three Bridges" started, but for Tongli people, Three Bridges symbolize auspiciousness and happiness.

V: Does this custom still exist now?

G: Yes. As time passes by, people endow walking across Three Bridges new connotation. Walking across Taiping Bridge people will be blessed with good health all around the year. Walking across Jili Bridge, people will be blessed with booming business. Walking across Changqing Bridge, people will be blessed with everlasting youth. There are folk proverbs about people of different ages to walk across Three Bridges. Walking across Three Bridges, the kids will be cleverer and make progress every year. Walking across Three Bridges, the girls will be born beautiful and slimmer. Walking across Three bridges, the young fellows will have a meteoric rise and be a promising man. Walking across Three Bridges, the elderly will live as long as the Southern Mountain and be healthy in old age. Walking across Three Bridges, the newlywed will have a complete meeting of minds and remain happily to a ripe old age. Now since you are here, you might as well experience walking across Three Bridges personally.

V: OK. I will have a try.

G: Of course. Go ahead.

Jiayin Hall

G: Now let's continue to visit a literary family—Jiayin Hall.
V: How old is it?
G: It was established in 1912.
V: Who was its first owner?
G: Its owner was Liu Bingnan. He started oil mill in Luxu at the very beginning, which made him rich, so he moved to Tongli to build this luxurious residence.
V: What is worth visiting here?
G: There are many beautiful elegant carvings here. These carvings on windows, roofs and so on will tell you many traditional customs in China.

Chongben Hall

G: Here is another famous residence—Chongben Hall.
V: Is it very old?
G: About 100 years old.
V: Whose house it is?
G: Its owner was Qian Youqin, a rich merchant, Tongli native, who ran the business of rice.
V: I see. Is there anything special here?
G: The group of architectures develops in depth revolving around the axle wire, with five entrances including the entrance hall, hall, front building, back building and kitchen.
V: I see. It is a very big residential house.
G: Right.

Task 4 Useful Sentences

1. Residents along the street will come out to view the occasion, extending their congratulations.
2. As time passes by, people endow walking across Three Bridges new connotation.
3. There are folk proverbs about people of different ages to walk across Three Bridges.
4. Now since you are here, you might as well experience walking across Three Bridges personally.
5. Its owner was Qian Youqin, a rich merchant, Tongli native, who ran the business of rice.

Task 5 Listening

You will hear five sentences. Listen carefully and put down the whole sentences.

1. _____ .
2. _____ .
3. _____ .
4. _____ .
5. _____ .

Task 6 Role-Play

Situation 1: Arrange a special travel plan of Three Bridges for the James, let the whole family enjoy the happiness of different culture by experiencing walking across Three Bridges.

Situation 2: The James comes to Suzhou from Australia to have a tour. You are the guide. The family has altogether 4 members, Mr. James, Mrs. James, their kids Tom and Kate.

- According to the itinerary, today you are going to visit Tongli, the famous water town in Suzhou.
- The James is to return to Suzhou after one day's tour. However, nowadays, there is a fashion for the travelers to experience living in Tongli for a whole day including sleeping in the local people's house for a night. The James is quite interested in spending a night in a local house.
- You arrange a local house for the James, and explain the cost.

Task 7 Translation

1. 谁也不知道走三桥的习俗何时开始的,但对同里人来说,三桥象征着吉祥幸福。
2. 走三桥可以让老人寿比南山,老年安康。
3. If someone celebrates marriage, the celebration group will walk across Three Bridges full of joy, accompanied by hilarious drum music and fireworks, praying aloud, "Peace, auspiciousness and everlasting happiness!"
4. These carvings on windows, roofs and so on will tell you many traditional customs in China.
5. The group of architectures develops in depth revolving around the axle wire, with five entrances

including the entrance hall, hall, front building, back building and kitchen.

Task 8 Supplementary Reading

Chinese Fans

No one knows exactly how fans in China were invented. The invention or rather the discovery of the fanning function could have been as accidental as follows: a primitive man irritated with lots of flies and mosquitoes, picked up a big leaf off a plant next to him to drive the pests away. To his delight, his effort resulted in cooling air movements.

Before long, fans acquired ceremonial significance. More than 3,000 years ago, fans were made with bird's feathers and were an outstanding characteristic in imperial pomp. They lent infinite gracefulness and charm to court dancers, who achieved the appearance of heavenly phoenixes. Along with the progress made in agriculture in the Han and Tang Dynasties, an ample supply of clothing material resulted. Silk and satin fans appeared and it became a fashion among scholars and artists to show their genius by writing and painting on fan surfaces. Fans soon acquired considerable social significance and became a part of the standard summer costume among the elite and the learned.

Tradition has it, folded fans were introduced to China from Japan and Korea about 1,000 years ago. They were usually made with fine paper mounted on bamboo. The scholars found it interesting to paint their poetic and artistic expressions on the surface. A great variety of fans have been produced in China; sandalwood, ivory, even gold, silver and jade have been used as material.

Of particular interest is the sandalwood fan. Its most outstanding characteristic is the pleasant, fragrant scent that comes from the wood. Even in modern air-conditioned environment, it will certainly enhance the elegance and femininity of the lady holding it gracefully in her hand. It emits subtle fragrance which is as enchanting and refreshing as any expensive perfume.

Palm fans were made in the Jin Dynasty (265-420 A.D.) and have been widely used by the Chinese people. They are very useful and welcomed by people of less expensive taste.

(Source: http://travel.chinavista.com/show_culture-8.html)

Questions:
1. What could be the cause of discovery of the fan?
2. What kind of significance did the fan acquire through history?
3. Did Chinese invent folded fans?
4. What are the materials that could be used for making a fan?
5. Could you briefly describe the sandalwood fan?

References

[1] 编写组. 饭店工作英语. 北京:中国旅游出版社,2006.
[2] 陈欣. 导游英语情景口语. 北京:北京大学出版社,2009.
[3] 关肇远. 导游英语口语. 北京:高等教育出版社,2004.
[4] 刘丽莉. 导游英语实用教程. 天津:天津大学出版社,2010.
[5] 陆志宝. 导游英语. 北京:旅游教育出版社,2003.
[6] 南凡. 旅游英语. 北京:高等教育出版社,2005.
[7] 姚宝荣. 模拟导游教程. 北京:中国旅游出版社,2004.
[8] 朱华. 英语导游听说教程. 北京:北京大学出版社,2006.
[9] http://www.travelchinaguide.com
[10] http://chineseteas101.com/
[11] http://www.china-travel-tour-guide.com/city-guide/suzhou.shtml
[12] http://en.wikipedia.org/wiki/Suzhou
[13] http://www.chinahighlights.com/suzhou/food/the-squirrel-shaped-mandarin-fish.htm
[14] http://www.suzhouculture.cn/list_en.aspx?id=37
[15] http://www.suzhouculture.cn/list_en.aspx?id=37
[16] http://travel.chinavista.com/destination-sight.php?id=167
[17] http://travel.chinavista.com/destination-sight.php?id=19
[18] http://travel.chinavista.com/destination-sight-17.html